6NP 1H29   1995

For Jack : another mentor, inspiration
and friend of my Soul.   MA.

No Plaster Saint

D1414484

Mildred Fahrni, National Secretary,
Fellowship of Reconciliation, Canada, 1948.

No Plaster Saint

The Life of Mildred Osterhout Fahrni
1900–1992

Nancy Knickerbocker

Talonbooks
2001

Talonbooks
P.O. Box 2076, Vancouver, British Columbia, Canada V6B 3S3
www.talonbooks.com

Typeset in Adobe Caslon and printed and bound in Canada by Houghton Boston.

First Printing: June 2001

National Library of Canada Cataloguing in Publication Data

Knickerbocker, Nancy, 1955-
No plaster saint

ISBN 0-88922-452-8

1. Fahrni, Mildred Osterhout, 1900-1992 2. Social reformers—Canada—Biography. 3. Pacifists—Canada—Biography. I. Title.
HQ1455.F34K64 2001   303.48'4'092   C2001-910191-0

The publisher gratefully acknowledges the financial support of the Canada Council for the Arts; the Government of Canada through the Book Publishing Industry Development Program; and the Province of British Columbia through the British Columbia Arts Council for our publishing activities. Publication of this book was also made possible by assistance from the Vancouver Historical Society.

I am not a visionary. I claim to be a practical idealist. The religion of non-violence is not meant merely for the rishis and saints. It is meant for the common people as well.

— Mahatma Gandhi

Contents

ACKNOWLEDGMENTS

It has been quite a journey from first to final drafts, and along the way many wonderful people have contributed to Mildred's story. Thanks go first to Mildred's nieces, Marion Irish and Beverley McMaster, who gave unique insights into her long life and complex character, as well as open access to her extensive personal archives.

The members of the Mildred Fahrni Project conceived of the idea of this biography, and their love for Mildred imbues every page. Special thanks to Frank Dingman, Carolyn Kline, the late Dick Legge and his dear wife Hazel, Jane Tennant and Frankie Tillman.

Members of the Canadian Fellowship of Reconciliation also gave generously of their memories and moral support. Thanks to the late June Black, Alice Coppard, Soonoo Engineer, Lydia Haythorne, Gail Raphanel and Daisy Webster.

Mildred's friends and fellow activists offered a fascinating personal and political context for Mildred's life. Warm thanks to Elizabeth Keeling, Frank McKenzie, Dr. Margaret Prang, Dr. Stanley Rowe, the late Mary Thomson and dozens of others who agreed to be interviewed.

For their early research, I am grateful to Dr. Carole Christopher, Barbara Evans, Irene Howard, Barbara Roberts, Marcia Toms and Dr. Meredith Wadman.

Former colleagues at *The Vancouver Sun*, Shelley Fralic and Ian Haysom, gave early encouragement, as did Lynne Bowen, my *sensei* in Sechelt. Jane Coverton's wisdom, editorial and herbal, helped too, as did Hilary Rose's exacting eye.

I want to acknowledge the B.C. Arts Council, the Boag Foundation, Peace Fund Canada, and the Vancouver Historical Society for invaluable assistance. Much gratitude to Wes Knapp and Kathleen MacKinnon of the VHS and to Karl and Christy Siegler of Talonbooks.

Above all, heartfelt thanks to my dear parents, Jim and Betty Ann, awesome children, Connor, Madeline and Max, and truly *querido compañero*, Chris Rose. *¡Mil gracias a todos!*

Brothers in ministry: S.S. Osterhout and A.B. Osterhout, circa 1900.

Chapter One: 1900

A PRAIRIE CHILDHOOD

Last century made the world a neighbourhood;
this century must make it a brotherhood.

— J.S. Woodsworth

On New Year's Day 1900, a thirty-four-year-old preacher's wife named Hattie Osterhout laboured to give birth to her second child. Outside the parsonage was the vast prairie and the Manitoba winter. Inside her soul was the memory of her firstborn, a baby girl who had died two years earlier. Hattie's heart contracted with the grief, still fresh. She thought of her own mother, who had born eleven children and died young.

Her family, the Smyths, had come from Great Britain to Canada, but they never really did put down roots on the Prairies. The hardship and bitter weather drove them to the United States, where they thought it was better to struggle in a fragrant orange orchard than over a quarter section of winter wheat. When her parents emigrated to California, Hattie chose to stay on as a frontier teacher. She started to remember the little school house in the village of Ninga, where she was teaching when the new preacher arrived in town.

Reverend Abram Berson Osterhout was a tall, elegantly-built man, impeccable in his grooming of body and spirit. He came from southern Ontario, one of six sons, United Empire Loyalists, all devoted Methodists. Hattie and Berson were married and moved to the town of Arden, Manitoba. There their first baby was born, and buried before her second birthday.

They had named her Grace. Grace of God. How small and light her body was when Hattie bathed and dressed her for the last time! She was grateful to the women of Arden who came to lend a hand and to weep with her. She shuddered to remember how Berson plunged into solitary mourning, shutting himself up in his study for three days and nights, closing her out. Oh, she was lonely then! But now all that was past.

Now a new era was being born and with it a new hope. Hattie laboured on, and prayed for her new baby. She was not afraid, for she always believed that she was held in God's care. Finally, on January 2, 1900, her second daughter came into the world, a healthy child of the 20th century. Hattie cradled her babe in her arms and slept peacefully.

* * *

In the year of little Minnie Mildred's birth, Queen Victoria sat upon the throne of England and ruled an empire that spanned a quarter of the world, including the vast Dominion of Canada, where Prime Minister Wilfrid Laurier's Liberals governed a population of more than five million. Many Canadians still willingly shouldered their colonial duty: seven thousand volunteered to help fight England's war with the Boers of South Africa. "Rule Britannia!" they cheered.

It was a time of innocence and optimism, of rapid progress and boundless possibilities. Immigration boomed and the railway opened up the land. The Canadian frontier was one of the last undeveloped wheat lands in the world, and the pioneers who came to homestead in the first decade of the century quintupled its grain production. In 1902 the first gasoline-powered farm tractor was manufactured. In some parts of the country the speed limit for motor cars was set at seven miles per hour.

Most Canadians still lived on farms or in rural villages. They had to co-operate to survive on the frontier, so their sense of community was strong. Everyone knew everybody else in town and it mattered what the neighbours thought. Family values were conservative; good children obeyed their parents and good wives, their husbands. Divorce? Unthinkable. Votes for women? Impossible. The Dominion Election Act stated that "No woman, idiot, lunatic or criminal shall vote." Sexuality was shrouded in secrecy, while drinking, smoking, gambling and dancing were also taboo. Folks knew white from black, and right from wrong. They worked from dawn to dusk, and observed the Sabbath.

By the turn of the century, the Catholic, Methodist, Presbyterian and Anglican churches represented about eighty-five per cent of Canadians. Methodism was the major Protestant denomination in a time when Christians hadn't yet found the ecumenical spirit. Fired by a passion for what was then still conceived of as "the white man's burden," missionaries ventured forth to the most remote parts of the Dominion.

Both Mildred's father and her uncle were among these fervent young men who believed that the road to Christian perfection lay in service to humanity. In 1893, the Osterhout brothers — Reverend Abram Berson and Reverend Smith

Victor and Mildred Osterhout, circa 1903.

Stanley — began their respective odysseys into the wilderness. Smith worked in northwest British Columbia, among the Nisga'a people of the Nass River Valley and the Tsimshean at Port Simpson. A gifted linguist, he dedicated himself to learning their languages. He wrote an early grammar of the Tsimshean language, and translated Methodist doctrine and hymns for their use. He loved these people and, by his example, convinced many to follow Jesus.

"The membership was increased one hundred per cent, and many trophies were won from heathenism to Christ," the Methodist newspaper reported. "He has a strong personality, a magnificent physique, a deep and orotund voice. He is an eloquent speaker, and in him the Church has a well-qualified and successful missionary, and the natives a firm friend and defender."[1] Then the church's youngest district chairman, S.S. Osterhout was at the beginning of a distinguished career.

Meanwhile, Berson, the elder brother, served the Inland Mission Service of the Manitoba Methodist Conference. He ministered with verve and dedication in remote pioneer towns and sod-hut homesteads throughout the southern part of the province. Roughly every four years he would pack his library and Hattie would bundle up the rest of the household goods and they'd move on to their next charge. From one simple parsonage to the next, the Osterhout family grew.[2]

Born in Rapid City, a village west of Portage-la-Prairie, Mildred blossomed into a chubby toddler with blonde hair and blue eyes. When she was two, the family moved farther northwest to the town of Birtle where her brother Victor Howard was born on July 11, 1902. They later moved on to Crandall, then to Gladstone and finally to Oak Lake.

One day when Victor was a baby Mildred's parents had to go out for a few moments. "Do you think you can look after your little brother?" they asked. Three-year-old Mildred looked up at her mother, all round and sweet-faced behind her spectacles, and her handsome father, so tall and dignified with his goatee neatly trimmed. She felt happy to be given such an important job, and proudly rocked Vic in his hammock until her parents returned and praised her for helping so nicely. Mildred often said, "There was always an atmosphere of goodwill and understanding in our family," and it began, for her, with this early memory.[3]

Her parents clearly loved one another, even if they were restrained in the ways they expressed it. As a family they went to ball games and on picnics in summer, skating and sleigh-riding in winter. Partly because they moved so frequently, Mildred and Victor relied on one another for childhood companionship. They teased and quarrelled between themselves, but they were good friends in an innocent time. As children, they knew nothing of hatred or violence, and had never even heard of murder. They were loved and cared for, simply but adequately housed and fed, and it did feel as though God was in His Heaven. They were free to roam the golden countryside, going swimming and riding horses. They'd wander down to the railroad tracks, where they listened for the lonely whistle and the comforting rhythms of the locomotives. Sometimes when a train pulled into town they'd sneak underneath to explore its inky underbelly.

Children of Mildred's generation also worked hard at chores. All work was segregated along gender lines. Women's work was in the home and garden, men's in the office and field. Mildred never forgot the time that her mother insisted she wash the dishes, while her brother was permitted to sit around reading a booklet they had both been given in Sunday school. She told her mother it didn't seem fair to her that she had to help out more often just because she was a girl. Hattie Osterhout may have understood her daughter's feelings, but in those days no mother raised her son to do dishes.

One of the first things Mildred's mother did when they settled into a new town was to plant her garden. Like most frontier housewives, she grew her own fruit and vegetables, and year by year, row by row, Hattie taught Mildred how to make things bloom. Kneeling together in the rich prairie soil, mother and daughter put down roots and nurtured a friendly, loving relationship. Every fall they preserved the harvest in preparation for the long months of winter — Hattie would stoke up the wood stove and set Mildred to work peeling and pitting the fruits of their labour. At the end of the day, they took pride in the gleaming jars of preserves on the pantry shelf. At night, they'd light the kerosene lamps and read, sew or mend.

The rhythms of the Osterhout household revolved around Sundays, but the Sabbath preparations began with the weekly Saturday night bath. In the winters Mildred shivered as she hauled in buckets of snow, which her mother set to melt on the wood stove. When the water was warm, they filled the tin tub in the kitchen and the family took turns scrubbing away the soil and sins of the week.

The next morning they put on their Sunday best and went to church. One of Mildred's earliest memories was of following in her father's footsteps through deep snow up to the church door, the light from his lantern swaying over the sparkling drifts. Gradually the congregation would assemble: the women in their bonnets and bustles, the men in bowler hats and starched collars and cuffs. When the time came and all was quiet, Mildred's father would take his place in the pulpit and begin speaking the words of the Lord.

Steeped in the revivalist tradition and fired by evangelical zeal, Reverend A.B. Osterhout preached salvation through faith in the atonement of Jesus. He praised duty and self-denial in the service of God and man. He warned against the sins of the flesh and the demon rum, and he practised what he preached. A lifelong teetotaler, he also disapproved of dancing, smoking, gambling and playing pool. His was a conventional faith, but one he sincerely strove to live in both word and deed.

Rev. Osterhout had a capable and gracious helpmate in his mission. He depended upon his wife in a great number of ways, and she never let him down. He respected her intelligence and counted on her to preach the sermon when he was ill. Because of her experience as a teacher and the depth of her own faith, it wasn't difficult for Hattie to feel confident and articulate in the pulpit. She was encouraged by the children, who would beam up at her from the front pew.

After the last hymn had resonated through the church, the worshippers often stayed to chat a while with their friends and neighbours, but the Reverend wouldn't linger. He'd hitch up his cart or, in winter, the sleigh, and be off on his rounds, spreading The Word to the farm folk on the remote homesteads and settlements. Some said he was like his Old Testament namesake, Abram, who also preached in the wilderness. "He was always faithful to his appointments," and sometimes that took real physical courage.[4]

On sub-zero Sundays, the family would wait anxiously for his return, listening for the whinny of his chestnut mare and the jingle of the sleigh bells. When he came through the door his beard would be frozen and his lips blue, but he would be smiling, his duty done for another week. Mildred would run to greet her Dad, and Hattie would pour him a cup of hot tea. The wind howled across the frozen landscape, but it was snug inside. The house was at peace, imbued with that special Sunday feeling, quiet and holy.

"I grew up with conviction," Mildred often said. "I was a believer in The Word." As a girl, she dreamed of someday becoming a missionary and helping people in a far-off land. It was an ambition that would have pleased her father, and she was eager — perhaps overeager — to please him. While Mildred clearly loved her mother and doted upon her little brother, she adored her father.

It wasn't easy being her father's daughter, however. When moving picture shows first came to Manitoba, they were all the rage among the young people but Father didn't approve of them and, despite her pleading, forbade Mildred to see them. He finally relented when a movie appeared about the life of Christ.[5] Mildred's father had high expectations, and sometimes she felt she had to earn his love. Of course, being the preacher's daughter in any small town imposed certain obligations, but at the same time, it conferred special status. On the one hand, Mildred was always welcome in the best company, but on the other hand she was supposed to set an example of girlish Christian virtue and be a paragon of propriety. Her tomboyish nature railed against these limitations.

"Come on, Vic, I'll race you!" cried twelve-year-old Mildred. Skates flung over their shoulders, sister and brother raced through the snow towards the frozen river, laughing and exhilarated. She triumphantly leapt first onto the river ice,

The Osterhouts visited Hattie's family in California, circa 1909.

but in an instant heard a heart-stopping crack and was plunged into the frigid waters. She struggled not to panic as she hoisted herself up, only to have the ice shatter underneath her again and again. With Vic's help, she finally clambered out and staggered, dripping and shivering, to the nearest farm house. There, kindly Mrs. Fahrni gave her dry clothes and sat her down by a blazing fire.

Swiss-born Christian Fahrni was the most successful farmer and rancher in the Gladstone district. He owned 900 acres of land and 150 head of cattle, as well as thoroughbred horses. Priscilla Fahrni was a mother of six and a leading member of the Methodist congregation. She always made sure her boys kept the Osterhout's barn well supplied with hay and oats, and that they took good care of the reverend's horse whenever he was away.

The Fahrnis grew Red Fife wheat, which was a fine variety but vulnerable to early frost. That meant they'd sometimes have a crew of twenty-five men working feverishly to bring in the harvest ahead of the weather. On one of those days Gordon, the eldest of the Fahrni sons, needed fresh horses for his binder team. The preacher's chestnut mare had been in the stable guzzling oats without any exercise, so Gordon hitched her up and put her to work. A while later he saw a tall figure striding towards him across the field. When Mildred's father found his horse sweating and lathered, he gave young Fahrni a dressing down he would never forget. Gordon called it "a ghastly event."[6]

Mildred and Victor loved to hang around the Fahrni fields to watch the men and horses hauling in the great wagon loads of grain. Up at the farm house, the women and girls had the enormous job of feeding two dozen hungry men three times a day, but Priscilla Fahrni always had huge pots of something savoury bubbling on the stove. She kneaded the bread, churned the butter and served it all fresh with either Johnny cake and molasses or berry pies for dessert. Sometimes Mildred helped Mrs. Fahrni pack up the baskets and bring supper to the men in the fields.

Walter, the youngest of the four Fahrni boys, was eleven years older than Mildred. He was a tall, good-looking fellow with clear blue eyes, a square jaw and hair the colour of straw. His brothers called him Buck. He liked the skinny girl with pigtails who helped his mother, and they often exchanged friendly words, but neither one ever imagined that more than thirty years later they would be married.

* * *

As the Osterhout children grew they became aware that their father's fine reputation was also growing, even beyond the bounds of their small-town lives. A.B. Osterhout began to take on a wider role in church affairs. He was elected president of the Manitoba Methodist Conference, and began making regular trips to Winnipeg for meetings. There he met and befriended another minister who became like a second father to Mildred, and who would begin to shape her most fervently-held beliefs.

Rev. James Shaver Woodsworth was a theological radical who had twice tried to resign from the church because he no longer believed in certain articles of faith, such as the virgin birth, original sin and miracles. Still, the church elders refused to accept his resignation by invoking the tolerant spirit of John Wesley, father of Methodism, who said: "For opinions, or terms, let us not destroy the work of God. Dost thou love and serve God? It is enough. I give thee the right hand of fellowship."[7]

Although Osterhout was far more conventional than Woodsworth in matters of doctrine, the two missionaries didn't let that get in the way of their friendship. One served on the lonely farms and the other in the city slums, but they both saw the hardship and injustice of the world. Both were convinced this had never been God's plan for his children. They preached the social gospel because they believed it was not enough for churchmen to mouth platitudes about saving souls for the hereafter — Christians had to be active in the world, building the Kingdom of God in the here and now.

Far from the Kingdom of Heaven, Woodsworth served in a part of Winnipeg that was more like hell on earth. The city's north end was overcrowded and filthy, a desperate ghetto where immigrants and refugees from all over Europe struggled to survive. Even children laboured ten-hour days in sweat shops, then trudged home through the muddy streets to their squalid shacks. Berson and Hattie Osterhout respected James and Lucy Woodsworth for their commitment to share the burdens of the poor by living and raising their children among them.

Occasionally the Osterhouts would clamber into the horse-drawn wagon or sleigh and make the trip east to Winnipeg to visit the Woodsworths, who lived with their six children in a little house next to the All People's Mission. Under the Woodsworths' leadership, idealistic staff and volunteers of the mission ran a baby clinic and kindergarten, offered housekeeping classes, gave away food and clothing in emergencies, taught English, and loaned out books. The All People's Mission trained a generation of Manitoba reformers, including the pioneer feminist, Nellie McClung. It was in Winnipeg's north end that Mildred first witnessed deep poverty, and she had the courage of heart not to look away. Indeed, she herself yearned to do just such work as the Woodsworths' someday. Also during these family visits, Mildred and Grace Woodsworth built the sisterly foundations of a life-long friendship and political partnership.

When the girls were in their early teens, both families left the Prairies and settled on the west coast. The Woodsworths were forced to uproot because James's growing radicalism made it impossible for him to conform to the dictates of church elders. Ultimately, though, it was his passionate pacifist convictions that compelled him to leave the ministry. In the years to come, Woodsworth's stand for peace would have the most profound impact upon Mildred's life, but would make him "an outcast from all the respectable and right-thinking people among whom he had grown up."[8]

Meanwhile the Osterhouts were transferred to a more affluent and cosmopolitan parish than they'd ever served. Now in his mid-fifties, Rev. Osterhout was no longer fit for the rigors of frontier preaching. In 1914, he left the Inland Mission Service and accepted a posting to the pulpit of Fairfield Methodist Church in Victoria, capital of British Columbia. At the age of fourteen, Mildred was thrilled at the prospect of leaving village life behind and heading for the city. The family moved into a large Edwardian-style wood frame house at 220 Moss Street in the leafy neighbourhood of Fairfield. There, the country girl soon snipped off her childish pigtails and began growing up a little faster.

The Osterhout family on the front steps of their new home at 220 Moss Street, Victoria, 1914.

Chapter Two: 1914

A TEEN IN WARTIME

As Mildred prepared to enter Grade Nine, Canada entered the Great War. The fateful day was August 4, 1914, when the trumpets sounded and the call to arms rang out across the land. To Mildred, the war was a distant, apocalyptic struggle between the forces of good and evil. On Sundays her father, like most other ministers, praised Canada's righteous crusaders against the German anti-Christ. Thousands of young men rushed off to fight for God, King and country. Mildred's cousin, Arthur Osterhout, enlisted and so did Walter Fahrni, her future husband.

Walter signed up with the Gordon Highlanders of the 16th Scottish Regiment, one of the first Canadian battalions to see action in France and Belgium. He was among those who experienced an excruciating landmark in the history of warfare: the first use of chemical weaponry. On April 22, 1915, a northeast wind carried a greenish-yellow cloud of chlorine gas across the Western Front at Ypres. In the Allied trenches, Walter and his comrades began choking and gasping in a muddy toxic horror. More than six thousand Canadians died in a week of fierce fighting. Walter suffered chronic lung impairment and would never regain his rugged constitution. More painful, though, were the emotional and spiritual wounds he suffered. His brother Gordon said that the experience "changed Walter's perspective on life, his whole personality."[1] It is clear that Walter's later pacifist convictions were rooted in the battlefields of Ypres, in Flanders.

Back home, Mildred remained only vaguely aware of the nightmare overseas. She certainly didn't question that going to war was the right and proper thing to do. She read the patriotic propaganda that rolled off the presses daily and the Methodist church jumped wholeheartedly onto the military band wagon, as had all the other denominations, with the exception of the traditional peace churches such as the Mennonites and the Society of Friends (Quakers). While Canadian pacifists were all but silenced by militant Christian patriots, some European peacemakers were actively working to prevent more bloodshed.

In 1914, an historic meeting had taken place between an English Quaker named Henry Hodgkin and a German Lutheran named Freidrich Sigmund-Schultze, then chaplain to the Kaiser. Both men pledged to work for peace although their countries would soon be at war, and together they founded the Fellowship of Reconciliation, an international pacifist organization that eventually spread to more than thirty countries, including Canada. After the Second World War, Mildred would play a key role in the Canadian FOR, but during the First World War she was only just beginning to see the personal and political implications of embracing pacifism.

In 1916, J.S. Woodsworth published his objections to conscription and so began his journey along what Gandhi called the "solitary path of peace." At once, he was fired as director of the Bureau of Social Research in Winnipeg. The Methodist Church of Canada similarly wanted nothing to do with him. In his third and final letter of resignation he wrote: "For me, the teachings and spirit of Jesus are absolutely irreconcilable with the advocacy of war. Christianity may be an impossible idealism, but so long as I hold to it, ever so unworthily, I must refuse ... to participate in war." In true patriotic spirit, the church that had earlier been so willing to accommodate Woodsworth's doctrinal radicalism now became utterly inflexible on his radical pacifism. His resignation was promptly accepted.

Then the Woodsworth family moved west. At first J.S. was unemployed, able only to get casual labour as a longshoreman in the port of Vancouver. He approached the work with verve, but it was gruelling and his health was frail. One evening, James, Lucy, and their six children came for dinner at the Osterhout's home in Victoria. During their visit, Mildred saw the shadows under Woodsworth's eyes, and read the concern on her parents' faces. As she passed the potatoes and urged seconds, she looked around the table at the children: little Howard, then Bruce, Ralph, Belva and Grace, the eldest, a good friend forever. "Dear God," she thought. "How will they ever survive?"

Mildred never forgot that evening, listening to Woodsworth over the dinner table, witnessing his integrity and conviction. She intuitively but firmly believed he was right, that the way of Christ was the way of peace. It seemed so clear, she was disappointed the clergy could be so blind and for the first time, she began to question her church. She saw the hypocrisy and politics that callously played with Woodsworth's fate, and she marveled at his willingness to accept suffering as the price of his beliefs. In later life she often said that "Woodsworth was the one who made the greatest impact on my thinking about non-violence."[2]

Mildred graduated from high school in 1917, the same year that the British Columbia Women's Suffrage Act was passed. She knew that she wanted to do some good in the world, but her options were limited to nursing and teaching. Like her mother, Mildred chose teaching. That fall she enrolled in the Victoria

Mildred in C.G.I.T. uniform, probably with her cousins, Edna and Delda Osterhout.

Normal School, where she took a one-year program that would earn her a certificate for both elementary and high school. That way, she'd be able to get a job and possibly go to university later.

In Dr. D.L. MacLaurin, founder and long-time principal of Victoria Normal School, Mildred found another important role model. "Mr. Mac," as he was affectionately known, gave his students a different outlook on their purpose as teachers, and inspired them with the nobility of their calling. In a time when teachers often strapped students, rapped their knuckles or boxed their ears, MacLaurin rejected such methods. He treated children with understanding, and taught alternatives to the authoritarian style of pedagogy. With Mr. Mac for inspiration, Mildred dreamed of being the kind of teacher who could really make a difference. At the end of term, "it was heartrending to say good bye to Mr. Mac. I'll never forget that wonderful man. He sure is an idealistic teacher."[3]

Mildred had a keen sense of fun and an easy laugh, but like many teenagers she worried a lot and felt insecure about her looks and capabilities. Although she was bright, earnest and hardworking, she criticized herself for not being expert in anything. She would never be conventionally pretty; she was too tall and her features were too strong, especially the famous Osterhout nose! But she was a striking young woman, with light brown hair, long legs and the grace of a natural athlete. She was very slim, but always fretted about her weight. She looked in the mirror, and scowled at a pimple on her chin. "I really must stop eating chocolate," she admonished herself in her diary.[4]

Mildred got good marks, taught Sunday school and outwardly behaved like a good preacher's daughter, but at this stage of her life she was mainly interested in boys and basketball. She was probably eighteen when she experienced her first kiss, which left her feeling quite disgusted. However, she was still captivated by the fantasy of romantic love — and where better expressed than on the silver screen?

"Eleanor and I saw Douglas Fairbanks in 'Headin' South.' Say, he's some high flyer. He made me feel so good I had to turn a somersault on the way home, while Eleanor in amazement held my hat."[5]

However, someone whose live performance made a more serious impression was Nellie McClung. A crusading teacher and feminist, she spoke at the Normal School in an appeal for young teachers to come and work in Alberta.

"Shall I go? Gee, just watch me if I get the chance," Mildred wrote. "Hats off to Mrs. Mc. She's somebody!"

A few of her girlfriends did go to Alberta and, as she bid them a tearful farewell, Mildred yearned to join them. She was angry with her father for refusing her permission, even though in her heart she knew he was right, that she ought to stay home with her mother. Still, it hurt that he was treating her like such a child, and she felt left out of all the fun her friends would be sure to have.

"I wonder if we'll ever get to Alberta," she sighed. "I sure want to go but hate to leave mother. She's been so sick again, poor dear, but I think she is on the home track now OK. Imagine Father saying that I'd cry my eyes out if I went to Alberta. I won't spill a single tear just for spite."[6]

As it turned out, Mildred's first teaching post was on Denman Island, one of the shaggy, evergreen islands between Victoria and the B.C. mainland. On the morning of September 4, 1918, she rang the bell outside the one-room school house and welcomed her first class — nine children at five different grade levels.

"Say, it is some stunt," she wrote. "Talk about hard work! It sure keeps you going … Have some of the craziest kids at school. Leo lisps and says plethant for present. Gilbert looks cross-eyed but never ventures a word."[7]

On the second day of classes, local parents began trying to impress upon Mildred "the necessity of a liberal use of the strap." Parents and most teachers of the day devoutly believed that to spare the rod was to spoil the child. But even after the Denman Island trustees admonished her for poor classroom management, Mildred stuck to Mr. Mac's advice and remained reluctant to use corporal punishment. This is not to say that she completed her teaching career without ever resorting to the strap — decades later she lashed out in one horrible incident that would haunt her for years — but certainly she did try to resist the prevalent policy of firm discipline enforced through frequent verbal and physical punishments.

One fall day Mildred was awaiting a visit from the school inspector, when she heard heavy footsteps outside the school house. She shushed the children, patted down her hair and opened the door, smiling nervously. Instead of the inspector, however, she found a large angry ram which charged into the classroom. Everyone shrieked! The children clambered over desks and tumbled out the windows. Mildred seized a broom and shooed the ram out the door, but he came back the next day, and the next. "It's some ram," she concluded.[8]

Portrait of Mildred, 1918.

Outside of school hours, Mildred often went to parties and on picnics, and was treated to ice cream or chocolates by some of the island's young blades. At eighteen, an age considered ripe for marriage, Mildred described herself as "an angelic old maid." She indulged in harmless flirting, but nothing more — at least, not until the new preacher arrived. Within a few Sundays, Mildred found herself intrigued by Reverend Jack Gibson because he related the Bible's teachings to current social problems.

At this time several international issues were felt uncomfortably close to home. All of Mildred's letters from the family were full of news of the Spanish influenza, transmitted by veterans returning home from the trenches. Worldwide, twenty-one million people died in the flu epidemic of 1918-19, among them about fifty thousand Canadians. In B.C., churches, schools and theatres were shut down in an effort to prevent the spread of the disease. Many of Mildred's friends and relatives were stricken, and she worried that her mother would also succumb. In November, the Denman Island trustees became so alarmed they decided to close the school. Mildred packed up in a rush and went home to Victoria, arriving just in time to mark the end of the war.

On the eleventh hour, of the eleventh day, of the eleventh month, the guns finally fell silent and jubilant crowds across Europe and North America streamed into the streets. "Peace celebration was fine," Mildred wrote. "Eleanor & I went downtown together and had a wild time in the crowd." However, while she sang and rejoiced that peace had returned, she still didn't understand the causes of the war and had no concept of the enormous toll it had taken.

Mildred returned to Denman Island and, on January 2, wished herself happy birthday: "19th to-day. Isn't it awful? Oh well, I suppose we must grow up," she told her diary. "The preacher called on me when I was out (worse luck) but he is coming again. Good night no. 19 & be a good girl forever." Being "a good girl forever" soon became rather more complicated than Mildred had expected.

At the start of the new term a new teacher, Miss Graham, arrived. She turned out to be lively and energetic, and played piano wonderfully well. "Miss G." and "Miss O." soon became fast friends. They decided to learn to drive, but had frequent engine trouble and quite a few close calls requiring assistance from young men. They soon earned themselves the disapproval of some islanders by careening all over the place in automobiles and staying out until dawn. A couple of the girls in their crowd even smoked cigarettes, but not Mildred. She didn't dance (although she wanted to) but she did play pool and billiards. "Some preacher's daughter!" she thought, ever-conscious of maintaining her own reputation and her father's as well.

Still, in some matters Mildred refused to be bound by convention. For example, she used to remove her long skirts and play basketball in her bloomers. What was worse, she played to win. "I can't help congratulating myself," she confided to her diary. "I made 10 baskets in 1 game. I checked Irvine 1st game & Miss Hood looked on in bloody silence. My life isn't worth a peanut."

Throughout the spring, folks also began to take note of the growing attraction between Miss Osterhout and Mr. Gibson who taught Sunday school together. He regularly went to her place for supper after church, sometimes meeting her after school and walking her home. He even said publicly that she'd make a fine preacher's wife. Far from fine, Mildred felt agitated, out of control, full of desires that shamed and repelled her. She was worried about her soul. Sundays didn't feel right anymore, they were so charged with nuance and repressed sexuality.

"4:00 a.m. Disgusting," she wrote. "Went to the concert & stayed to the dance. Mr. G. & I sat & looked on. He wore my ring all evening. Home was never like this ... Feel wicked still."[9]

When Jack finally declared his feelings, she panicked.

"April 2. He loves me!!!! Oh Jack how could you? What will I do? ... He broke the awful news & I (influenced by the moon) half gave in. Oh dear, it's the limit. I really don't love him & perhaps never can. He made me promise to try."

Mr. Gibson's impetuous behaviour around the young school mistress sparked quite a lot of talk — even talk of dismissing him. Mildred was marking exam papers when one of the local fellows "came in radiant with the news that Mr. Gibson is fired." Mildred was incredulous. She couldn't believe they had actually done it. "Hang, hang, hang them all!!!" When she heard all the unkind gossip that had been circulating, she blushed hot scarlet with anger and embarrassment. The moment Easter holidays came, Mildred fled the island. "Oh joy! Just think HOME tomorrow."

Back in Victoria, though, nothing was the same. Vic met her with the solemn news that Father had gone on the train to bring Mother home because she was so ill she couldn't travel alone. Three months earlier, in the hope that some fine weather would help her get "a little more blood tonic," Hattie had gone to visit her father and sister, Grace, in southern California. While there, she suffered a terrible "attack," which Aunt Grace described in frightening detail. Mother, on the other hand, tried to reassure the family.

> My Dear Ones …
> I am not worrying, so don't you about the travelling. I have been in God's keeping all my life, except when I went away from Him, and am just resting in His care from day to day.[10]

Mildred tried to take consolation from her mother's firm faith, but she missed her and needed her counsel. With a heavy heart, she returned to Denman resolved to break up with Jack, who, it appeared, was truly smitten.

> Poor Jack … It's really too bad you love me but I can't help it & I don't love you. Surely you can get over it though. We went down Pickles road for a walk and there I made my feelings (or lack of them) quite plain. Jack really has it bad & I'm sorry but that's all. I guess I am rather mean. I told him I could dance at his wedding tomorrow. He groaned. He says he can't forget. It's too bad, Jack.[11]

It was a signal of her independent nature that at the perfectly marriageable age of nineteen, Mildred decided not to marry a very nice young minister like "dear old Dad." She chose not to follow her mother into the role of a preacher's wife and, instead, began educating herself for a larger role in life.

Mildred and friend Laura Cashore in Benton, Alberta, Summer 1920.

Chapter Three: 1919

COMING OF AGE

With "the war to end all wars" finally over, Canadians struggled to cope with their losses: 59,544 dead and another 172,950 wounded. The thousands of returning servicemen received an enthusiastic heroes' welcome, but immediately were confronted with a new enemy: unemployment. Post-war recession hit hard. The loss of military and industrial jobs put thousands of workers onto the streets. Rum-running became a lucrative business after the U.S. declared prohibition, but times were tough for those who just wanted to make an honest buck. The pain of widespread joblessness was compounded by rampant inflation and a nation-wide shortage of affordable housing.

Because they had so little hope of finding work, many young soldiers took advantage of veterans' assistance to attend university. "We owe much of our initiative and progressiveness to the large number of returned men," Mildred's classmates wrote in the 1920 Alumni Annual. "Some of the vim and vigor of the warrior's life they have infused into our favoured class, until we are ripe for deeds of derring-do."

Mildred was able to attend university largely due to her father's belief — not universally held at the time — that daughters deserved to be educated just as much as sons. Father gave over his study to her and paid her fees. In fact, access to post-secondary education was remarkably open. When she entered the University of British Columbia in the fall of 1919, there was no tuition per se, only fees such as registration and Alma Mater Society that totalled $20 for the year.

Mildred's class was the university's largest ever, and UBC was ill-equipped to meet their needs. Faculty and students struggled to teach and learn in woefully decrepit old army huts known as the Fairview Shacks, located near the Vancouver General Hospital at Oak and 12th Avenue. Lectures were held in the shacks, but also in tents, a church basement, attics and nearby homes. Roofs leaked and rats inhabited some classrooms. In the overflowing auditorium, students sometimes even sat up in the rafters.[1]

By 1922, UBC students began agitating in earnest for government to build the university at Point Grey, where construction had begun but been halted by the war. "All aboard for the varsity crusade," cried the campus paper. The students launched a petition and got more than 56,000 British Columbians to sign it.[2] They then staged the famous protest march now known as the Great Trek. About 1,000 students, including Mildred, marched across town carrying placards that read "Point Grey Or Bust!" They had to hike over a horse trail to the site of the future campus. Soon afterwards, Premier John Oliver announced $1.5 million was to be given for construction to begin. It was "the best news since the armistice," the campus newspaper declared.[3] Mildred always remained an active UBC alumnus, and was quietly proud of the small part she played in founding the university.

After the weird and wonderful initiation rites for freshmen, Mildred met a group of new friends and was elected to the class executive as vice-president of women. She was officially enrolled in the Faculty of Arts, but she also took the requisite science courses to keep her options open for medical school because she still dreamed of serving overseas as a missionary doctor. She commuted by train and streetcar from New Westminster, where Reverend Osterhout had been transferred to serve in the pulpit of Jubilee Methodist Church.

In 1920, the Osterhouts acquired their first family car, the same year B.C. drivers changed from the left-hand rule of road to the right. Radios and telephones came into common usage, as did all kinds of electrical appliances that promised housewives new freedom. Even respectable women bobbed their hair and wore skirts that showed their knees. It was the Jazz Age, when young couples danced the Charleston and the fox trot. As always, the new music and dancing provoked cries of outrage from the pious. Mildred yearned to dance, but hesitated to do so against her father's wishes. Watching her friends on the dance floor, she questioned whether such good fun could really be sinful in the eyes of God. Finally, she told her mother that she intended to give it a try. "You'll break your father's heart if you do," was the reply.

After her first year at UBC Mildred wanted a respite from her parents' overly-protective concern, so she leapt at the chance to teach in Benton, Alberta. She would have nine grades in a one-room school, and be paid $120 for the summer. She arrived full of excitement and almost immediately "fell in love" with her roommate, Laura Cashore. The two young women developed a passionate, and sometimes possessive, friendship. They slept in the same bed, shared silly worries about their weight and complexions, told one another all their romantic secrets. They were both fun-loving and flirtatious and, if the truth be told, more than a little too daring behind the wheel of a car. They went to the country fairs and swooned over the barnstormers who looped-the-loop and barrel-rolled across the huge prairie sky. "Oh, for an aviator!" Mildred sighed.

At this stage her life resembled nothing so much as a romantic comedy, and she was having a wonderful time playing the lead role. She even experimented with make-up and costume. One day she wore her petticoat for a skirt, but was disappointed when no one noticed the difference. According to the breathless confessions in her diary, Mildred and Laura had many beaux.

> Slim ... made various attempts to get me to go to dances, picture shows, etc ... but then I was with Floyd. He is so divinely tall! I adore his height ... [Later] I piked off with Allan for a ride. Fluttering heart be still! but how can you? — Floyd is so tall and stunning! Laura landed something rather cute that night too.[4]

Soon enough, Allan Denton won out over handsome Floyd and the others because he was "a ripping good sport & not least he's so beautifully unsentimental."[5] Allan and Mildred had a playful relationship. He dunked her in the water barrel; she took off with his car. Because Allan drove his own car, he and Mildred often ended up sitting in the front seat making conversation while the couple in the back seat was free to kiss unobserved. It's possible that this arrangement suited Mildred just fine, although she admitted that she and Allan sometimes "spooned on the hill."

Once again people began to ask Mildred about wedding bells, but she never seriously considered the idea of marrying and settling down in Benton, a town she called "a hole." Instead, with great mock solemnity, she bet Laura that she would be the last to marry. She signed with a "trembling pen, Mildred Osterhout (forever thus).[6] At summer's end Mildred was less sorry to leave Allan than Laura.

In the end, though, he got the last laugh. For her twenty-first birthday Allan sent a diary and an enlarged photograph of Mildred in her dressing gown. "Horrors! It's a shocker!" she wrote. One can imagine Mildred's frantic efforts to hide the scandalous picture from her father. Perhaps she wasn't able to, because they quarrelled that evening. She didn't record the reason for their argument in her diary, but she closed with this postscript: "P.S. Just one thing more. Self-pity is weakness! Don't forget."[7]

All summer long, underneath the laughter and gaiety, Mildred had been fretting about her mother, almost afraid to commit her fears to paper. "I'm so worried about my dear mother. I can't think of anything to write. She was sick again & oh my I can't help worrying to-night some way but I do hope she is better. It's awful!"[8]

In fact, her beloved mother's condition was deteriorating and the X-ray treatments seemed to be no help. She was suffering from cancer, but Mildred did not name the illness in her diary. It is possible that her parents didn't reveal the frightening diagnosis. Perhaps she blocked it out, blinding herself to the obvious ravages of the disease. Hattie Osterhout suffered terribly before she died in the summer of 1921. From Mildred's diary:

> Aug. 11 — Mother taken to hospital.
> Aug 12 Operated on, 26 adhesions.
> Aug 17 Wed — Gone
>   20 — The funeral
>   Oh ——————————
> He knows & loves & cares
> Nothing this truth can dim
> He gives his very best to those
> Who leave the choice to him.

These were the last words Mildred wrote in her diary for many months. Like her father, who had mourned alone for baby Grace, she held her pain inside. Incapable of expressing her grief in her own words, she copied out the little poem of affirmation and acceptance. The simple verse reflects a naive, child-like faith, but Mildred could remain a child no longer. A whole host of adult responsibilities were suddenly thrust upon her, and she shouldered her burden as the woman of the family.

In those days, the politics of housework were simple: men took for granted that women did it all. So, on top of her studies, Mildred did the cleaning, shopping, cooking, baking, washing, mending, gardening, laundry and all the many other small tasks that go into making a home. She served as companion to her father, and hostess when he had visitors. She also was responsible for her brother, Victor, who was attending UBC but "having trouble applying himself." Vic was an intelligent, handsome young man who loved his sister dearly, but he was no help whatsoever on the home front — not that Mildred expected him to be. With two men to cater to, she became even more reluctant to marry and add a third man to those already under her wing.[9]

Her mother's death and her own independent nature effectively cast Mildred in the role of merry spinster. Vic would later marry and Aunt Mildred would dote upon his three children, perhaps all the more so because she would never have children of her own. By remaining single and childless, she was free to work and to explore the world in a way that few women of her generation could, but she was still tied to the domestic sphere and there was always Father waiting at home. On the first anniversary of her mother's death, Mildred wrote: "It was the longest, hardest day of my life, but it brought relief to terrible suffering & I

Mildred and Dr. Henry Burton Sharman at SCM camp, B.C., early 1920s.

won't complain." Apparently she never did. Instead, she returned to UBC carrying a double load, but determined to do so with a cheerful heart.

The following summer, Mildred accompanied her father on a sentimental journey to Manitoba, to the towns where he had ministered and where people remembered Hattie fondly. They laid flowers on little Grace's grave, and Mildred longed for the big sister she had never known. After two weeks of train travel, father and daughter arrived in his home town of Frankford, Ontario. The trip strengthened Mildred's family connections, and it helped her to grow out of her teenage self-centredness. One day she chatted for a couple of hours to "an interesting feller" on the train who provoked some soul-searching. "He thinks I'm terribly narrow and prejudiced, I know. I wonder if I am. I'll have to give myself a housecleaning I guess," she wrote.[10]

In this reflective frame of mind, Mildred arrived at Elgin House on Lake Muskoka for a week-long seminar offered by the Student Christian Movement. The SCM was founded in 1920, partly in reaction to the conservatism of the Young Mens' and Young Womens' Christian Associations.[11] The founders, including many war veterans, shared a deep commitment to the social gospel. They believed that the Bible called them to put their faith into action on behalf of the poor and meek. For them, the message of the Sermon on the Mount was that socialism and Christianity were inextricable. In a time when the various denominations of the Christian church maintained strict separation, the SCM was ecumenical in spirit and in action. As the vanguard of a new modernism, SCM members were labelled troublemakers by the institutional church, but were tolerated because they were young and it was thought they would one day outgrow their radical notions. Perhaps some did, but not Mildred.

On the contrary, the SCM spurred Mildred to take the first crucial steps on her path to intellectual and spiritual liberation. It also freed her from her father's profoundly conventional faith. For example, because she grew up with a literalist approach to scripture, Mildred believed that Eve actually was created from Adam's rib. When fellow SCM members suggested that such stories could be interpreted symbolically rather than as fact, she went home and very carefully counted her own ribs.[12]

At Elgin House, Mildred participated in a Bible study group led by Dr. Salem Bland of Wesley College in Winnipeg, one of the great Methodist leaders of the time. However, it was the extraordinary teaching of Dr. Henry Burton Sharman that had a lasting impact. Sharman was the first chairman of the SCM and his *Synoptic Gospels* were used for decades in study programs across Canada. His method was simple. He presented the life of Christ as told by Matthew, Mark, Luke and John in columns down the page, so that students could easily compare and analyze the different gospel stories. While he occasionally contributed out of his vast knowledge of Biblical languages and literature, Sharman typically withheld his own views because he believed it was the duty and right of students to discover Jesus for themselves. For thousands who participated in his seminars, Christ emerged as a real man, one whose life and teachings had new relevance for the 20th Century.[13]

For Mildred, the week at Elgin House was "a stirring up time … It makes me feel so small & inadequate yet fills me with the thought that I must get busy think & live & work. It was great to meet so many fine girls & men all filled with Christian aims & trying to find the way."[14] Sixty-five years later, Mildred still believed that "of all the insights into the way of Truth and Love, Dr. Sharman's incisive questioning was the most challenging."[15]

Back at UBC for her fourth year, Mildred served as vice-president of the Women's Section of the SCM. Victor also joined the movement, and it became central to their social as well as their religious lives. They hosted discussion groups in their home and Vic met his future wife, Connie Smith, at an SCM conference. The UBC chapter met regularly on campus and for retreats at Horseshoe Bay, Deep Cove and Copper Cove near Vancouver.[16]

An avid swimmer and hiker, Mildred thrived at camp. Once, on one of their many walks in the woods, the campers came across a hummingbird's nest full of tiny chicks cheeping in the dappled light. They stood back, breathless at the wonder of Creation. In these moments Mildred saw God in everything — a nestling, a flower, a mountain. She also loved camp because some of the best discussions took place there, sitting around the campfire or watching the waves. Their debates were earnest and animated, charged with each young person's faith, fired by their experience of war. Like many in the movement, Mildred was as deeply affected by the intellectual challenge of the SCM as by any of her university courses.[17]

As her spiritual life broadened, her political awareness grew as well, inspired by the example of J.S. Woodsworth. After he was dismissed from the church for his radical pacifism, Woodsworth essentially became an outcast from "respectable" society. However, he soon emerged as a leading advocate for the unemployed and the union man alike. In the summer of 1919, he arrived in Winnipeg a few weeks after the start of the famous General Strike. It began as a dispute over collective bargaining in a few machine shops, but the strike soon spread throughout the labour movement until it became "a trial of strength between the workers and the owning classes of Winnipeg."[18]

As the weeks passed, hysterical claims that the workers aimed to Bolshevize the country caused tensions to escalate and violent clashes erupted. Woodsworth addressed mass meetings and wrote for the strike bulletin, urging a negotiated settlement. The government finally broke the strike by ordering the arrest of Woodsworth and other labour leaders, and charging them with seditious conspiracy. Among the allegedly seditious writings were two quotations from The Bible.

Mildred applauded Woodsworth's courage and rejoiced when he was elected to Parliament for the first of many times in Winnipeg North Central. In the same election of 1921, Agnes Macphail became the first female Member of Parliament. It was a landmark for Canadian women, who still would not legally be "persons" under the constitution until the end of the decade.

Mildred's other significant mentor at this time was Dr. Theodore Boggs, economist and faculty advisor to the SCM. His course on "Capitalism, Socialism and Communism" gave Mildred her first opportunity to study these concepts. Back in Benton, she had been to a lecture by the British suffragist Emmeline Pankhurst, who "gave a splendid address on the great need of unity to overcome the rising unrest & Bolshevist principles."[19] Six months later, she went to "a socialistic meeting" at UBC which "was quite different from the lecture I heard by Mrs. Pankhurst. She described things [in the Soviet Union] as deplorable but [the UBC lecturer] pictured Bolshevism as an almost perfect condition to live under."[20] Mildred had heard so much conflicting opinion that she entered Dr. Boggs's class full of questions and misconceptions. Fortunately, he was a courageous professor who encouraged his mostly middle class students to see for themselves, to go to the union halls, to listen to the workers and learn about the human cost of economic policy.

By 1920, nearly 10,000 Vancouverites were unemployed. Seeing the desperate hungry people in the bread lines moved Mildred's heart, while the dignity and passion of those on the picket lines stirred her too. She was especially drawn to the Industrial Workers of the World, the "Wobblies." Banned in 1918 under the War Measures Act, they went underground and kept on organizing, even under threat of violence and death. They called for the abolition of the wage system and the state itself. They believed in the general strike as the means to revolutionary social transformation, so for them the defeat in Winnipeg had been a terrible blow.[21] Mildred responded to the Wobblies because she, too, had a sense of mission.

"Oh, I remember the determination of those men," she recalled. "And we, of course, wanted to join them in bringing about a better system. Naturally, they were labelled Communist, as all of us were later on."[22]

While she began to dream of building the revolution, Mildred had more mundane tasks at hand, such as packing up the parsonage. After decades of service to the church, Reverend Osterhout was retiring. She was truly devoted to her father, but Mildred found that in retirement their roles gradually reversed and he grew increasingly dependent upon her, as he had been upon her mother. The dual responsibilities at home and on campus began to weigh upon her.

> Now I'm halfway through my 4th and heaviest year. Oh, the Chemistry & Physics & I'm a senior with a gown but still feel like a know-nothing & life is the same mad rush. Will rushing ever cease? And I must go to bed to get ready to start it again to-morrow. Oh, to do it nobly & cheerfully![23]

Mildred graduated from UBC on May 10th, 1923 with her Bachelor of Arts in English and philosophy. Her photo in the Varsity annual shows a serious young woman with bobbed brown hair and a determined chin. The caption reads:

> Open my heart and you will see
> Graven inside of it, Chemistry.
> Mildred is so energetic that she can find time for animated discussions of S.C.M. debating and the Players' Club. Her sympathy, gaiety, and ready wit will long remain in our memory.

Claude Campbell, president of the class of Arts '23, remembered Mildred with warmth and respect. "I liked her. She was very level-headed," he recalled.[24] Perhaps it was her level-headedness that made her decide to give up her childhood dream of serving overseas as a missionary doctor. The course of study in medicine was too long, and she was realistic enough to know that the demands of home and hospital would be too heavy.

In the fall of 1923, Mildred enrolled in the Master's program in the department of philosophy. Bent over her books at her father's desk, Mildred explored some of the questions of personality development. "Habit as a Factor

UBC graduation, 1923.

in Conduct Control," was the topic of her thesis. The following spring she graduated with first class honours in two of her courses. The Dean of Women wrote an unsolicited letter of reference saying: "Miss Osterhout was a thoroughly 'all round' student ... I was impressed with her careful attention to details, her ability to work with other people, her unfailing good humour under testing circumstances, her resourcefulness and tact."[25]

Despite this and other glowing references as well as her M.A., at first Mildred could not get a teaching job in the Vancouver public school system. She did find work at the YMCA as "Industrial Secretary," a position that put her in charge of five clubs, the girls' lunch room and the Y's summer camp. The next year she moved to the position of Girls' Work Secretary at Canadian Memorial Church. Both these jobs reinforced Mildred's growing conviction that the Canadian economic system was fundamentally unfair. Seeing the plight of these unemployed girls and women on a daily basis caused Mildred to feel deeply discomfited by her own relative privilege.

They were by no means affluent, but the Osterhouts' economic situation was secure. They already owned a family car and, in 1925, Rev. Osterhout bought his first house. Father, daughter and son moved out of their last parsonage and into what would remain the family home for the next 70 years: a modest wood-frame structure at 4536 West 8th Avenue in Vancouver's Point Grey neighbourhood. The location was still relatively remote from the city centre, but it wasn't far from the beaches and the site where work was at last beginning on the new university.

In the fall, Mildred got a job at Langara Elementary School, on West 15th Avenue not far from home. It was a delightful teaching assignment because so many of the students came from well-educated families,

Vic Osterhout with motorcycle, circa late 1920s.

and there was an active and supportive Parent-Teacher Association. For the next five years, she taught the intermediate grades and supervised the school library. She kept a family of canaries in her classroom as well as a white rat, and she often took the children tramping through the woods or combing the local beaches during natural history class. She was a popular teacher because of her lively, friendly manner and gentle approach to discipline.[26]

"All the staff adored her," said Kathleen Barrett, who taught Kindergarten when Mildred taught Grade 7. "She was such a warm, loving person" — the sort of person who would open her home to a colleague who had no family and nowhere to celebrate her wedding. "The teacher and her fellow got married in the Osterhout's front room, and Mildred's dad performed the ceremony." Unlike some, Kathleen never found Reverend Osterhout to be stern or forbidding. One day when he happened to walk past her kindergarten class, one of the little girls ran, all wide-eyed, to tell Mrs. Barrett that Jesus had come to school! "With his beard and his dignified manner, Mildred's dad did resemble the typical image of Christ," Kathleen said, chuckling to remember that child's sweet naiveté.[27]

As Mildred became more confident in the classroom, she grew increasingly frustrated with the authoritarian, impersonal structure of the school system. She wanted to incorporate counselling and social work into her teaching practise, and took a special interest in children whose behaviour hinted there was trouble at home. Sometimes, despite the formidable barriers of social reticence and convention, she won students' confidences. She was such an empathetic listener that her tact and skill in resolving conflicts became well known. Once the principal even asked her to mediate his discussions with a boy about to be expelled.[28]

Sometimes, though, Mildred found herself dealing with serious emotional disturbances for which she had no training. For example, she got to know a young woman who was struggling to cope with the sudden deaths of her father and sister. Her mother, who had previously suffered a nervous breakdown, could offer little help. The girl was deeply withdrawn, inarticulate, fearful and in despair. Mildred saw her almost every day for three years, offered her friendship and eventually helped her get started in a nursing career. Mildred recounted the case in her application for an international scholarship to Bryn Mawr, the elite women's college near Philadelphia.

> Because I understood and accepted her, she was able to make known to me what she was unable to express to anyone else. I consulted with a psychiatrist who approved my method, but I felt the need of a deeper understanding of the technique of dealing with such a delicate problem. My experience in this situation helped develop my interest in Psychiatry and I am determined to know more of it.[29]

In another part of the application, she described herself this way:

> I am of a fairly even temperament, tending to the phlegmatic type, but with a capacity for a great deal of activity and a lively participation in life. I am apt to be self-conscious before superiors and reticent about expressing myself before those of outstanding intellectual ability …

> I am so concerned about making right choices that I put off making a decision as long as possible. I am very sensitive to the opinion of others and perhaps too easily influenced by them … I find it difficult to accept my limitations and feel impatient when unable to achieve my ideals.

> I have some ability to make people feel at ease, can discern their difficulties and have faith in their ability to overcome them. I am quite reliable and conscientious and enjoy giving time to other people in a constructive way.[30]

Bryn Mawr granted Mildred the scholarship as an International Fellow for the academic year 1930-31, a year which prepared her for the most transformative experiences of her life. In the eloquent study, *Writing a Woman's Life*, Carolyn G. Heilbrun notes that in the lives of exceptional men and women "there is a time when the individual appears, before the age of thirty, to be getting nowhere, accomplishing none of his aims, or altogether unclear as to what those aims might be. That person is, of course, actually preparing for the task that, all unrecognized, awaits."[31] Clearly Mildred was approaching the end of what Professor Heilbrun calls the "moratorium," the crucial period of preparation for one's life work. What was the great task awaiting her? Nothing less than peace on earth.

Chapter Four: 1930

HEARING THE CALL

Considered one of the finest women's colleges in the United States, the stately campus of Bryn Mawr is set in rolling countryside northwest of Philadelphia. From the start, Mildred was grateful for the opportunity to study there, but ill at ease with the privilege it conveyed. She was assigned to Radnor Hall, an ivy-covered graduate residence with "60 students, 9 maids and 2 menservants under its roof."

"I feel so cramped and confined, hedged in by traditions and customs and paralyzed," she wrote. "Here we sit in stiff chairs and are waited on by coloured maids who also make our beds. I feel a million miles from home or a homey feeling. Damn!"[1]

On the other hand, at Pendle Hill, the new Quaker college nearby, she found "the most gorgeous friendly free atmosphere." Her first experience of a Friends' meeting was "a real joy." Her mentor, Dr. Sharman, was there with others that Mildred instantly warmed to and respected. Her heart and soul told her she belonged at Pendle Hill, but her head insisted on Bryn Mawr, especially after she discovered her fellowship would be wasted if she reneged.

"And now as I stay I determine to put my life and energy into the work & associations here. A sense of calm has come over me and I feel that with the presence of God in my heart, life will be rich anywhere."[2]

She enrolled in the department of Social Economy and Social Research. Her courses in Social Change, Social Case Work and Statistics were all taught by female professors. In a time when few women went to university, let alone graduate school, they were blazing trails in their chosen fields. Intellectually, Mildred found the work to be highly challenging, and her classmates to be bright and hard-working.

Among the international students, Mildred found a life-long friend in Riek Lieseveld from the Netherlands and Grace Rhoads from New Jersey. She loved and admired them both: Grace because she was honest and independent, and Riek for her "faith in the Infinite with a ready ridicule for the superficial." Together they discovered the museums, theatres, shops and restaurants — first in Philadelphia and later New York. They marvelled at such urban wonders as rapid transit, the Empire State building and fast-food cafeterias. She wrote to the family:

> I've just had a hasty lunch in an Automat. When you drop in your nickel and press the button, the door pops open and you take your bun, or pie, or if you are a well brought up girl like me, your salad, then you knock someone off a chair and sit down and eat it hurriedly so you won't be deafened by the noise.[3]

Mildred's friend, identified only as Bessie, and an unidentified male friend at left. Mildred with Reginald Singh on the right. Bryn Mawr, Philadelphia, 1931.

Group travelling photo, circa 1930. Mildred is in the centre of the frame.

Perhaps because she lived in a community of women Mildred felt physically free and uninhibited at Bryn Mawr. With the wind in her hair she strode around the campus in a storm reciting Romantic poetry at the top of her voice. She warned her father that she planned to take "natural dance" with a friend. "We run around the campus in the early mornings or late night and pretend we are little leaves or a flower's dream or some such," she wrote. "It's great having a lovely big campus with grassy lawns and huge shade trees that give you a sense of protection and apartness from the big noisy city."[4]

Bryn Mawr was truly a world apart. The students dressed up for dinner, and some were active socialites with as many as a dozen ball gowns in their closets. If they returned to campus after dark, they were greeted by the "lantern man," an avuncular Scot whose job it was to escort the young ladies back to their residences. Some of the enormous estates that graced the surrounding country-side belonged to alumnae, generous ladies who often invited the international students to teas and parties. Mildred had never imagined such abundant delicacies, elegant clothing and jewelry, sumptuous furnishings, superb artwork, burbling fountains, fields of irises and peonies, fragrant woodlands alive with firefly light. It was both enchanting and disgusting.

> I went with some international students to supper in the grandest house to-night that I have ever been in ... Everything was luxurious and the supper they served was better than most wedding feasts ... Needless to add I came home more of a socialist than ever. Why is it possible for one family to have so much luxury heaped around them when at least 120,000

in Philadelphia are dependent on charity and barely getting enough to exist? When I go to do my case work tomorrow I'll find homes where they have nothing to eat or perhaps tea & bread only.[5]

Mildred volunteered one and a half days a week in Kensington, a poor neighbourhood of Philadelphia. She was supposed to do "personality adjustment work from a psychiatric approach," but sheer survival issues were more important to her clients as winter approached. "I feel when I'm down there that no one has a job," she wrote home.[6] Mildred had a keen eye and a compassionate heart, and her correspondence painted an evocative picture of the street life in Kensington:

Dust, filth, garbage in the streets. Dirty, unshaven dejected unemployed slouching on the stoop. Fat, lurid proprietors filling up dark doorways. Thin, careworn women with drooping shoulders arguing by the open front markets. Ragged children with armloads of pretzels crying their wares. Lean black cats slinking out to search the garbage."[7]

Pickets patrol the doorways of industry with strikers' badges on their arms, some with vigorous rebellion, others with bitter antagonism and some with resigned depression on their faces ... [A man] grabbed a pack of potatoes off a vegetable cart and ran down the street followed by a policeman who went in to find a hungry family stewing kittens."[8]

The whole picture forms such a contrast with that of the wealthy district in which I am spending the rest of my time that I am in a continual state of irritation regarding the mal-distribution of bread and butter and cake. The strain is increased because of one's helplessness and inability to do anything about the condition.[9]

Early in the New Year, though, Mildred met a woman whose work in the slums of London held out great hope for the people of Kensington and poor communities everywhere. She came to speak at Pendle Hill and afterwards asked Mildred the most important question of her life. She was the British pacifist and social worker, Muriel Lester.

Muriel had grown up in London in a devoutly Christian and exceedingly wealthy family. The Lester children went to the best schools and vacationed on the Riviera, but did not share their parents' class consciousness. At nineteen, a rebellious Muriel went to a party in "the famous East End of London ... the disreputable haunt of thieves, drunks and hooligans."[10] Far from looking down on East Enders, Muriel felt at home with them. She was drawn back again and again to her new friends, until she could no longer bear the contradictions between her life of leisure and theirs of struggle.

Unlike most young ladies of her class, Muriel saw all people — rich and poor — as children of God, equal in His sight. Her sister, Doris, and brother, Kingsley, shared that belief. They had such a strong will to live their faith, both in word and deed, that they moved into a slum district called Bow. There they embraced voluntary poverty and began building the community. Muriel and Doris grieved deeply when young Kingsley died soon afterwards, at the age of twenty-six. In his will, he left all his money to his sisters to use for the benefit of the people of Bow. With additional financial help from their father, they bought an old Baptist chapel and named it Kingsley Hall in memory of their beloved brother. It became the centre of a network of neighbourhood services including a nursery school and childcare, youth and seniors' groups, Bible study and worship hall. Muriel wrote:

> Day and night my mind was set on this job of getting a little community in East London to function as servants and lovers of their neighbours, co-operating with God by restoring their birthright to His dispossessed children, the birthright of music, art, poetry, drama, camps, open-air life, self-confidence, the honour of building up anew social order, the Kingdom of Heaven, here and now in Bow.[11]

Muriel's practise of voluntary poverty — which she contrasted to the "compulsory want" suffered by the masses — offered a compelling model to Mildred, who felt so deeply ambivalent about living in luxury and working amidst desperate need. And whereas Mildred felt she had nothing to offer the poor in Kensington, the work Muriel was doing in Bow seemed to empower people to help themselves and, in doing so, to change their lives. Muriel spoke the language of the social gospel, and she was a persuasive speaker. Muriel must have sensed Mildred's keen interest because, before she left Pendle Hill, she looked Mildred straight in the eye and asked: "Why don't you come to Kingsley Hall and help us? We've never had a Canadian volunteer before." She explained that ten international volunteers came each year. They were not paid, except for pocket money, but they received room and board at Kingsley Hall. Everyone shared in the work of running the hall and offering service in the community.

"I am interested in it because it is both idealistic and practical," Mildred wrote to her father: "They try to put the ideals of Jesus into real living with & for the people & it seems to me that is a better way than doing a superficial job from the outside."[12]

In later years, Mildred often commented that saying "yes" to Muriel Lester was the most important decision she ever made. With characteristic indecision, though, she took months to make up her mind. Her letters home throughout the first half of 1931 were full of procrastination and apologies. She was hampered in her decision-making by her devotion to her father, and her feelings of guilt at having left him alone for a year. Although she relished her independence, she also missed him deeply. Once she woke in the middle of the night, imagining that she had heard his voice. She later wrote, asking if he had been thinking about her that particular night. She wished she could talk things over with him — especially since her love life had taken such an interesting turn. One afternoon over tea at the International Club, Mildred had met a romantic Anglo-Indian named Reginald Singh. He was instantly attracted to her and began calling daily and sending chocolates and flowers. She didn't return his ardour, but she was certainly surprised and pleased by all the attention. She confided in her diary:

> Roses! Carnations! Gladiola! Trimmings! Reginald, how could you? I am overcome! After just meeting you! Flattered of course! Thanks a lot, but really you shouldn't! I wonder about the weekend. Not too fast … It's rather fun though, being rushed after 30.[13]

Reginald also wrote her ardent letters and poems, including a saccharine "Sonnet to Osterhout," which he signed "Consuming love, R.A. Singh." His emotional exuberance was quite overwhelming to Mildred, who was undemonstrative by nature and by training. It's worth noting that Mildred wrote quite openly to her father about Reginald, even though she knew he wouldn't approve of her dating an Indian man.

Mildred, however, delighted in crossing the cultural barriers imposed by her upbringing. She had had so little contact outside White Anglo-Saxon Protestant culture, she was ignorant of any other religious traditions. Reginald, however, moved in much more diverse circles than she had encountered, and he provided an exciting glimpse not only of Indian culture, but of an intercultural community. Reginald introduced her to some of his Jewish friends who welcomed her into their home and taught her a little about the custom of keeping kosher. Except for two former students, Mildred didn't know any Jewish people. She was fascinated to meet a young dentist and his wife, who gave her "quite an insight into the feeling of suppression that the Jewish people have, and the discrimination that is still shown, even here where they have become well established, and have been [living] for so long."[14]

Mildred's cultural horizons broadened even further after her final exams, when she moved off the campus of Bryn Mawr and into the inner city of Philadelphia. She lived in the Music Settlement House, an inner-city centre where leading musicians offered free music lessons. She found it "quite exciting" living in "the foreign district where there are all kinds of black, yellow and white people." Although she bore nothing but goodwill towards people of colour, she still used freely a type of language that offends modern sensibilities, language that reflects the depth and pervasiveness of racism in her society. For example, she used the term "Jew" as a noun meaning cheapskate, and as a verb meaning to cheat someone. She called the local Chinese restaurant "the Chink's," and sometimes called black people "niggers" although she typically used the term "coloured." One day out of curiosity she took a walk through the black district of Philadelphia, an area which she and everyone else called "Niggertown." She regarded the people as though they were fundamentally different, yet her attitude was open and friendly.

> I'm immensely interested in all the varieties of size and colour one sees amongst them as well as the size of their lips, the gaiety of their clothes and the 'debonair' manner of some of them. One young swain flashed me the glad eye and kept turning back to see the effect as he walked down the street. Needless to say I was all of a flutter — my widowhood at Bryn Mawr cutting me off from such contacts.[16]

While Mildred was thrilled by the notion of an inter-racial relationship, she hastened to assure her father that she had no intention of becoming Mrs. Singh. "Don't be alarmed," she wrote, "I am beyond the susceptible stage." She had turned down previous offers of marriage, and Mildred knew she would turn this one down too. She left Reginald not because of his colour, but because she was much too independent to allow a crush to alter her life course. She enjoyed her time with him and thought he was a dear, "but rather youngish, and a bit sentimental."[17] Inevitably, parting was more difficult for Reginald than for Mildred.

"Darling," he wrote. "It is really very hard to be without you — if you would only say yes — However I shall always be waiting ... By Jove, I'd give a thousand to see you and clasp your hands in mine again ... "[18]

Two weeks before she was due to sail for London, Mildred was elated to be reunited with her father in New York. Together they went back to the Osterhout family homestead in Frankford, Ontario, where they enjoyed a great visit with their many relatives. When it was time to say goodbye, it was Mildred's turn to feel like weeping.

"What a grey world when the train pulled west with Father! It's easy enough to orate about the firm chin & stiff upper lip *but* it's harder to fix them on the face," she confided to her diary.[19]

Mildred and Camille Soloman on the roof of Kingsley Hall, Autumn 1931. Gandhi's cell is in the background.

Chapter Five: 1931

A HERO(INE) EMERGES

On a golden day in August 1931, Mildred stood at the rail of the SS *Duchess of York* with the breeze in her face and "that glorious free feeling" in her heart. Bound for London's industrial slums, she intended to have a wonderful time en route. Almost immediately, an exciting prospect for ship-board romance presented himself.

"The first male attendant works fast — sentimental songs in the moonlight, cabin visitings, petting advances, good technique," she confided to her diary.[1] A bout of seasickness briefly dampened the flirtation, but not Mildred's poetic sensibilities. "A poem brought my nice German boy to comfort me in my distress. Rather a pet." She soon found her sea legs, and spent the rest of the voyage indulging in late-night rendezvous: "There's that man tapping again. Ought to have something to play with a man like that."[2] Of course she didn't yet know it, but within a fortnight Mildred was destined to meet another man who would spark in her an entirely different sort of feeling. His transparent love for everyone would touch her heart and soul, and his dynamic action in pursuit of truth and justice would always fire her political work. He set her life on a heroic, rather than romantic, course.

As she made the transition from ship to shore, Mildred tried to focus her mind on the task ahead: six months of mission work and social service in an East London community centre. She felt sheepish as the cabbie deposited her in front of Kingsley Hall. Really, she chided herself, how could anyone serious about serving the poor arrive with such an embarrassing amount of luggage? There was no time to worry about such things, however, because right away she was surrounded by a lot of people who all smiled and greeted her in a variety of British, American and European accents.

"Say, Mildred, can you cook?" asked one of the young men who helped haul in her bags. "Um, yes, a little," she confessed. A loud hurrah went up from the group. "She cooks! She cooks!" Before she could protest, they appointed her "big chef," handed over the kitchen keys, and led her off to the local markets. "It was rather fun but terribly confusing, and all that night 'tuppence, ha'pence, thrupence' etc. whirled around in my brain," she wrote back home.[3]

She would be cooking for a "family" of ten volunteers who came from all over Europe and North America to work with Muriel Lester at Kingsley Hall. A three-storey brick building with arched windows overlooking Powis Road, Kingsley Hall was a kind of "teetotal pub" where neighbours could drop in for a chat or to play cards, chess or billiards in an environment free of alcohol. It also boasted a large gym, a sanctuary and several meeting rooms. Other services included a nursery school and child care, programs for mothers and youth, Bible study and worship hall. Besides her duties in the kitchen, Mildred was assigned to work with the elderly in the community and in hospital.

She and the other resident volunteers were housed in simple brick "cells," as they called them, up on the roof of Kingsley Hall, which afforded them a marvelous view of the patched and leaky rooftops of Bow. Some of Mildred's Canadian friends in London told her she should get out of the East End and find herself some better-situated digs, but she had no intention of moving. Much to her surprise, she found she had moved into the centre of the most important news in the British Empire.

Mohandas K. Gandhi was coming to London for the Round Table Conference on Indian independence and he would be staying at Kingsley Hall, in one of the cells just adjacent to Mildred's. The British government had offered him posh lodgings near Parliament, but he declined in favour of the invitation to stay in Bow among the poor, his chosen people. Mildred happily rolled up her sleeves and got caught up in Muriel's whirlwind of preparations for the *Mahatma*, the Great Soul.

In 1926, Muriel had travelled to India on behalf of the International Fellowship of Reconciliation and spent almost a month at Gandhi's ashram, or community. She implored him to come to England, but he demurred saying there was nothing he could teach the English. She protested, urging him to come not so much for what he could teach the English, but for what he could learn from them! The Mahatma, astonished by her audacity, laughed heartily and agreed to come some day.

Mildred readily sympathized with Gandhi's cause but, like most people, she knew more about the peculiarities of his diet and dress than about his philosophy and politics. For example, at that time his vegetarianism was a curiosity, and some people insisted that he had sailed to England with his own goat — which he had milked himself! She wrote:

> Everybody talks Gandhi — when he will come, what he will eat. The pub men all asked if old Gandhi were there yet.

Kingsley Hall, London, 1931. Gandhi is seated in the centre of the second row, Mildred is on the right of the same row.

"If he was," said one, "I'd come & drink his goat's milk."[4]

The local boys liked to tease that Muriel and Mildred were keeping a goat (or even a flock of them) up on the roof of Kingsley Hall. In the kitchen, the Gandhi gags were flying. The British approved of the Mahatma's punctuality, but they were amused that he wore his famous dollar watch around his neck. One of the young women draped herself in towels and hung an alarm clock around her neck in imitation of his exotic garb.

The press came and went, snapping dozens of photographs of Bow, of Kingsley Hall, of the cell where Gandhi would sleep, of Muriel, of Mildred, of practically everyone. Mildred's picture appeared under the boldface headline: "Gandhi, Idol of Women." The article began by breathlessly questioning whether Mahatma Gandhi would exert the same influence upon women in England as he had in India.

[At age 62,] he is the very extreme antithesis of all that men ordinarily consider magnetic for the other sex ... a wisp of a brown man, a mere wraith. Yet, he is a magnet for the other sex. How does he do it? ...

He has seized the hearts of his brown sisters because he has made himself their bold, outspoken champion ...

And this same tug of the little brown magnet that is Gandhi has proved irresistible to white women too.[5]

Accompanying him to London, for example, was Miraben, formerly Miss Madeleine Slade. She scandalized London society by renouncing title and fortune, shaving her head, and becoming one of Gandhi's most devoted disciples. After the death of her father, Admiral Sir Edmond Slade, she became Gandhi's adopted daughter. The caption under Mildred's picture read: "Two American mission workers will serve Gandhi during his stay in London. They are Mildred Osterhout, who will prepare food for the little Indian leader, and Miss Camille A. Solomon, who will wait on the Mahatma." Evidently the British press felt it was perfectly all right for Indian women to adopt Gandhian ideals, but for English ladies to do so was quite improper. A white woman serving a brown man? The British colonial mind recoiled at the thought.

On the day he was to arrive, hundreds of people queued up for hours in the pouring rain, waiting for a glimpse of Gandhi. School children and grandmothers, reporters and cameramen, police and security officials, working men and women — everyone cheered loudly when the car finally pulled up. The Mahatma's party included his son, Devadas, two male secretaries and, of course, the ever-faithful Miraben. Mildred told the story to her father and Vic in a letter.

> I was in the dining room arranging the last grape when suddenly the door opened and there was the great little man. Muriel introduced me and I clasped my hands and bowed in good Indian fashion, having been taught the art the day before, and then they went upstairs, and we saw no more of Gandhi until about 10 p.m. when he came down to the hall and talked with various members of the Joy Nights club, picking up babies and smiling at all.
>
> Next a.m. I bravely arose at 4:15 to go to prayers *à la Indienne*. We sat on a rug while the Indians chanted and one of them read by candle light, but I am afraid I didn't get it all as I was a bit sleepy and I never did know my Sanskrit very well.[6]

After first prayers, Gandhi always took a pre-dawn walk. Mildred managed to struggle out of bed and join him about three times a week. The cobblestone streets were dark and quiet as they set out, usually about a dozen pilgrims following the white-clad figure. Always bringing up the rear were three detectives assigned by Scotland Yard. The security men had no need to worry, though. The British people, unlike their government, opened their hearts to Gandhi. It was one of the many paradoxes of his political career that his steadfast commitment to the powerless people was the very source of Gandhi's power.

His physical appearance — bald, skinny, gap-toothed and always smiling — endeared him to everyone in Bow, especially the mothers. Wherever he went in the neighbourhood, a crowd of children and admirers followed along. Although his clothing provided scant protection from the damp autumn chill, he refused all offers of overcoats or shoes. One day a saucy little boy cried out, "Hey Gandhi, where's your trousers?" He laughed heartily and made a joke that was soon cabled around the world: "Well, you wear your plus-fours and I wear my minus-fours."

The first Sunday of Gandhi's stay, he was scheduled to preach over the radio from Kingsley Hall to all of England and even as far as North America. Technicians bustled about for hours getting set up. However, by the time all the connections were established Gandhi was in the middle of supper. "The world can wait," he said, and went on eating his fruit. So Muriel filled the air time with a little preamble on Kingsley Hall while he finished. Finally the Mahatma sat on the floor in front of the microphone and arranged his homespun blankets about himself. Speaking in a low voice, he began by observing that prayer is common to all religions of the world.

> If we believe in God, it follows that we must pray to Him. I have said so often that prayer to the soul is what food is to the body and that, as a matter of fact, prayer is far more important to the soul than food is to the body, because we may at times go without food and the body may feel all the better for the fast.[7]

He also spoke of the "gnawing of the heart" and the sense of uneasiness he felt on days past when he believed that he had such important work to do that he could miss his prayer times. For Gandhi, daily prayer was essential. "What is prayer?" he asked. "Not a muttering of the lips or a muttering at all, it is really a longing from the heart."

Whatever her expectations, Mildred certainly wasn't swept away by Gandhi's words of wisdom; she called the sermon "a simple little talk." She was shy before the legendary Mahatma, but not in awe of the man. She could see that although millions called him *Bapu*, or Father, he did not really understand his youngest and most loyal son, Devadas.

"We all adore him [Devadas], but have resigned ourselves to the fact that he is nearly married," Mildred wrote. "He wears narrow homespun trousers and shirts and a good hefty overcoat, and even stepped out in a pair of gray European trousers the other day when we met him in town."[8] Mildred felt awful for him when simply dressing for the weather elicited public criticism from his saintly father.

> At a meeting [Gandhi] was addressing on voluntary poverty, he expressed his joy on being released from all material possessions, and when asked if

his family agreed with him he said, 'My wife, poor woman, she still has her struggles. My eldest son does not agree with me at all and with the other three the spirit is willing but the flesh is weak!' We thought this rather hard on Devadas who sat in the audience and who is such a dear even if he does wear more clothes than his father.[9]

As she got to know the rest of the members of Gandhi's entourage, Mildred learned about their particular foibles too. Here's how she described the group:

Mahadev Desai the chief secretary is an awfully fine chap but one wonders when one looks at the cut of his trousers if his spirit is not a little weak too. He lives in the ashram and is married and has one son … He likes his tea hot, if you should be entertaining him.

Pyarelal (commonly called Parallel) is supposed to be a clever and well educated man but he is not quite so entertaining as the others. He is very absent minded …

Miraben … who used to be Miss Slade until she went to India 6 years ago and fell at the feet of Gandhi where she has remained ever since, so to say, is a very interesting person. She is dark, and shaves her head and wears an Indian sari so easily passes for a Hindu, and in some respects is really more so than the others. She is very strict about all observances and leads in some of the Sanskrit prayers. She does her 314 yards of spinning as conscientiously as Gandhi himself every day, but I think the others slip up sometimes.

They are not so fussy about their vegetarian diet either. In fact we think they like to fall for something with egg in it if they can do so unconsciously.

Anyway they are jolly and it's good fun having them, but how we wish they'd come on time for meals.[10]

Mildred's role as cook for the Mahatma turned out to be minimal. "We soon discovered that he eats nothing cooked. All I do is extract the goat's milk from the milkman," she shrugged. "But when it comes to the rest of the party I am on hand and I certainly do some hopping to fill them up as well as our own crowd." Her biggest problem was getting ahead with her supply of goat's milk. She had a terrible time trying to camouflage it in puddings for the family: "… in spite of sugar and spice very often the goat will out, and sometimes he comes out strong."[11]

Working in the kitchen, Mildred became familiar with Gandhi's theories of nutrition and soon began considering vegetarianism herself. From Miraben she also learned about his weekly day of silence, his discipline of daily prayer, walking and spinning, and many other details that Miraben juggled with faithful efficiency. Sometimes the two women sat together up on the roof while Miraben did her spinning and told of her travels with Bapu: the clamouring crowds of devoted peasants, the Untouchables who flocked for his blessing. She explained how besides independence for India, the other great cause of Gandhi's life was his crusade for the outcastes, who he called *Harijans*, children of God.

Like the Mahatma, Miraben was celibate, and wore her hair shorn as a symbol of her vow. Gandhi took his vow of celibacy in 1906 at the age of thirty-seven. The concept of *Brahmacharya*, the learning of God, is fundamental to Hinduism and means ultimate self-control and an abnegation of sensual appetite.[12] Steeped in the prim traditions of Methodism, Mildred could understand celibacy as a way

Mildred and Gandhi's youngest son, Devadas on the roof of Kingsley Hall, London, 1931.

to heightened spirituality. She even briefly imagined herself in the role of chaste devotee, and warned her father: "don't be surprised if I come home with my hair shaved off and 6 yards of homespun draped around me for clothing!"

Most days, though, Mildred was more actively struggling with basic questions of gender and freedom. As a single woman (a spinster or an old maid, some would have said) society expected her to be celibate. But at thirty-one, Mildred was questioning the conventional boundaries of expression. She dreamed of sex, her fear of it, and her yearning for it. Fascinated by new developments in the emerging field of psychology, she began keeping a special diary, in which she explored the latent and manifest meanings of her dreams. One night, for example, she dreamed she was going to the countryside, and was concerned about how to transport a lot of tiny black beetles in her bag so that no one would see them. Upon reflection she identified the beetles as her "dark, unsatisfied desires," and felt that the dream expressed her conflicting need for sexual fulfillment with her repression. She had been thinking of her developing awareness of sexuality, and her growing acceptance of it.[13]

It is remarkable that Mildred expressed herself so openly in these diaries because these were not matters she spoke of, not even with her closest friends. In an undated note saved with her letters home from Kingsley Hall, she asked herself:

> What do you demand of a man before you go out with him? What must he be like? When should you kiss or pet?
>
> Do you think every man expects you to yield to him? How are women to be free?
> — equal mental strength
> — economic equality ...
> — demand respect

On the first and last counts, Mildred could easily hold her own. She was confident of her equal mental strength, and her honesty and integrity quickly earned her the respect of both men and women. Economic equality, however, was more difficult to achieve. Mildred was able to pay her own way in London only because her father continued to send her significant sums of money. For example, in one installment he sent more than the other volunteers earned in forty weeks. Kingsley Hall was in such desperate financial straits that Mildred couldn't in good conscience accept the seven shillings a week that was given to the volunteers. She knew that, for some, those few shillings were more money than they had ever had at one time. Her father's largesse was an embarrassment of riches, but she wasn't about to turn it down. In a letter thanking her father for fifty dollars, Mildred wrote:

> It makes me feel like a wealthy Canadian to realize how little these people have. I try to be careful but I don't live within my $1.25 [a week] and I don't feel quite fair about it. But when I have my day off I feel I must take advantage of the chance to go places and do things, for I must know something of London. So the check will be carefully but gratefully used.[14]

On her first few days off, Mildred had "a jolly time" exploring Piccadilly Circus, Westminster Abbey and Kew Gardens. She explored the National Gallery with Riek Liesveld, her Dutch friend from Bryn Mawr who was also visiting London. They met for lunch and then viewed masterpieces including "ugly sensual Reubens" and "lovely Rembrandts."[15] She got one invitation to see the sights of London and another invitation to the Policeman's Ball from a couple of the Scotland Yard detectives assigned to accompany Gandhi. She often stopped in at Canada House on Trafalgar Square to write letters or pick up news from home.

Whenever she could, though, Mildred spent her free time with young Devadas Gandhi and "the older, more interesting," Mahadev Desai. They took her to the East Indian Students' Union, where for the first time she "tasted the heavenly mango." Eating fiery, fragrant curries and dousing her throat with glass after glass of water, Mildred felt challenged and alive, full of hope and a sense of the historic moment. Hungry to learn all about the independence struggle, she also enjoyed the intercultural subtleties of non-violence. One day at lunch a Mrs. Cheesman unthinkingly killed a mosquito, despite the Gandhians' known reverence for all living things. Fortunately Miraben was not at the table, so there was apparently no need for a fuss.

Gandhi walking in London, 1931.

On the day the Mahatma was to take tea at Buckingham Palace, everyone wondered whether he would change his costume in any way, but apparently not. "Gandhi makes elaborate preparations before going to see the King — turns over his shawl! Ah, but it was a royal sight to see Mahadev in his white suit," she sighed.[16] It was Devadas who first suggested that Mildred should come to India, but she was most attracted to Mahadev, perhaps as a romantic foil to the ascetic Gandhi. Just as much though, she was attracted to the drama of the independence struggle and the principles of justice and equality it embodied.

Only a year earlier, Gandhi had launched his most dramatic challenge yet to the power of the British Raj — the famous Salt March of 1930. In defiance of English laws which made the manufacture and sale of Indian salt a government monopoly, the Mahatma announced that he would walk the 240 miles from his ashram to the Arabian Sea. Once there, he would make salt. Day by day, thousands of devotees joined him along the way. After ritual bathing and prayer, he knelt and picked up some of the sea salt caked on the shore. In Gandhi's hands, those few simple grains became a potent symbol of British injustice.

It was a classic demonstration of his only weapon: *satyagraha*, truth force. Elegantly simple and clearly practical, Gandhi's plan sparked massive civil disobedience. Within a week, millions of people all over India were making their own salt. The British responded with mass arrests — estimates range from 60,000 to 100,000. Soon the jails were overflowing with prisoners, including Gandhi himself. The administration was crippled. Revenues fell sharply. Even some of the most staunch British colonialists were beginning to see that force would never silence Indian demands for *swaraj*, self-rule.

The Labour government of Prime Minister Ramsay MacDonald had convened the Round Table Conference and was prepared to accept Gandhi on equal terms, but others opposed him every step of the way. Winston Churchill, for example, declared that he was revolted by "the nauseating and humiliating spectacle of this one-time Inner Temple lawyer, now seditious fakir, striding half-naked up the steps of the Viceroy's palace."[17]

The day Gandhi was to speak to the House of Commons, Muriel led quite a large group from Bow into the crowded visitor's gallery. Mildred was so moved, she was practically speechless. "Imagine the thrill of hearing Gandhi tell the Labour party what he wanted for India & why," was all she wrote that night. After weeks of meetings, Gandhi saw that the Round Table Conference held out little promise of real political gain, so he concentrated on communicating with the English people and preparing them for the idea of an independent India. He spoke to every kind of audience, and met with all sorts of famous people including George Bernard Shaw, Lloyd George and Charlie Chaplin.

It was Gandhi's way with everyday people that touched Mildred most, though. One of the members of the Kingsley Hall community who she visited regularly was John Morriss, a blind old man who was paralyzed and had been confined to hospital for more than seven years. One day he asked whether she thought Gandhi might come and visit him. Mildred replied that she doubted it, really, because there were so many demands upon his time and he rarely slept more than two or three hours a night as it was. John urged her at least to ask, so Mildred promised she would. Gandhi didn't immediately respond to her request, so after a few days she thought he had forgotten all about it. But early one morning as they set out to walk, he announced that today they would visit John Morriss. Mildred was a bit flustered because she realized the hospital would have preferred notice of Gandhi's arrival instead of an impromptu visit in the pre-dawn hours. Nevertheless, she happily showed the way to John's bedside.

Gandhi was known for his exceptional nursing skill and the healing power of his hands, which had long, slim fingers and an intuitive touch. Many miracle cures were attributed to those hands. When Gandhi grasped John Morriss's hand in his, and spoke gently to him, the old man was overwhelmed. Tears welled in his sightless eyes and he said, "Mr. Gandhi, this is the happiest moment of my life."[18] Mildred would always remember the encounter with a flood of love for them both, two humble men meeting as equals despite barriers of race and the Raj. In Gandhi's transparent compassion and respect for John, Mildred saw reflected his love for everyone — rich and poor, brown and white, noble and untouchable.

People naturally loved him in return. On his birthday, October 2, the friends at Kingsley Hall gave him a party. Everybody enjoyed themselves immensely, and understood that he would not eat any of the cake. During the festivities, the nursery school children presented Gandhi with some of their own toys, which he gratefully accepted for the children at his ashram school. Mildred loved the way Gandhi valued the toys as the children themselves did, and honoured their sweet spirit of giving.

As the weeks went by, life gradually returned more or less to normal in Bow. The crowds receded, the numbers of policemen decreased, the journalists went on to other assignments, even Devadas and Mahadev stopped making the long commute from the city centre to Kingsley Hall. Only Gandhi and Miraben came back every night to their rooftop cells.

Mildred's days began with the rhythmic chanting of his prayers and ended with the soft whirring of his spinning wheel. At first it had all seemed too exotic to grasp, but slowly the chants began to sound less foreign, still incomprehensible but somehow meaningful. She began to dream of India. Someone, perhaps Devadas, gave her a little charm of an elephant. Its message to her was that she could be of use in India. She went to Canada House and inquired about returning home via the Orient.

William Shirer, who first met Gandhi while covering that same Round Table Conference for the *Chicago Tribune*, later wrote:

> I count the days with Gandhi as the most fruitful of my life. No other experience was as inspiring and as meaningful and as lasting. No other so shook me out of the rut of banal existence and opened my ordinary mind and spirit, rooted in the materialist, capitalist West as they were, to some conception of the meaning of life on this perplexing earth. No other so sustained me through the upheavals and vicissitudes that I lived through in the years after I left India.[19]

Like Shirer, Mildred was shaken "out of the rut of banal existence" by Gandhi's message, and she found that profoundly liberating. Here again, Carolyn Heilbrun's analysis pertains. She notes that while men are encouraged to pursue an epic quest plot, women are expected to live a traditional love-and-marriage plot. For women like Mildred who desire the heroic quest, "some event must be invented to transform their lives, all unconsciously, apparently accidentally, from a conventional to an eccentric story."[20]

Autographs from Gandhi's group at Kingsley Hall, 1931. Devadas signed first and the Mahatma last.

It is at precisely this juncture that Mildred now found herself. Meeting Gandhi was the "accident" that set her life on a heroic course, and freed her from the confines of a conventional western woman's story. She knew that Gandhi's way demanded comprehensive commitment, and that was a spiritual and political challenge she couldn't resist. From now on, her life would be forever entwined with that of India and its quest for freedom — not only freedom from Great Britain, but also from hunger, sickness, racism, the caste system and war itself. It would be a heroic struggle, and Mildred longed to throw herself into it, heart and soul.

Before Christmas 1931, she wrote "a penny novel" which she mimeographed and sent to people back home in lieu of gifts. She cast herself as the heroine, although a rather meek and hapless one. Mahatma Gandhi, of course, is the hero about to sail out of her life and back into the battle for his homeland.

Already the heroine feels the impending separation, for the Round Table Conference has ended rather hopelessly," she wrote. "With the leisure of the East and the poise of one who works for eternity, Gandhi says, 'What matter if it does not come now? It must come in time.' And so he will return to re-open negotiations and perhaps to plunge the country again into *Satyagraha*, feeling that a demonstration alone will prove his earnestness to those who will not listen to reason …

And so the heroine is left wondering — wondering about India, about voluntary poverty, about the economic situation here, there, and everywhere, wondering about democracy, about God, wondering if her Western education has developed in her such an attitude of wondering that she is too inhibited to take action … Am longing to go to India. Shall I?[21]

It was a cold December dawn when Mildred took a last walk with Gandhi through the streets of Bow. Afterwards, she went to his cell while he sat alone at breakfast. She brought him water and then knelt before him on the floor. This would be the first, but not the last time she appealed to him as a supplicant, a pilgrim seeking his light to direct her path. Both times, it seems his response left her wanting something more.

"Bapu, I want to come to India," she said. "If I do, may I come to the ashram?"

"Of course, of course," he said, "but you should not wait too long."

"Many think this is a bad time," I said.

"On account of the present situation?" he asked with a quizzical non-committal shake to his head.[22]

When she went to help Miraben finish packing, they came across the collection of used toys from the nursery school children. Someone suggested that Gandhi wouldn't want to carry such a lot of junk all the way back to India. On the contrary, he replied, "Every bit of it is going."[23] Mildred smiled as she tucked a Winnie the Pooh bear and a stuffed rabbit into the last basket.

The good people of Bow turned out in great numbers to give Gandhi and his crew a proper sendoff. Many wept as they waved farewell. One motherly neighbour, a Mrs. Potts, wiped her eyes saying, "I hate to see him go. I just want to tuck him in." Mildred and a few others went down to the train station with the luggage and said their last good-byes. Then the shrill whistle blew and they were gone, leaving Mildred with more questions than answers.

On the morning of her last day at Kingsley Hall, Mildred shivered as she struggled out of bed and dressed for morning prayers. Later that day she was in a reflective mood:

> I don't know that the universe has responded to my outreach but I have felt that as I opened myself to all the stimulation of life the reaction has been an experience of life flowing in & through me. I have felt I touched the outskirts of the great current of vitalizing life surging through all things. I believe in a great onward thrust in the universe but I feel I have lost my "personal God."[24]

Mildred toured Russia and experienced its revoloutionary changes with a group from the London School of Economics, Summer 1932.

Chapter Six: 1932

THE QUEST BEGINS

In this uncertain state of mind, Mildred moved into her own flat in West Central London. It was small but cozy and, at sixteen shillings a week plus gas, it was within her budget. Mind you, the landlady was a stickler. At night she would cough not-so-discreetly outside the door, until Mildred got the clear message it was time for "lights out." The old soul was ever-friendly and talkative in the extreme. She often repeated the stories of her dear husband's death and other family tragedies, so that Mildred was relieved when another boarder moved in and began to absorb her share of the poor lady's loquacity.

She enrolled at the London School of Economics, founded in 1894 by the socialist Fabian Society. Named for a Roman general who owed his success to cautious rather than brilliant campaigning, the Fabians espoused evolutionary rather than revolutionary change. They believed in "the inevitability of gradualness," and their philosophy was aimed at forging a democratic, pluralist state. "What they wished to establish was a society where merit would be rewarded not by materialistic gain but by service to the community."[1] Among the Fabian Society's most influential leaders were George Bernard Shaw and Sidney and Beatrice Webb. The Webbs were writers, researchers and socialist visionaries whose legendary partnership shaped the British Labour Party and the English welfare state in a very fundamental way.

With their pragmatic approach and their focus on service, the Fabians had a deep impact upon Mildred's thinking. She read G.B. Shaw's *The Intelligent Woman's Guide to Socialism*, and recommended it to her brother and father. Her courses included "Methods of Sociological Research" taught by Sidney Webb, and "Political and Social Theory" with Harold Laski, another brilliant socialist whose penetrating intelligence was combined with great wit and a gift for teaching. "Laski is such a famous person here & such a marvellous orator they say to get a degree from the LSE you must speak three languages English, French, & Alaskan," she told the family.[2]

Mildred attended lectures at the LSE but didn't spend too much time studying because there was so much more to be learned outside the classroom. She attended speeches or readings by T.S. Eliot, H.G. Wells, Edith Sitwell, Walter de la Mare, John Galsworthy and many others, including Jawaharlal Pandit Nehru, future prime minister of an independent India. She joined the International Students Club because it hosted excellent lectures and concerts, and at tea-time an interesting mix of students congregated there, many of them Indians.

Letters from her Gandhian friends offered glimpses of the Mahatma's enormous impact on the European leg of his tour. One young missionary wrote: "People on the continent are very like Indians — sentimental, enthusiastic. The English are courteous & respectful but they did not run after Bapu like the French and the Italians." Mildred read all the press reports of events after his return to India and attended large demonstrations opposing the latest British crackdown on the independence movement. The headlines read: "BEATING OF PICKETS IN MADRAS, Government Admits Use Of Excessive Force."[3] She received one letter recounting Gandhi's arrest in Bombay which so moved her that she wrote it out in her own hand for her father and brother to read:

Suddenly, like the coming of a dream there was a stir & a whisper, "The police have come." We started up & I saw what I will never forget — a fully uniformed commissioner of police at the foot of Bapu's bed, & Bapu just waking, a little bewildered, looking so old, fragile and pathetic.

"Mr. Gandhi, it is my duty to arrest you." A beautiful smile of welcome broke out on Bapu's face ...

Mrs. G. with tears running down her cheeks said, "Can't you take me with you?"

Everyone in turn touched his feet ... He was full of joy and laughter. As the tiny figure got into the car it was a wonderful tribute to India's non-violence that the few policemen could stand in the midst of the crowd without fear or danger.[4]

Gandhi's influence upon Mildred began to deepen. In *The Moral Basis of Vegetarianism*, he wrote: "I do feel that spiritual progress does demand at some stage that we should cease to kill our fellow creatures for the satisfaction of our bodily wants." Mildred decided to stop eating meat in the spring of 1932 after she had a "revolting dream of seeing an animal killed."[5] She wanted to live the life of a *satyagrahi*, and was prepared to make the kind of fundamental personal change to do so.

Keeping her materialist desires in check was another struggle. She planned to head for the Continent, but her anticipation was dampened by her acute awareness that in five weeks of travel she would spend more than people in Bow could earn in a year. She asked the family:

> Doesn't it sound ridiculous for one who lived in a semi-state of voluntary poverty for 5 months to be talking so glibly of spending so much on herself? I looked at every penny I spent in Bow with much consideration before I spent it and thought of many people who needed it worse than me. But Bow seems a long way in my past now and I rationalize with very little trouble from my conscience that anything that I spend would make jolly little difference in alleviating the distress among the poor. I don't think it is that I have become indifferent but I see more clearly the futility of effecting any advantage through one's individual effort … One feels so helpless in the need of such stupendous change.[6]

These and other writings from early 1932 show that Mildred was feeling overwhelmed and confused. She was learning so much about the world situation — which was bleak — and her mind was opening up so rapidly, with so many different perspectives constantly emerging, that she didn't quite know what to believe. Certainly the final words here contradict the life she lived, which was founded in the passionate belief that individual effort was not for a moment futile: on the contrary, it was essential. Not only that, but Mildred could see all around her, in Muriel Lester and other new friends in the Fellowship of Reconciliation, individuals who didn't allow themselves the luxury of helplessness precisely because the need for "stupendous change" was so terribly urgent.

Whatever doubts perplexed her, the people Mildred met in this period laid the foundation for her lifelong dedication to the Fellowship of Reconciliation. She had attended an FOR meeting under the great dome of Albert Hall, where she heard the inimitable Maude Royden's plea for the formation of a Peace Army. Envisioned as a sort of "moral force" under the banner of the League of Nations, the Peace Army would be made up of pacifists willing to work and, if necessary, to die in non-violent service to humanity. More than three hundred people had signed up so far. Through the pacifist movement, Mildred found other people with the courage of their convictions. Just as in Gandhi's circle, here were people willing to lay down their lives for peace and justice.

Spring came and Mildred launched off across the English Channel. She was subdued as her train chugged away from Dunkirk and across the peaceful countryside, still pocked with evidence of the Great War. Her eye was drawn to "the old tree stumps, the overgrown trenches & the cemeteries with their white place stones and one huge cross." Once in Paris, though, her spirits lifted.

"Mes Chères," she wrote home. "Je vous aime, je vous adore. Que voulez vous encore? I think I could learn French if I stayed here for the rest of my life." Her

French was pretty atrocious, but she was able to understand the basics most of the time and her sheer enthusiasm to communicate won her much help. The sights of Paris continued to delight Mildred, but she was most fascinated by the work of the sculptor Auguste Rodin.

> You get a wonderful sense of the unity of man & the elements in his life-like figures emerging half-formed from the masses of rocks. And yet it is not simply a material unity but a spiritual one. The spirit of man as truly as his physical form seems to be yearning — struggling for expression — not freedom from the clay … but expression in it.[7]

Perhaps Mildred was touched by Rodin's art because she too was in the process of emerging, struggling for definition and expression of her inner self. She too was seeking freedom and communion in her daily life and a sense of unity or harmony in her spiritual life. Mildred had left England feeling a sense of loss for her "personal God," but on the Continent she saw glimpses of Him once again. She saw Him in the Rodin sculptures, felt His presence at a Catholic mass and worshipped Him in Quaker silence.

She arrived in Geneva in time for a beautiful Easter Sunday. That evening she went to the park in front of the League of Nations. Established by the Allies after the First World War in an attempt to unite the countries of the world in peace through collective security, the League was headquartered at the stately new Palace of Nations. The stars were glittering between the lacy branches of the trees, and everything felt "calm and quiet and living," she wrote, "… God — breaking through."[8]

While Mildred was moved by the great potential for good the League of Nations represented, she knew the political reality remained far from ideal. The founding Covenant of the League enshrined the principles of arbitration of international disputes, arms reduction and open diplomacy. As well, it established the International Court of Justice. U.S. President Woodrow Wilson was one of the chief founders, but the United States never actually joined; this fact seriously weakened the League. Given its weak response to Japan's invasion of Manchuria, "people here have pretty much lost faith in its ability to do anything," she wrote home.[9]

At the League building, Mildred saw huge piles of petitions that had been sent from all over the world as part of a disarmament campaign by the Fellowship of Reconciliation. As well, the FOR organized a Peace Crusade in which young people from all over Europe were walking to Geneva for a disarmament conference. Mildred regretted that her trip hadn't coincided with the dates of the conference, but she paid a visit to the Canadians who would be there. The head of the Canadian delegation, Dr. Riddell, was only cautiously optimistic about the disarmament conference — "not that he thought they would accomplish much, but he thought a little would be a lot. Total disarmament is at present a sentimental impossibility to him." Mildred tried to shrug off his "rather depressing attitude" with a walk down by the lake, where she saw "a perfect double rainbow … full of beauty & promise."[10]

In Zurich, she was welcomed by a member of the Swiss Fellowship of Reconciliation, Gusti Schultz. Despite the rain they went for a long hike in the Alps, glorying in the mountains and sky. Later, Mildred gave a talk on Gandhi to some students and professors, the first of many. Over the years, this talk came to be called: "I Walked with Gandhi," and throughout the rest of her long life she would tell and re-tell the story to any group or individuals who were interested. Mildred moved many hearts and minds with that telling.

She moved on to Vienna, a city economically depressed but historically the centre of fascinating new research by Sigmund Freud, Alfred Adler, Carl Jung and others who were laying the foundations of modern psychology. The Austro-American Education Bureau helped Mildred arrange visits to schools and treatment centres. She applauded the progress made by the socialist government, especially the affordable housing projects and integrated system of quality public education from early childhood on up. After a tour of one pre-school, she wrote: "I long to see such [schools] established in London's East End and Philadelphia and all the other places where the children have no place to play but the street."[11]

Another day she visited a "child guidance clinic" run by a woman psychologist named Dr. Holub. A couple of evenings later, she was enjoying Vienna's lively cafe society and chanced upon Dr. Holub sipping espresso with her colleague, Dr. Alfred Adler. Mildred was welcomed to the table, and enjoyed the meeting immensely. In contrast to the strict confidentiality demanded by the Freudians, Adler pioneered the concept of group counselling, and treated children in the context of their families and schools. Mildred wrote:

Dr. Adler is a nice old boy whose attitude to life is friendly & optimistic. Everybody is good & capable of anything. All people need is encouragement.
"I always praise them" — even when they are not doing well? "Especially then."[12]

Behind the gaiety of the elegant cafes and smokey beer cellars, Mildred sensed pervasive fear and social insecurity. The streets were full of beggars, the shopkeepers were careful to lock up tight every evening, and people headed straight for home. Still, she often broke the 10 p.m. curfew at her boarding house and had to pay a fee for waking the surly night porter to let her in.[13]

Across the German border, Mildred felt a sudden and dramatic change in atmosphere. Here it was harder to travel alone as a single woman. The military

Mildred in Munich, 1932.

dominated society in a way she had never seen before and the police had a distinctly unfriendly attitude. In Munich the men were aggressive, calling out in rough voices as she passed by on the street. Prostitution was legal and prevalent. The people seemed desperate and without hope. It was said that some Germans were actually starving.

Although Germany is so poor, the taxes so heavy, & the unemployed so numerous, ... the people seem to be very brave in carrying their burdens ... The policemen all wear warlike helmets with much silver and look very military — they almost make me frightened but the people one meets are not military at all.[14]

Mildred was glad to leave Munich and head for Holland, home of her ancestors. In Rotterdam, she enjoyed enormous hospitality from Riek Lieseveld, her friend from Bryn Mawr. Riek's family was in the coffee business — "if anyone can be said to be in business in this terrible depression." She also met some natives of the village of Osterhout, and was surprised to learn that the Dutch Osterhouts were staunch Catholics! As her train chugged across the verdant springtime farmlands, Mildred reflected upon her heritage.

> I tried to imagine myself as the first Osterhout who tilled the soil & milked the cows until the restless yearning for adventure called him from the lowly land to seek his fortune in the West. I wonder if he looked down the future and thought of us and what life would be like in our time. Well, it's fun to think about him anyway. I wonder if he took his wife with him or married a Westerner.[15]

On the last leg of her journey across Belgium, soldiers crowded onto the trains and she was again struck by the ever-present unease created by a heavy military presence in the streets and at border crossings. It gave her "a sense of the futility of civilization and the stupidity of man. Soldiers, passports, customs, even more than language difference show the barriers between us — worse because imposed, artificial and unnecessary."[16]

On the Dover to London train, Mildred conversed with an Austrian gentleman who predicted another war unless the countries of Europe could find a new spirit of unity to heal the fractures of the First World War. The only hope, he said, lay in "the leadership of a young man of great mind & heart born of the present suffering generation whose will could shape his vision into reality. Either this, or Europe must break." Neither Mildred nor the sad-eyed Viennese imagined that only months later, in January 1933, Adolf Hitler would be elected Chancellor of Germany.

In February, the Nazis would burn the Reichstag and accuse communists of the arson. In spring, Hitler would issue the first of more than four hundred anti-Jewish laws and decrees. He would outlaw trade unions and all political parties except his own. By summer, he would muzzle the free press and establish his propaganda machine. He would wipe out individual rights and give the Gestapo sweeping powers of arrest and imprisonment without trial. While the Third Reich had only just begun its catastrophic rise, Mildred had a terrifying dream of the impending conflict and of being buried alive.

> War preparations
> 2 ropes drawn across no man's land.
> I wept at their stupidity
> Went down road to await results
> — somewhat fearful
> — hid in large covered wagon
> — huge truck of dirt went by & as it towered above my hiding place I closed my eyes & felt the horror of it falling & crushing me. Then felt I must get out & crawled through small hole landing by horse which was restless — but got down over its head.
> No action in the battlefield.[17]

Mildred's interest in dreams offers a unique window on her intimate thoughts. Not surprisingly, her father played a large role in her dreams, reflecting a deep daughterly love underscored by guilt and a strong desire to rebel. Her analysis of the different layers of meaning to a recurring dream reflects this ambivalence:

> Vivid dream about getting ready to go away on train.
> Got delayed missed train was in terrible mix up.
> Often dream about being held up when planning to go somewhere.
> Manifest — connected with delays causing habit of being late
> Latent — indecision, can't make up mind definitely. Always reconsider, never like to make decision final & irrevocable

Explanation — Too much control by family — conceding to wishes Father final authority.[18]

In contrast to her diary, Mildred's letters reveal the tender side of her relationship with her father. In early November she wrote: "If Sunday evening finds you sitting quietly at home at 9:30 you must not think you are alone for I am there too."[19] After more than a year and a half away from Vancouver, Mildred was beginning to feel homesick. She missed her father and her brother, who was by then teaching at King Edward School in Vancouver and spending all his spare cash on a car and later a little boat called *The White Heather*. Mildred knew home was months away and many adventures still lay before her, but she was beginning to look forward to her return to the sea and the coastal mountains.

She still longed to go to India, but was also fascinated by the idea of seeing Soviet Russia. When a space became available on a tour group from the London School of Economics, Mildred jumped at the chance. The LSE was abuzz with the latest from the Soviet Union because Sidney and Beatrice Webb had just returned from "a kind of pilgrimage." Out of it came the Webb's final epic, *Soviet Communism: A New Civilization*. The book was "monumental in conception, in scope and in error of judgment." It sang the praises of the regime, then one of the most oppressive in the world, and even asserted that Josef Stalin "has himself very explicitly denied any such personal dictatorship." Like many less perceptive observers, the Webbs were so terribly mistaken because they saw only the model villages, schools, prisons, factories, and hospitals. Most of all, they wanted to believe in the revolution.[20]

Mildred, too, set off for Russia with high hopes that she would find an alternative to the capitalist vision, which was so cruel and unfair. Like the Webbs she saw much to applaud in the communist vision, but unlike them she did not blind herself to the injustices committed under Stalin. Her group left London in late July 1932 and sailed right into a storm on the North Sea. One passenger even offered five hundred dollars to be put ashore! It was an enormous sum for the times but the captain stayed his course and by the next day they were slipping smoothly through the calm waters of the Kiel Canal. It felt like a magical journey and Mildred wished the boat could go on and on endlessly through the midnight sun. The Soviet ship had a distinctly more egalitarian approach than other liners. Even though she was travelling third class, Mildred had free access to all the decks and lounges and could mix with the first and second class passengers. The crew members were mostly Russian speakers, and were able to teach Mildred at least one friendly word: *Tovarish*, Comrade.

In the port of Leningrad Mildred sat on her suitcase and scribbled letters home. Later they chatted with some people who wanted to know whether they

Mildred's snapshots of Russian places and people, 1932.

were proletariat or bourgeoisie. "They seemed to feel there is no hope for us until we have a revolution," she wrote.[21] The next day they visited the summer palace of the Czar, which struck Mildred as "the most gaudy display of wealth you could imagine. It is little wonder the people starved while royalty lived so extravagantly." That night Mildred slept well in a third class coach on the overnight train to Moscow, where they had "a splendid guide" who kept up a gruelling pace from the Kremlin to the co-ops, the youth camps to the model prison. By turns, she was fascinated, saddened, inspired and confused by what she saw.

> There are still very hard conditions in Russia. Labourers whom we talk to often complain about lack of food. A Chinese who had been here 3 yr. said he wanted to go back to China, that conditions were worse here than when he left home. Many complain that for a month at a time there is no butter or perhaps no sugar. All the youth who have caught the spirit of the New Russia bear these hardships without complaint but with a wonderful enthusiasm for the state that they are building. The devotion & sacrifice of so many of these young people makes one think of the zeal that inspired the early Christians — & still inspires some.[22]

The LSE group visited a special camp and school for underweight children considered susceptible to tuberculosis. There Mildred was amazed by the teenagers, who "started quizzing us on the most complicated political and economic questions ... What is our attitude to disarmament, about the U.S.S.R., evolution, Darwin, the Bible ... etc." She viewed the clean, well-equipped kindergartens and schools with approval, but was uneasy about the omnipresent portraits of Lenin and posters praising Stalin's first Five Year Plan.

> Children are being conditioned so thoroughly from the cradle ... to look at life from the Marxist viewpoint, that one wonders if they will ever be able to see any other. This indoctrination of the young with the theory of the class struggle, the inevitability of revolution, the economic factor as being completely determinative, is so narrowing that it prevents freedom of thought, and limits the extent of intellectual development ... The kids sing revolutionary songs, and one feels very much that the whole system is impregnated with propaganda.[23]

After their whirlwind tour of selected sites in Moscow and environs, the group boarded the train south to Kharkov, in the Ukraine. They travelled for thirty hot, dusty hours over the vast prairies, rich in harvests. What seemed a thousand miles later, they were finally able to see the object of their long journey: the largest dam in the world. Among other dry facts, Mildred and the group learned it generated 84,000 horsepower in each of the nine turbines. "It was most interesting but we did feel we had come a long way just to see a dam & the uncompleted structures of what is to be a great industrial city. However we had a swim in the Dneiper & altho we did not see all of Russia we saw all of some Russians," she quipped in a letter home.

On the return voyage, Mildred and her fellow passengers appreciated anew the abundance Westerners often took for granted. Discussions were lively around the dining tables, as passengers who had been on different tours shared their experiences of the Soviet Union. There was an enormous range of opinion, and Mildred was impatient with some self-styled "experts."

> I was confused enough by what I saw but with such a medley of impressions from others it is all the more difficult to clarify one's viewpoint ...

> Some of the passengers were wildly enthusiastic after a three-week tour, there was one who was sadly disillusioned and upset after eight weeks ... I'm waiting for my ideas to shake down a little bit before I write my book but just between you and me I'll give you a few tips as to what things are really like in Russia.

> Russia is under the most stringent dictatorship — even if it is of the proletariat. There is not freedom of speech & thought must be confined within the limits of the system. But on the other hand the dictatorship is working definitely for the improvement of living conditions, & social & educational opportunities for the masses of the people ...

Economically things are bad … One hears harrowing tales of the poverty amongst the peasants & in the small villages but one must remember that before the revolution the people suffered terribly & many starved … And one is painfully reminded of the boycott that all the countries have put on Russia. … The blood of Russia's peasantry is on our Capitalist heads! …

However it turns out, this is the greatest revolution that has ever taken place & will remain a great spectacle on the pages of history for all times.[24]

Months after her return, Mildred remained deeply moved by the spirit of sacrifice and discipline she witnessed among the youth, who were "giving themselves to the task of building a new society with enthusiasm and unselfishness. This spirit so permeates the group that it transforms the monotonous factory job, or the tiring farm labour into an act of service." Whether they were inspired by the social gospel or the communist revolution, Mildred always loved that sense of excitement generated by people working together with a shared dream. She was awed by the transformative power of selflessness. She saw it reflected in the dedicated young Komsomols, but that spirit of giving had shone most brilliantly in Gandhi. Her encounter with the Mahatma deepened her commitment to a life of peace, and her studies and travels gave her much more to offer in the cause of justice for all. As she prepared to leave England, Mildred dreamed of Bapu, and of serving him once again.

In the two years since she left home, Mildred's intellectual and spiritual growth had been phenomenal. How she would express these deeper values and more passionately-held convictions, she wasn't yet sure. Her vision was broader and her goals more radical, but she knew her daily life would be more constrained. She had grown and changed so much, she wasn't sure how she would fit back into the family again. She wondered about her relationship with Vic, who also appeared in her dreams. She sailed from London via Cherbourg to Montreal, then travelled across Canada by train. Stepping onto the station platform in Vancouver, she made a transition from the vagabond life of a student and traveller back to the static role of housekeeper and caregiver, dutiful daughter and sister.

Portrait of a young socialist: Mildred proudly wore her CCF pin on her lapel, Vancouver, 1933.

Chapter Seven: 1933

INTO THE FRAY

Dear old Father and her "cher frère" Victor, handsome Uncle Smith and Aunt Amy with all the cousins, and many friends and neighbours were waving on the station platform to welcome Mildred home. She disembarked into their loving arms, and made her way home to hot tea and friendly chatter, a warm bath and a deep sleep in her own bed. Ah, bliss.

After two years abroad, Mildred's ear was accustomed to hearing many different, often indecipherable languages. In the first days at home, she listened to the rhythms of street life in amazement. Everyone was speaking English, in an accent that was familiar and comprehensible! At first Mildred watched her fellow Canadians with a strangely objective eye, but soon she relaxed back into the West Coast sensibility. Together she and Vic swam, sailed and climbed local mountains, glorying in the autumn colours. But, even though her father had a good pension, her brother had full-time work and the family was secure, she couldn't avoid the ugly truth: the Great Depression had hit home.

Overeducated and unemployed, Mildred at least wasn't alone. Among the jobless were many of her friends, capable young university graduates who sincerely wanted to make their best contribution to society. Yet there seemed to be no place for them. During an interview with the superintendent of the Vancouver School Board, she enthusiastically elaborated her ideas about progressive education. He listened for a while and then interrupted her to ask: "My dear, don't you realize there's a Depression on?" It wasn't only blue collar workers who were suffering. Vancouver teachers were having to take pay cuts to keep their jobs. The superintendent suggested that she would be lucky to get a regular classroom job, let alone to implement any sort of new program, no matter how worthy.

Mildred got busy "trying to paint Vancouver Red." She began a new job as a social worker in the downtown core. Funded by the Young Women's Christian Association, the Business and Professional Women's Club and the University

Women's Club, her position involved helping unemployed women and girls. The group operated a clubhouse in the Burns Block on West Hastings, beside the old B.C. Electric Building and the Pantages Theatre. Mildred did her best to create a homey feeling for the girls, who were in their teens and early twenties. Because most of their families were on relief, they scrambled for any work they could get, usually in laundries or factories. The club offered friendship and moral support, recreation and free entertainment. Members could take piano or painting lessons, and often could pick up tickets to whatever show was in town that hadn't sold out.

Ever a believer in the benefits of fresh air, Mildred organized camping trips. Then nineteen years old, Evelyn Harris was among the unemployed girls who helped put on a bazaar which raised "the princely sum of $36" to fund these outings. One time Mildred took about ten girls on an overnight trip to North Vancouver. "She wanted us to see nature," Evelyn recalled. They slept out under the stars and got terribly damp and shivery. "I was cold, and Mildred offered me her sweater, and I slept in it. I never forgot that, how she loaned me her sweater."[1]

Mildred enjoyed herself too, but had mixed feelings about spending her time organizing these adventures. Certainly she was never the sort of doctrinaire socialist who couldn't have a good time. On the contrary, she was more like the anarchist Emma Goldman, who said, "If I can't dance, I don't want to join your revolution." Mildred firmly believed it was important to give these young women a chance to get together and have fun, but that wasn't enough. What they really needed were jobs and justice, not teas and tickets to the movies. Their plight touched Mildred's heart and clarified her political goals.

In the early years of the Depression, almost nothing existed of the universal social safety net that Canadians today take for granted. Back then unemployed married men with families could get some relief, but it was woefully inadequate. Single men and women were ineligible even for that small measure of assistance. Women who held down jobs were often criticized for taking work from male breadwinners. Homeowners who were unable to pay their mortgages or taxes ended up on the street, and hundreds of families were evicted en masse from rental housing in downtown Vancouver. Everyone on relief was made to feel ashamed for needing it, and people held out against asking for it until finally the hunger became too much. Some jottings from Mildred's journal:

> Last month 110 pupils stayed away from city schools part time because of insufficient clothing ... Boys sentenced to Oakalla prison for 6 months — but given 48 hours to get out of town for the crime of being without employment! ...

Hospital Case — Woman, 24, Has 4 children — Septic abortion followed by abdominal abscesses. Wife of longshoreman. Many women unaware of birth control methods, driven to desperation by pregnancy, try to bring on abortion & often become infected.[2]

Poverty, unemployment, racism, sexism: all these ills cried out for remedies, but Mildred was still searching for her way to respond. She was broadening her personal vision of socialism, "which was ethical, humanist and Christian in nature."[3] At this time she became involved with the League for Social Reconstruction. Modelled on the British Fabian Society, the LSR was founded in 1932 by Frank Underhill of the University of Toronto and Frank Scott of McGill. Their thinking was fundamental to the origins of the Co-operative Commonwealth Federation; indeed the movement's maiden statement, the Regina Manifesto, was largely their work. The League grew to include many intellectuals and educators, who together became the "brains trust" of the fledgling CCF.

Through the LSR, Mildred came into contact with Dorothy Steeves, a lawyer, and Juvenile Court Judge Laura Jamieson, a teacher, suffragist and peace activist. With Lucy Woodsworth, Laura had founded the Western Canadian chapter of the Women's International League for Peace and Freedom. Both Laura Jamieson and Dorothy Steeves would be among the first female members of the B.C. Legislature, along with Mildred's old friend Grace Woodsworth. While Mildred had been abroad, Grace married Angus MacInnis, Independent Labour MP for Vancouver South. The ceremony marked the beginning of a great love match and a political partnership that lasted to the end of their days. Angus and Grace spent their wedding night aboard the train bound for Ottawa and the next session of Parliament.[4]

In the spring of 1933, the call went out for activists to come to Regina for the first national convention of a new movement united against capitalist injustice. Canada's major socialist, labour and farm groups were uniting under the leadership of J.S. Woodsworth to build a new social order, a co-operative commonwealth. Right away, Mildred decided that somehow or other she was going to get to Regina. Fortunately, Dorothy was also determined to go, and they could borrow a car from her husband. R.P. Steeves was an affable high school principal affectionately nicknamed Steevie, who got his old jalopy back on the road and bid adieu as his wife and her comrades drove off in it. Bound for Saskatchewan along with Dorothy and Mildred was a young lawyer from North Vancouver named Frank McKenzie, who would serve the CCF for many years with distinction.

The journey was an adventure. It took place long before the Trans-Canada Highway was built, so the pilgrims had first to drive south and then head east through the United States, without benefit of a road map. "The first thing that

Group photograph of the first annual convention of British Columbian CCF groups in Vancouver, August, 1933. Mildred is seated in the second row, second from the left.

happened was the tires started to go pop," McKenzie recalled. "It was a common affliction in those days."[5] One by one, all four tires blew. The friends hadn't counted on having to buy a new set of tires enroute, so they were all practically broke by the time they arrived in Regina, he said. However, they soon forgot their troubles, listening to the convention secretary read aloud the proposed Manifesto of the Co-operative Commonwealth Federation.

Besides the overthrow of capitalism, with its inherent injustice and inhumanity, the Regina Manifesto outlined a program for economic planning, co-operative institutions, socialized health care, constitutional changes, a labour code, taxation and socialization of finance, agriculture and external trade. The sections of special interest to Mildred concerned protection of fundamental freedoms, promotion of social justice and foreign policy to foster international co-operation. "Canada must refuse to be entangled in any more wars fought to make the world safe for capitalism," the Manifesto declared. It concluded: "No CCF government will rest content until it has eradicated capitalism and put into operation the full programme of socialized planning which will lead to the establishment in Canada of the Co-operative Commonwealth."[6]

As those words were read aloud, Mildred, Dorothy, Frank and the other delegates and visitors all leapt up as one. Cheering and laughing together amidst the thunderous applause, their ideological differences were dispelled in the optimism of the moment. Over the next three days, however, the Manifesto was debated section by section. The delegates represented such a broad segment of the political spectrum that discussions were pulled first one way and then the other. Besides the Fabian intellectuals like Mildred and Dorothy, the British Columbia group included Marxists whose views were in sharp contrast with the rural delegates, who were suspicious of Communists and other "congenital rebel, crypto-anarchist" types.[7]

There were few women among the 131 delegates to the CCF founding conference. They met as a caucus just once, and Agnes Macphail naturally dominated the discussion. The only woman in the House of Commons, she was part of the Ginger Group, which supported Woodsworth's initiatives in Parliament. Mildred later reported their discussions this way:

> From the majority came the strong protest that women's activities should not be separated from men's, that fundamentally their problems are the same. Agnes McPhail [sic] put the case most emphatically and dramatically (being Agnes) when she stated, "I am sick and tired of hearing about special committees on education and health for women. Don't men want to be healthy and don't men want to be educated?"

> She said, "I have never asked for anything in parliament just because I am a woman, for if I can't get what I want by my own personality, brains, courage, and determination then I don't want it at all."

> Miss McPhail declared, "We must win our recognition as persons not as women. We have no separate problems. We are all interested in the social reconstruction of Canada."[8]

The social reconstruction of Canada: there was no one else more worthy and able to lead the people towards this goal than J.S. Woodsworth. For his acknowledged leadership and integrity, the MP for Winnipeg Centre was overwhelmingly acclaimed leader of the new federation. The poet and law professor F.R. Scott later wrote that Woodsworth "gave the new movement a quality of leadership which at once lifted it above mere party politics." In his speech to the delegates, Woodsworth said: "I am convinced that we may develop in Canada a distinctive type of Socialism. I refuse to follow slavishly the British model or the American model or the Russian model. We in Canada will solve our problems along our own lines."[9]

During the conference, Mildred greeted Woodsworth with warmest respects from her father, and inquired after the well-being of Mrs. Woodsworth and the rest of the family. She always felt fortunate to have had such a long friendship with the Woodsworths, and often said that J.S. had the greatest impact on her thinking about non-violence. Mildred related to Woodsworth her experiences with Gandhi, and felt sure that the two would find in one another kindred spirits. After all, they were alike in so many ways.

Both Gandhi and Woodsworth were tiny men, frail-looking but with great physical stamina, rigorous in their self-denial. Both were active seekers, travelling thousands of miles throughout their countries, riding along with the people in third-class coaches or walking the dusty by-ways. Both were free-thinkers, never fettered in their love of humankind by artificial barriers of religion or race, caste or class. Both affirmed the fundamental unity of the human family, and found God through service to the least of His children. On opposite sides of the world — Woodsworth at the All People's Mission and Gandhi in the slums with the Untouchables — the two men were living out the same message. It was the message of the Sermon on the Mount.

In J.S. Woodsworth and the CCF, Mildred found the Canadian expression of her Gandhian beliefs. Regina was a political turning point, but it was also a spiritual watershed. For Mildred, the Regina Manifesto was like a blueprint for building the Kingdom of Heaven on Earth. She always spoke of this as an evangelical time in her life, and of the movement as being rooted in Christian pacifism. As soon as she got back to Vancouver, she took to the airwaves with a new focus and sense of mission. On August 8, 1933, she told listeners of Radio CKMO: "I have come back from the convention at Regina more than ever convinced that in the Co-operative Commonwealth Federation lies the hope of economic and spiritual freedom for the people of Canada ..."

The CCF appealed to Mildred partly because it demanded an intellectual commitment. It had a rational program of social planning and believed in the ability of common people both to understand economic problems and organize in order to solve them. The movement was an educational crusade as much as a political party. As Walter Young pointed out though, members of the CCF needed that intellectual commitment to outweigh the social stigma of being labelled a "Red." In that way, the movement really demanded the courage of one's convictions, and that's exactly what Mildred wanted to express. She wanted to be part of something that expected the best of her, something that required the kind of dedication and self-sacrifice she had seen in Gandhi and his disciples.

In the best Osterhout tradition, Mildred launched into her mission with verve and dedication. Although she spoke into a microphone and not from a pulpit, she was a preacher nonetheless. Like her minister father and her missionary uncle, she felt called to give her all. She strove to live out the CCF vision of social justice: "From each according to his ability, to each according to his need." She was a very able young woman with a lot to contribute, and a willingness to keep her own needs strictly in check. She called upon her deep faith and her revivalist heritage and threw herself into the movement, heart and soul.

"We were so committed and stirred up," she said. "I think Father's evangelical approach came bursting through, for I couldn't wait to get up on any platform that would have us."

The movement soon faced its first big challenge. A provincial election was called for November 2, 1933. The CCF fielded a full slate of novice candidates including two women: Dorothy Steeves in Point Grey and Mildred Osterhout in Vancouver Burrard, which was then a two-seat riding. Mildred's running mate was Tom Sidaway, a railway car conductor. Their chief opponent was the Liberal incumbent, the formidable Gerald Graton McGeer, an establishment lawyer (a King's Counsel, in fact) and a wily campaigner. They were two among twelve candidates for the seat.

> The political climate was so chaotic that [Mildred] must have felt like Alice stumbling into the Mad Hatter's tea party. The Tories and Liberals were vying for popular support with a dozen splinter parties, scores of independents and the CCF, which had already split into two factions, one rallying around the official party colours and the other proclaiming itself as an Independent-CCF. The press and the opposition saved most of their invective for the CCF, condemning it as Bolshevik, fascist, syndicalist, selfish, and un-Christian — sometimes all in one newspaper editorial.[10]

Possibly because the political arena was still so hostile to the participation of women, Mildred seems to have adopted a more serious style of dress — not severe, but definitely more sober than in later stages of her life. As always, she was tall and slim. Her hair was ash blonde, very short, parted on the side and combed sensibly back. She wore no make-up. In a passport photo of the time, she looks steadily into the camera lens, just barely smiling. But a great warmth is in her eyes and her earnest face is open, almost vulnerable. She wore her heart on her sleeve and a CCF pin on her lapel.

She was naive, of course, and didn't understand how to work with the press. As well, she was scrupulously honest, so she said things more experienced politicians would not have. For example, during an all-candidates meeting sponsored by the Parent-Teacher Federation, she made a costly blunder in response to a tricky question. The next day boldface headlines reported:

SCHOOL SOCIALISM
C.C.F. WOULD 'FIRE' DISAPPROVING TEACHERS

> Miss Mildred Osterhout, C.C.F. candidate, was asked what the C.C.F would do with teachers who refused to conform to the teaching of Socialist principles in the schools.

She said that anyone who refused to co-operate would naturally have to be dismissed, but it was intended to hold night schools for the purpose of training the teachers in the ideals and principles which it was desired that they should impart to their pupils.

Asked whether 'God Save the King' would be sung, she said this had not been considered, but it would be her own idea that some song suitable for both parents and children would have to be written giving expression to the idea of love and co-operation for which the C.C.F. stood.[11]

As reported, Mildred's comments were too controversial to merit only one-day play. Even *The Globe and Mail* picked up the story, and *The Vancouver Sun* ran an editorial urging voters to do whatever necessary to defeat the CCF, "with all its chaotic and radical implications."[12] Neither McGeer nor the press would let the issue sleep, repeatedly compelling her to justify statements she'd never made. A few days later, in a speech at the Hotel Vancouver, she fought back:

When I explained to a group in the Kitsilano School what I meant by socialized teaching, in which children would have an opportunity to work under the guidance of teachers in small groups where they could learn the important lesson of living as contributing members of society, I was quoted as having said we should force the teaching of socialism in the schools.

The lengths to which the old-line parties will go in criticism is shown by the fact that one of my opponents in Burrard, Mr. McGeer, stated on a public platform that he had an affidavit to prove these statements regarding the teaching of socialism. If one had time to challenge such a libellous statement even the redoubtable Gerry might be forced to an apology.[13]

The campaign got even dirtier. Mildred and other CCF candidates struggled to debunk the many stereotypes and epithets that were hurled at them and their movement. Despite the Red-baiting and ugly accusations of anti-Christian sentiment, they tried to keep to the moral high road, stressing the CCF as the ethical choice over the corrupt and greedy Tories and Grits.

On election day, "the big question in everybody's mind was: How big is the C.C.F. vote?" The *Sun* also reported that "a notable feature of the election was the number of women taking part."[14] However, when the votes were counted only one of the five female candidates was elected: a Mrs. Paul Smith. (Her own first name was not reported in the paper.) A Liberal, she ran in Burrard alongside Gerry McGeer, Mildred's nemesis. His picture was in the paper, headed VICTOR. He garnered 9,572 votes, followed by Mrs. Smith with 8,832. Third in the polls, Mildred won 6,491 votes and her running mate, Tom

BURRARD

VOTE

Co-OPERATIVE Commonwealth Federation

Vote for both with a X

OSTERHOUT Minnie Mildred Osterhout, of Vancouver, Social Worker	**X**
SIDAWAY John Sidaway, of Vancouver, Street Railway Conductor	**X**

You vote at...

Your number is......... ....

Voting card of CCF candidates for the November 2, 1933 provincial election.

Sidaway, got 6,249. (Mildred and Tom may have taken some consolation in that McGeer's brother, Manfred, lost in Vancouver East to the CCF.)

It was a very respectable showing indeed, especially considering that, as predicted, the election was a Liberal landslide. T.D. "Duff" Patullo swept into the Premier's office with 30 of 41 seats. But, with six seats going to the CCF, the big news of the '33 election was the astonishing success of the new party in its maiden campaign. The CCF caucus included the dynamic father and son, Ernest and Harold Winch, who were both elected for the first of many times in Burnaby and Vancouver East respectively. E.E. Winch was a respected trade unionist and Harold was the youngest person ever elected to the Legislature. Like Mildred in Burrard, Dorothy Steeves made a strong showing in Point Grey, but was defeated. A few days later, Mildred wrote a long letter reflecting on her first election and on the personal and economic costs of entering the political arena. She had no illusions that because of taking the CCF stand she had irrevocably closed the door in terms of her potential employment as a teacher or social worker.

Dear Comrades,

And now it is all over, shouting included, and the Liberals have won. And yet in a sense we have won too ... we are on the map, are the official opposition, and are on the way to building a strong organization.

83

Altogether it has been a great experience running as a C.C.F. candidate ... I wonder if this political move was just a sidestep for me and if I shall be back into the social work field again or if I have stepped too far ... too far to go back. Probably the door has closed behind me as far as remunerative work in Vancouver goes, either in the teaching or social work profession.

I don't feel the same security in my home town that I used to. True, I have made many friends, but I have built up a line of critics and resisters too ... and I never had these before. Crowds of people who did not know me from the proverbial hole in the ground now think of me as that awful red who wants to teach socialism in the schools, etc ... Someone even said she would not have me in her house — a W.C.T.U. [Women's Christian Temperance Union] woman too ...

Other things in the campaign hurt me far more, being refused five minutes to speak at the Neepawa picnic, and again turned down by the Presbytery, and ... then to be rejected by a member of the family. Yes, one of my cousins sat on the Liberal platform and had it announced that he wanted it known he was not a brother of mine ...

Still, it was great to get to know some of the old timers who have been in the movement for years ... and are still undaunted. I hope I'll have the faith to carry on as they have done.[15]

Of course she had, and did. Mildred always found great strength in the movement, and great joy in collective struggle. "I understand better now what being a communist means in the way of personal submergence in the party," she wrote. This new political understanding coincided with Gandhi's teachings on selflessness, and finding oneself through losing oneself in service to others and to God.

Mildred used the microphone of CJOR radio as a pulpit from which to preach the gospel of the Co-operative Commonwealth. Broadcasting from the old Grosvenor Hotel in downtown Vancouver, she did a weekly program called "The Woman's Point of View," which addressed topics including peace, progressive education, socialist economics and women's rights. She advocated wages for housework and real economic independence for women. She predicted that with the CCF's plan of socialized medicine, women would be infinitely healthier and happier than under capitalism.

Not surprisingly, her opinions were not shared by the owners of CJOR radio. In May 1935, she received a letter from G.D. Chandler, the station manager, announcing that "any material ... station officials are inclined to question will be submitted to our solicitors ... IN ORDER TO TAKE CARE OF THIS PROCEDURE IT IS *ABSOLUTELY NECESSARY* THAT ALL

PROPOSED MATERIAL BE SUBMITTED TO THE STATION IN TYPEWRITTEN FORM NOT LESS THAN ONE FULL BUSINESS DAY PRIOR TO THE PROPOSED BROADCASTING TIME."

Mildred shrugged off this attempt at prior censorship, co-operated with the new deadlines and kept right on telling the CCF story, which soon began to attract more and more voters. "I think on the whole the movement is advancing quite well," she wrote. "There are over 200 CCF clubs in the province now and new ones are forming all the time, while the older ones are expanding their activities."16

In 1934, Dorothy Steeves won a by-election in North Vancouver and became the first CCF woman elected to the provincial Legislature. A brilliant debater, she was eloquent in her crusade for mother's allowances and a minimum wage for domestic workers. As an MLA for the next eleven years, she championed disability pensions, holiday pay and housing assistance for the working poor, and promoted the early credit unions.17

That year, Mildred and Dorothy organized the first CCF Summer School at a camp on Saltspring Island. The registration fee was one dollar, while food was five dollars per week. They scheduled meetings for morning and evening, but left afternoons free for swimming, beachcombing, skits and reading. The syllabus included seminars by J.S. Woodsworth on the Regina Manifesto, Arnold Webster on "Fascism and Communism," W.W. Lefeaux on "Marxian Economics," and Frank Roberts on "How to Study Dialectics." Grace and Angus MacInnis and Harold Winch rounded out the list of speakers. For Mildred, summer school combined the joys of nature with the comradeship of co-operative life and learning. Everyone shared everything and pitched in. Men were expected to do their own dishes, and they did. As the brochure promised, it was an escape from household routine — and that was something Mildred cherished.

The civic election of December 11, 1935 was the next opportunity to increase CCF representation. This time Mildred ran for one of two vacant positions on the school board, and she won! In fact she almost topped the polls, being beaten only by an incumbent trustee named James Blackwood, who got 8,502 votes to Mildred's 7,816. Gracious in victory, Blackwood sent a warm note saying, "If you enjoy the work on the School Board as much as I have done, then you have a very enjoyable and interesting two years ahead."

"Just a note to congratulate you on your fine victory," one friend wrote. "You deserve to win for many reasons, but not least that you represent advanced educational theories and CCF ideals in the city," wrote another. Some quipped that the election had changed Mildred's relationship to her brother, then a secondary school teacher. "When the returns came over the radio that night

Jack's first reaction was, 'Why, Mildred will be Victor's boss!' Don't be too hard on him."[18]

Several of her correspondents expressed their regrets that there was no salary attached to the office, particularly considering Mildred's already heavy load of CCF duties. "Would you rather receive my sincerest lamentations?" inquired Jack Dick, writing from Whonnock. "I shouldn't think the job would be all beer and skittles, judging by the way the board here gets it in the neck from doting parents!" Despite the many obstacles they knew she would face, all expressed highest confidence in her abilities.

With this wave of best wishes that flooded Mildred's mailbox came a long letter in the familiar angular penmanship of Walter Fahrni, who got the good news while aboard a ship anchored off Port Alberni.

"CONGRATULATIONS LADY! And so you are now a member of that august assemblage known as the School Board — Good work Mildred. I wish I could have had a small part in getting you elected with such a comfortable majority. No doubt this will add considerably to your responsibilities ... Whatever you do tho [sic], don't let it interfere with our A.B.C. meetings."[19]

To Mildred and Walter, "A.B.C." stood for "A Big Change," which was precisely the point of their reading and study group examining social and economic policy from the CCF perspective. Often called the "black sheep" of the Fahrni family, Walter shared Mildred's socialist convictions, and wanted to convince others of their rightness as well. He once asked Mildred to do him the favour of introducing his brother, Roy, to some of the CCF leaders. Roy was a newspaper publisher in the interior town of Kaslo, and Walter thought he "would be a mighty good socialist if he gets a chance to hear it put up in a logical manner."

From Walter's perspective, the most logical argument for radical social change was the struggle he witnessed among the working men in ports up and down the coast. Mariners and fishermen, labourers and longshoremen — they were all desperate to find work, no matter how dangerous or poorly paid. Walter's own experience of being overworked and underpaid also sharpened his convictions. He knew pretty well everything there was to know about the massive new diesel engines that powered freighters working the Pacific northwest, but he had no formal credentials so the size of his pay cheque never reflected the responsibility he carried.[20] His brothers always urged Walter to do an engineering degree but he never did, just picked up skills through correspondence and on the job."He was the smartest of the bunch of us," recalled his elder brother, Gordon. "He was always inventing things, could fix anything."[21]

Fulfilling the role of ship's engineer but lacking the university degree to claim a professional salary, Walter was in a vulnerable economic position. He wrote to

Walter Fahrni at sea, undated.

Mildred at home, circa 1930s.

Mildred about having "sent in an ultimatum to the Company several weeks ago — more pay and better working conditions." When the deadline passed with no response, Walter packed up his gear and was getting ready to head ashore when he decided it would be really satisfying to to call the boss (collect, of course) to tell him "just what I thought of him and his lousy Company."

However, the smooth varlet beat me to it and took all the wind out of my sails by saying, "Hello, old chap. I'm glad you called me up. We have decided to give you the increase in pay you asked for and if the job doesn't easy up by the first of the year we will put an additional man on the boat." So what can you do with an outfit like that — when they even take away your principle grounds for nursing a grievance — [22]

Such unscrupulous ways of dealing with others would have deeply offended Walter's sense of decency and dignity. He was a person who always treated others with respect and expected the same in return. He was the chief engineer when Paul Hucal, "an orphan lad of 18," signed on board. Paul never forgot how Walter showed him the ropes and treated him like a son. "We sailed together for about two years," Hucal recalled. "We'd go on shore leave together, and Walter knew all the best Chinese restaurants up and down the west coast from Alaska to San Diego. He spoke some Chinese and he'd order the real stuff, not just chop suey." Hucal summed up his mentor and friend this way: "Walter was a good individual, fair and square. He was just as honest as they come, and his word was his bond. They don't make them like that anymore. He was a real gentleman who never spoke ill of anyone."[23]

For all these qualities, it's easy to see why Mildred would have loved and respected Walter, but she was reluctant to marry him — or anyone else. He courted her for several years but, because he was so often away at sea for months at a time, it was easy for her to continue delaying a commitment to the relationship. He proposed to her many times but she always turned him down, insisting that her first responsibility remained at the side of her aging father. Over a period of days in the spring of 1936, more than five years before she finally did agree to marry him, Walter wrote Mildred a long letter in which he tried to assuage her doubts about marriage. In broaching issues of denial, honesty, love, sex, fidelity, careers, money and her mission in life, Walter appealed to Mildred's intellect and to her emotions.

> Aboard the M.V. *Salvage Princess*,
> Port Alberni, B.C.
> April 9th/36

Mildred Dear —

... I really believe that in many ways, you are attracted to me as strongly as I am to you, just as the magnet that attracts an object is itself attracted to that object. It must be so. It is incredible to me that you, whose attractive force is so great, should not feel a strong answering pull. I think we are both of a more than normally emotional nature — you even more than myself — yet we rarely allow our emotions to dominate our reason ...

You believe that nothing should be allowed to interfere with your mission in life. You have the personality, the energy, the ability and the training to do a great deal of good in this world and your first duty lies in that direction. You have seen many promising careers wrecked by unwise marriages — you can see that marriage entails giving up a part of your freedom that is so vitally important to your work — it means dividing your interests and under even the most favourable circumstances, confines you in many other ways ...

I feel too that your public career is of paramount importance. You have so much to give and you are so well equipped to be a real benefit to the world, that I would have a very poor opinion of any man that tried to monopolize you — that would try to make your interests secondary to his own. I would be very unfair to submerge you in so much domesticity that your work would suffer ...

I have not mentioned financial matters at all. Probably that is one of the problems I am trying (subconsciously) to evade. It is a large one ... I am afraid that my mental attitude toward work for work's sake does not agree with the copy book axiom ... If financial success or even a reasonable degree of security involves scrapping of all my standards and ideals, then I fear that I am doomed to obscurity and poverty (in capitalism) for I can't do the things that seem to be required to ensure success along conventional lines ...

It rather shocks me to realize that I am not so self sufficient as I had thought. It would be humiliating to admit to anyone else that I required a love interest to prod me back into reality & activity. You see love, more than any other emotion, is the one that I feared. I didn't know that until recently — I preferred thinking that I scorned it.

Thanks Mildred Dear — It has been just grand being friends with you. Whatever else happens I want to keep that up. Love, Walter.

This remarkable document is both Walter's love letter to Mildred and his manifesto for a radical relationship. He acknowledges the legitimacy of her doubts about marriage, but assures her that he wouldn't expect her to be a traditional wife. Similarly, he left her with no illusions that he would necessarily be accountable as a provider like a traditional husband would — he was too much the dreamer, inventor and idealist. He often felt unable to express himself, but Mildred surely was moved by Walter's emotional courage as, for the first time in his life, he put aside his male pride and opened himself up to honest dialogue about love and companionship in life.

At this time, Vic was also getting ready to marry. At an SCM camp in the summer of 1936 he met Connie, a graduate of the University of Alberta who served as girls' work secretary for the Religious Education Council of Alberta. Within six months of meeting, Constance Evelyn Smith and Victor Howard Osterhout were married in Edmonton. When they returned to Vancouver in January 1937, Mildred hosted a tea for her brother's beautiful bride. It was the beginning of a life-long friendship, as Connie became like the sister she never had.

Mildred shared with Vic and Connie her concern for Reverend Osterhout's health. At age seventy-five, he was close to his brother, Smith, and he still corresponded with friends and relations back east. He was a member of Point Grey United Church, down the street. He also liked to bake, and gave his own home-made sweets as Christmas gifts. Mildred tried to interest him in different hobbies, and eventually got him hooking rugs. Still, she worried that he spent a lot of time alone.

Meanwhile, Mildred was serving not only on the Vancouver School Board, but also on the CCF provincial executive and women's central committee, and was helping organize a winter school to complement the summer one. Often, as she dashed out the door to yet another meeting, Mildred felt guilty. Despite all her hard work, she was not earning a penny to contribute to the family coffers, and so was economically dependent upon her father. She felt she ought to be spending more time with him, yet she also knew that he — better than anyone — understood that nothing he could do or say would stop her. She had her mission, just as he had had his. Her zeal and depth of commitment were his legacy; he had set high standards of service. When society treated her as an outcast and scorned her deepest beliefs, she always found refuge from the pressure of politics at home.

By January 1937, Mildred was exhausted and badly in need of a break, so she readily agreed when her father suggested a visit to California. Father and daughter were both nursing colds when they boarded the train. Mildred read some Marx and the *Reader's Digest* along the way. They settled into a seaside cottage at La Jolla, where Mildred counted upon the sun and ocean to reinvigorate her body and spirit. She consulted the woman at the local health food store about her sense of physical depletion and came away with a book about the latest "health diet." In this bourgeois town of tourist shoppers and restaurant diners, Mildred felt "very far away from the struggle." That distance was exactly what she needed. "Gorgeous sunset walk with Father — filled me with 'an ecstasy of bliss' +100."[24]

Mildred had recently adopted a habit of noting fluctuations in her emotional and physical well-being in her diary: zero indicated a neutral, calm state of being, and plus or minus figures indicated more extreme states. For example, after an argument in defense of some striking workers, she wrote: "Feel +100 when I protect the exploited." Later in the month: "Felt terribly cross -200. Took a walk ... Felt -300." Or: "Father -100 when I returned." And another day: "More talk with Miss Grey about children ... Tired, head thick -100. What *is* wrong?"

It's interesting to speculate upon the conversation Miss Osterhout and Miss Grey had about children, which would have been a pressing issue at this stage. Exactly when Mildred decided that she would not bear children of her own is unclear, but it was a conscious decision and one she did not regret. Mildred was always involved with other people's children — nephews and nieces, students, friends and neighbours. She loved them and babysat them, but retained her personal and political freedom in a way no mother could have. Perhaps Mildred believed she was not meant to be a mother; in any case, it is far from certain that she could have conceived a baby had she wanted to. About this time she lost fifteen pounds and stopped menstruating altogether, a condition that would last almost ten years.[25]

After two months in California, Mildred looked forward to getting back into gear, but all too soon she felt "the old strain returning." The incessant rain wore her spirits down, and the squabbling within the movement gave her headaches, according to her diary. Her depression came through in her speeches: "My C.C.F. story sounds sad!" Mildred felt so tired and disillusioned, she decided to pull back from politics.

After a provincial election was called for June 1, 1937, Mildred declined a nomination, but the party didn't want to take no for an answer. Weeks later she was still feeling pressured to run. In mid-May the CCF Members of Parliament came west to campaign in support of the provincial candidates. First to arrive was M.J. Coldwell, who would later succeed Woodsworth as national party leader. Mildred hosted a supper for him and spent a week driving him around to various meetings. Woodsworth arrived a few days later, and Mildred was delighted to have him on her radio show and to chair a meeting for him. She rushed around madly all morning cooking and cleaning house before serving luncheon in the garden to J.S. and Lucy, Angus and Grace, and her sister, Belva.

On one of the campaign days, Mildred and Grace were scheduled to speak together in New Westminster at what was supposed to be "a huge women's rally." Something went wrong with the organizing, though, because they arrived to find an audience of only twelve women! Of course they spoke to the twelve, and then kept on speaking all around the province. The pace was hectic right up until election day. Mildred worked as a scrutineer and at the end of the day was too exhausted to go to the dance. The work paid off, though, with seven CCF members elected. Unfortunately, the Tories captured eight seats, making them the official opposition.

Mildred's "innards" had begun to act up in the last few days of the campaign, so she decided to fast. Perhaps it was the impact of Gandhi's asceticism, but she often criticized herself for overindulging — not only in tea and cakes, but even something as basic and nutritious as cheese sandwiches. Her diary does not reflect any spiritual motivation to this first extended fast, but rather that she considered it a sort of cathartic cure. Three days later she was definitely hungry and, by the ninth day, she was "more & more tired & hungry." By June 15th, when Vic and Connie left for a year in Europe, she still had not broken her fast. On the 19th, she ate her first solid food in eighteen days — some vegetables. A few days later she still felt "unpleasantly toxic," but her appendix was "not so naughty."

If Mildred was in less than good health, it seems that so was the CCF. For more than a year the party in B.C. had been fractured by bitter internal feuding. Debate at the annual convention was "acrimonious." In her journal, Mildred asked herself, "Why do nice people argue so nastily?" When it was all over, Mildred was happy to retreat to the quiet pleasures of summer in her back garden.

She was next persuaded to run for office in the spring of 1938. The riding of Dewdney, vacated by the death of Conservative MLA Dr. Frank Patterson, was not considered very strong CCF territory. Other potential candidates, including Grace MacInnis, Arnold Webster and Billie Mandale, the local party secretary, had already declined the nomination so everyone agreed Mildred was a real brick to take it on. She was encouraged when Canadian Pacific telegraphed a message from CCF headquarters in Ottawa. It read:

Victor, Reverend Osterhout and Mildred in the back garden, Vancouver, 1935.

Congratulations on your excellent choice of candidate stop British Columbia needs Miss Osterhout at Victoria stop Send her there with an over-whelming victory stop Every wish for success stop

J.S. Woodsworth and Federal Members.

Mildred went to work with Billie Mandale as her campaign manager. Her dad had given her free use of the family car, so they were able to kick off the campaign by plastering their posters all over the riding:

C.C.F. RALLY
Legion Hall, Mission City ...
Come and Hear The Peoples' Representatives

The peoples' representatives sharing the platform with Mildred included MLAs Dorothy Steeves, Lyle Telford, Sam Guthrie and Len Shepherd, as well as party president Arnold Webster, always a popular speaker. It was raining hard, but more than seven hundred people attended, making it one of the largest political rallies ever held in the Fraser Valley. In her speech, Mildred said:

I have looked into many faces since entering this campaign, faces telling of economic hardships and suffering. They are clear, poignant reminders of the necessity for a change, and it is you and I, friends, together with our movement, the C.C.F., who must make this change. Society must be built on a co-operative basis not, as at present, on the maintenance of privilege and the exploitation of man.[26]

Billie came up with a pamphlet called "Introducing *Your* Candidate." A black and white photo of Mildred was captioned: "Vote CCF for PEACE and PLENTY!" Its message was heavily punctuated for emphasis: "Poverty must be abolished in B.C.! Plenty must be shared! A chance to make a decent living must replace unemployment! Security must overcome insecurity! Creative leisure must be assured!"

Mildred's opponents took out advertisements in the papers. Liberal D.W. Strachan's asked, "Who's Best for Dewdney?" The ad for the Conservative candidate, Reeve W.A. Jones, answered "JONES is Best for Dewdney." Both men were middle-aged, balding and bespectacled, wearing crisp white shirts with conservative suits. Compared to these solid types, Mildred was at a disadvantage. She was too capable and well-educated to be dismissed merely for being a woman, but she was young and attractive — and single to boot! The CCF paper had fun with the way the mainstream press didn't quite know what to make of Mildred.

> Then — of all things — they have a woman candidate this time! As the *Victoria Times* says: Imagine a splendid woman like Miss Osterhout getting mixed up with poor people — those CCF'ers! Why, she could be a Liberal cabinet minister any day! They say she has made more friends in Dewdney in one week than her opponents have made in six.[27]

With Billie's extensive contacts and Mildred's growing confidence on the campaign trail, the campaign progressed so well that they began to think she actually had a chance of winning the seat. Certainly the local supporters were working overtime to help. "Why, the local CCF'ers have already laid down a barrage of raffle tickets which is simply impregnable," reported the party paper. Then, just days before the vote, disaster struck in the form of "help" from rival Communist Party pamphleteers.

> Our dear friends, the Communist enemy, with good or ill intent ... I'd like to know which, came swarming over the countryside two days before the election, and showered the country with dodgers, calling on the people to vote for the defender of freedom, democracy, bread, butter, cake and pie, the People's candidate, Mildred Osterhout. And signed themselves on behalf of the struggle ... The Communist Party of Canada.[28]

The CCF'ers were outraged. They knew, as Mildred and Billie knew, that it was "the kiss of death." Ironically, while she had been so busy fighting the right wing, she was betrayed by the left. On election night the victorious Liberal candidate congratulated Mildred on a good, clean fight. When the count was done, David Strachan had won with 2,034 votes. Mildred was third in the polls with 1,648 votes.

> 3:01 a.m. The night of defeat & victory! The shouting is over — the Liberals have followed the bagpipes down the street & left us quiet & sad. But we have taken it on the chin. In words of courage we have accepted the task of the job ahead & have determined to carry on.

> "I didn't know I wanted to win so much. But the faces ... [29]

Here the journal entry ends abruptly. Perhaps Mildred broke down in tears, thinking of the brave faces of the dear people who had worked so hard on her campaign. Maybe she just was overwhelmed with fatigue and nervous let-down. In any event, that was all she wrote on election night. A few days later, though, she wrote a long letter reflecting on the campaign, and the difficulties of being a single female candidate:

> Dear Comrades, ...

> Well, my dear friends, it was a glorious defeat ... but who could call it anything but a victory when we gained 400 votes?

> But of course you are not interested in all the lurid tales of the by-election in Dewdney. So I'll just let you in on the scandal. That Osterhout girl ... you know ... she has broken her father's home and heart. She has a shady past ... Of course she is a Communist ... and you know she ran all around the country with her campaign manager ... and well, shh ... its too too to mention in public. Women have no business in politics anyway. She should be married and raising a family of half a dozen young voters if she wants to make a contribution to the country ...

> Up gets [Liberal Premier Duff] Patullo, and spreads his massive front across the platform, and talks of his noble heritage, his long family tradition, his triumphant achievements to be perpetuated in a never ending line of putting Patullos. And he asks with great scorn ... what has Miss Osterhout to offer in the line of descendants to this country? Ah me, I forsee that before the next election I must grab a husband and give birth to a couple of sets of quintuplets.[30]

Mildred felt heartened to receive a letter from Ernest Winch, written in his angular hand on the blue-crested stationary of the Legislative Assembly:

> The tumult & the shouting dies,
> The candidate to her kin departs.
> Still for that glorious cause to fight
> With loyal and courageous heart.

Congratulations to a fine comrade for a good fight & a great victory.
Ernest E.

P.S. Of course next time I see you I'll be full to overflowing with much needed and greatly appreciated (?) criticism. E.E.

Mildred chuckled, her sense of humour never far from the surface. But she needed to step back from the political life and search more deeply on the spiritual side. She was still yearning to go to India, and the opportunity arose almost right away. Muriel Lester was taking a group from England to the Mahatma's ashram at Sevagram, and she wondered if Mildred could meet her there and help out as a sort of Gandhian tour guide? Yes, of course she'd love to. But could she afford it? Yes, thanks once again to her father's generosity. An insurance policy matured and Rev. Osterhout gave Mildred the money to go seek her prophet. By fall, she was off on her first pilgrimage to India.

Chapter Eight: 1938

PILGRIMAGE TO INDIA, PRELUDE TO WAR

Mildred flung open the porthole of her third-class cabin aboard the *Keian Maru*, bound for Yokohama. It was Halloween time in Vancouver, and the air was heady with the sting of sea spray and the aroma of roses — a farewell gift from Walter. She met her friendly Norwegian roommate, unpacked her fanciest dress (a borrowed taffeta) and went up for dinner which turned out to be a wonderful four-course feast. But soon her head began to pound, and she felt that queasy greenish feeling rising around the gills. She endured the next two days heaving in her bunk. When she finally found her sea legs, she surfaced in a stiff breeze and tottered a mile around the deck. After that, she was in her element. "Few people go out, but I put on my leather coat & helmet and wade right into it — so I'll have refreshing memories when I get to the tropics," she told the family.[1]

Throughout the trip, Mildred wrote regularly to "Dearest Father, Vic and Connie," whom she called "my very dear and only sister." They saved each letter, more than thirty in all, mailed at ports from Tokyo to Cairo. The Pacific Crossing from Vancouver to Yokohama took thirteen days. Mildred passed the time reading Nehru, and tried to follow his non-violent example by "declaring an armistice with the cockroaches." Not to give the wrong impression: everything was ship-shape.

There was one serious catch, however: Mildred was appalled to discover that her ship was owned by the Japanese government. Like most Canadians of the time, Mildred opposed Japan's illegal invasion and occupation of China, and she would never have booked passage on this line had she known. She campaigned against selling scrap metal to Japan and supported the boycott of Japanese goods called by the Women's International League for Peace and Freedom. She saw Japan as a fascist, militarist, imperialist state and she shuddered to think of even a penny of hers going into its coffers. Halfway across the ocean, she was still "nourishing sentiments of resentment against the Japanese & feeling unhappy about the boat!"[2]

Another little thing, but one that really irked Mildred, was how the crew persisted in trying to get her to eat Japanese food for breakfast. She was by nature a culinary adventurer, and during the journey she tasted oysters, eels, sukiyaki, sushi and other Japanese delicacies. But "a huge bowl of rice & bean soup to say nothing of a smoked fish & a young octopus on top of some bamboo shoots just isn't my idea of a breakfast."

Meal-times were even less satisfying in terms of conversation. Her dinner companions included a Russian mother and daughter "who are loquacious on one subject only — food & its deficiencies," and two "greyish" Free Methodist Missionaries. "We all study our menus intently & wish we'd ordered anything but what we called for. If an idea ever got loose at the table I'm sure the furniture would fall down under the weight of it."[3]

Within a few days, though, some interesting passengers surfaced from their sickbeds. There was a charming doctor from Siam (as Thailand was then called) and a delightful woman from Oregon, who had lived four years in Madras and loved it. Her enthusiasm about India contrasted with the attitude of the "missionary ladies," who exuded a smug sense of cultural and religious superiority.

The third day at sea was the birthday of the Japanese Emperor Hirohito. All the passengers and crew were made to assemble on deck, and the captain made a long patriotic speech. Then all the Japanese bowed towards Tokyo and sang their national anthem with pride. Mildred found the ceremony disturbing. "As I looked at the fervent faces and listened to the devoted chorus, I could not help praying, 'God save China from the passionate nationalism of this Imperialist-dominated people.' They are so filled with love of country that they could not bear the disloyalty of one critical thought."[4]

On board the *Keian Maru*, the only news passengers received came in the form of daily "radio sheets" that provided only sketchy details, mostly about developments in Japan, Germany and Italy. After watching a movie about Tokyo, Mildred wrote: "Talk about propagandists — these Japanese fairly gloat over their country & describe its glories to you. They seem to feel it a waste of time to go anyplace else."[5]

While Mildred despised the Japanese government, she tried to understand the Japanese people. Whenever possible, she struck up conversations with Japanese passengers or crew who spoke English. One day she talked with a young man who explained that the principal characteristics of the Japanese people were simplicity and unselfishness within. She asked how he could possibly correlate unselfishness with his nation's aggression towards China.

"War is very destructive," he said, "but out of it may come great spiritual triumph."

"No!" she cried. "War destroys spiritual values."

Mildred found it astounding that the Japanese actually believed they were "fighting for the spiritual triumph of the East!" "Well," she shrugged, "all the world is mad so why not Japan."[6]

It was the sort of sentiment that might have driven some people to drink, but not Mildred. She was a teetotaler, born and bred. She did go into the bar one day, where she sat and sipped a ginger ale, but "that was the extent of my indulgence in spite of invitations to join in parties to imbibe more potent fluids. Can't get away from my training!"[7]

Whether in the bar or on deck, the subject of tropical insects and diseases came up frequently in conversation amongst the passengers — especially those who, like Mildred, were still getting inoculated en route. After her last typhoid injection, she jealously guarded her sore arm as she bumped and zig-zagged her way about the ship. "I thought we were in for fine weather, but here we go loupy lou again to-night," she wrote. The storm hit soon after:

> … huge waves crashed with terrifying thunder against the side of the ship, threatening our timbers & joints. We were tossed from side to side in our bunks while our luggage played dash and dodge about the floor …

> When we tried to walk the decks torrents of water dashed over the sides to trip us in our stride. The sight of mountainous waves rising & tossing their snowy crests in endless succession was glorious.[8]

Finally a couple of days later, two other ships were sighted on the horizon and a small bird flew out to meet the *Keian Maru*. "Tomorrow I shall put my foot on the land of the Rising Sun," she wrote. They sailed into Yokohama harbour on November 11, Armistice Day, 1938.

One person she most looked forward to meeting was Dr. Toyohiko Kagawa, a visionary and poet who had achieved fame with his work "Songs From The Slums." Born out of wedlock to a geisha who was abandoned by her wealthy lover, Kagawa endured great deprivation in his childhood. He converted to Christianity as a young man, and lived out his faith in a slum area of Kobe known as Shinkawa, the "pest hole of the Orient." Kagawa and his wife were practically idolized by the Christian missionaries in Japan due to their extreme self-sacrifice.[9]

They graciously welcomed Mildred as a friend of Muriel Lester's. When Mrs. Kagawa offered her a pair of slippers, Mildred realized that yes, she really should take off her shoes when entering a Japanese home. By the end of her first conversation with Dr. Kagawa, Mildred could tell that he and Gandhi were motivated by the same spirit. Later he took her over to their Fellowship House, where she stayed for a few days while she visited some of their co-operative efforts: a settlement house, rice husking mill, nutritional food kitchen, consumer store, bank and pawn shop. Mildred was especially impressed with the kitchen, which turned out about 1,500 meals daily for hungry people.

Mildred's most vivid impression of Japanese society was the intense nationalism, although visible signs of the war were strangely lacking. There seemed to be no shortage of food among the wealthier classes, and the streets were full of young men who asserted they would be glad to go to war because it was such an honour to die for the emperor. Students wore uniforms of white shirts and red caps, symbolic of the Rising Sun flag. They were proud to support a national austerity program and eat the Rising Sun lunch — nothing more than a box of white rice with a red plum in the middle. The people regularly demonstrated in the streets to celebrate victory in battle, and the children were taught to sing songs with lines such as, "We shall quench our thirst in the red sea."

Mildred couldn't stand the thought of continuing to support such a belligerent regime, so she inquired about changing her ticket. She was told it would cost seventy-five dollars to leave the Japanese line and switch to P&O. At first the amount seemed prohibitive, but the more she thought about it, the more it galled her. Once again, Mildred had the freedom to take a principled stand because of her privileged economic position. Because of her father's steadfast support she could afford to simply take the loss and book herself aboard the *Rawalpindi* bound for Shanghai.

First, though, she spent a fascinating day with the family of J.S. Woodsworth's younger brother, Dr. Harold Woodsworth, then head of the department of English at the university near Kobe. Harold had started his mission in Japan in 1909 with the YMCA, and so his understanding of the culture was decades deep. Mildred appreciated his considerate interpretations of the political situation as it was unfolding in Japan. She wished she could have spent more time with the family, but she was scheduled to depart.

Sailing up the Yangtze was a shock: " ... past buildings shattered by bombs, in between warships flying the Japanese flag — we ploughed through the dirty water." Unlike Tokyo, Shanghai showed Mildred the human face of war. Homeless people slept in the streets and alleys, in doorways and on window ledges. Babies died like flies and were left in the street, "40 bundles often picked up on one night," she was told. A big truck trundled past, and Mildred was horrified to realize it was loaded down with human bodies. Victims of a bomb attack, they had been tossed in such that the arms and legs stuck out awkwardly on all sides.

At St. Luke's, a free hospital run by the Anglicans, the three hundred beds were always full and many patients had to be turned away daily. Doctors and nurses there had seen children abandoned, blinded by malnutrition, suffering from beri beri, dysentery, bayonet wounds and worse. They introduced her to a pregnant woman who had just been rescued from behind enemy lines. Japanese soldiers had poured kerosene over her body and set her aflame. The woman was horribly burned and profoundly terrorized. Her baby was stillborn. Mildred was shaken: "I've heard so much about atrocities in China that I'm almost ready to fight the Japanese myself so I may be a violent pacifist by the time I get home."[10]

She visited a refugee camp situated beside a filthy creek. Driven into exile by the Japanese invasion, the seven hundred ragged inhabitants were crowded together with only makeshift structures and straw bedding. They survived on thin vegetable soup and rice. Despite the atmosphere of drab destitution, Mildred got a hopeful feeling from the smiles of the women at their knitting or children at play. The refugees had even organized their own school, although books were scarce and students often lived eight or ten to a room.

She admired the quiet resistance of the Chinese: "You can't conquer people whose spirits will not be crushed." Still dignified and free in spirit, some Chinese people told her, "We are used to eating bitterness."[11] Mildred felt humbled by their resilient morale, and guilty that the West was "adding to the suffering through pouring munitions into the hands of the aggressor. The stain of such blood money must remain a disgrace from which we cannot escape until we stop the traffic in armaments."[12]

Mildred felt an instinctive sympathy for the Chinese but, as in Japan, she found the religious practices primitive. Visiting a Buddhist temple, she found it "lined with ugly dirty Gods," soiled by "the smoke of hundreds of candles & scent of thousands of incense sticks ... It's all very ugly & barbaric." This rather ethnocentric attitude would surprise people who knew Mildred later in life, when her awareness had transcended such judgmental pronouncements.

Outbound from Shanghai Mildred boarded the *Conte Verde*, an Italian ship bound for home port with stops in Hong Kong, Singapore and Colombo. From the capital of Ceylon (as Sri Lanka was then known) it would be only a brief ferry ride to India. "We have a lot of Italian soldiers on board, some of them in khaki & some black shirts. To see them raising their hand in open salute & strutting about like the conquerors of the world is certainly an appalling thing. Certainly one should be glad to live in Canada away from all this war hysteria."[13]

Meanwhile, the South China Sea was brilliantly blue and the gaily-coloured flying fish flashed in and out of the waves as they sailed the coasts of Vietnam and the Malay peninsula. In Singapore, Mildred toured botanical gardens luxuriant with ferns and fragrant orchids. Friendly monkeys leaned down out of

In "the Pearl of the Indian Ocean," 1938.

the palms to be fed by hand. Later she visited a leper colony up on a hill outside of the city. The colony was home to three hundred people, "some with horrible sores and deformities, decaying fingers & toes." Mildred's concern about disease and wellness was broadened in Asia, where public health issues were much more critical than in Canada. She felt great compassion for the lepers, but she could not have worked among them. "Between the lepers & the monkeys I've developed a scratching complex," she wrote home.

Arriving in "the Pearl of the Indian Ocean," as Sri Lanka was then called, Mildred felt "a great sense of contentment, as if I had arrived." She tasted papaya for the first time and relished an omelette with coconut and red peppers. She rode an elephant, swam in the surf and visited the Cinnamon Gardens, spicy and colourful with hibiscus and bougainvillea.

Mildred found much to delight the eye and empty the purse in the market places of Asia. In Tokyo she was tempted by the glossy lacquer ware and brilliant silks. In Shanghai she "went on a frantic shopping expedition" and ended up having to buy another suitcase to carry her tea pots, kimonos and other trinkets. In Colombo she couldn't resist a garnet ring and bracelet. At last in India, she was immediately assailed by the crowding, the pitiful beggars and the enormity of the people's need. She felt sinful to have done so much shopping in the midst of such poverty.

As planned, Mildred met up with Muriel Lester in Madras. They were booked into the YWCA, where she arrived to find "Miss Muriel" ill in bed, but well enough to dispatch her niece, Dorothy Hogg, on multiple errands. Dorothy gave the clear impression that their tour was "singularly up in the air." Mildred wondered: "Am I on a wild goose chase or just a lame duck hunt?"[14]

Their first destination was an ecumenical conference in Tambaram, south of Madras. Neither Mildred, Muriel nor Dorothy was registered, but given the nature of the gathering they hadn't anticipated a problem in joining the 470 people from 70 countries assembled there. Unfortunately, the proceedings were closed and delegates were "kept as closely locked in as we are kept barred out." Mildred decided not to even try to gain access to the meetings, but she did go to a reception held in the garden at Government House. She didn't have an invitation, but was able to borrow that of a Mrs. Foley, who had departed India the previous night. "I quite surprised Mr. Foley by announcing my adoption of him as a husband," Mildred wrote home. She enjoyed the colourful pageant of seekers in traditional Chinese, Japanese, Malayan, Indian and Western costumes. The Governor arrived in state and paraded between the red-coated soldiers to the head table under a canopy in the garden, "whereupon we all rushed to the food & fell upon the sandwiches & cake with great gusto."

In Madras, Mildred felt lucky to have the chance to meet Sarojini Naidu, a leader of both the All India Women's Conference and the Congress Party. She was a woman "whose radiant personality shines through the whole Gandhian epic and is forever remembered in India."[15] Mrs. Naidu gave an eloquent talk on the role of women in creating the new civilization: "Liberation from the sense of inferiority is our great need. Inferiority is only an illusion — we must stand up & say 'I am free.'"[16] Afterwards, the women had tea and other Indian and English delights: "spices rolled in a leaf, curry roll, sweet sausage, fruit salad, ice cream and cake." Remembering the meals in London curry houses with Devadas Gandhi and Mahadev Desai, Mildred thought, "How jolly to see chapatis again!"

Mildred soon discovered that Muriel hadn't changed a bit in the seven years since they last met and hence their friendship remained tinged with ambivalence on her part. She wrote:

> Muriel is her delightful, stimulating, impulsive, aggravating, disconcerting self. I'm very lucky Dorothy is here to get the brunt of her disturbing inspirations. We have a quiet haw haw on the side over her many impulses — but she is a vivid soul and stirs people profoundly.[17]

Within a few days Mildred decided to head out on her own. After all, she hadn't come all the way to India just to have tea or go shopping (although she did get wonderful cobra and python belts for only one rupee from a peddler at the door of the Y). But she seemed to spend so much time waiting for Muriel that relations between the two were sometimes quite tense. Finally Mildred just got "fed up with Madras & decided to start my tour a week before Muriel's with a visit to an ashram." Off she went to visit a missionary named Mary Barr at Nidibula.

She bought a ticket for the 7:45 a.m. train, boarded a third-class car designated "Ladies Only," and settled in to enjoy the ride. It began pleasantly enough, but it turned out to be "rather a disastrous trip." First the train ran into a buffalo and killed it. As if that was not bad enough, it later struck and killed a blind man. As they chugged away from the scene of the accident, Mildred only had eyes for the "miserable half-blind beggar child" left with five rupees in one hand and his father's dead body at his side. It was Christmas Eve, 1938.

Despite the deaths, Mildred arrived at her destination only one hour late. Too late to find the ashram, she stayed with the family of an American doctor who ran a Salvation Army Hospital. That evening they witnessed a lamb being taken to slaughter in preparation for Christmas feasting Indian style. "As I go to bed the beating of drums tell the story of another death — the lamb," Mildred wrote in her diary. "Altogether it was rather a killing day."

Next morning Mildred felt so homesick that she became very weepy at the ashram, thinking of her empty chair by the fireplace. She told her father, Vic and Connie: "At first I felt very sorry for myself & missed you all very much. But I read your letters again & looked at your pictures & decided to be happy. And really it has been quite an interesting day."

She learned something about political diversity within the Indian National Congress from "a lean, unshaven youth," an ardent Congress supporter. He explained that the socialist sector in Congress readily accepted Gandhi as its leader and was willing to co-operate on the immediate goal — the overthrow of British imperialism. However, the Communists did not accept non-violence as their creed, only as a political strategy peculiarly suited to Indian conditions and psychology. He also explained that the left wing of the Congress Party opposed Gandhi's program of village industry because they did not believe it would solve India's economic injustices. To go back to the old homespun ways, as Gandhi advocated, was a step backwards, he said, not forward into the bright future of an independent India. "They believe in the socialization of machinery, not the return to medieval society," he told Mildred.

She talked with another youth, "a devout follower of Gandhi's who believes completely in non-violence and soul force. He is convinced that nothing would hurt him because his love goes out to all things — he does not fear even snakes or tigers. He is a very sweet person & gives a great sense of peace." He touched Mildred with his loving forms of address, first calling her "sister" and then "mother."

Late in the day, the ashram people all sat in a circle on the ground to enjoy Christmas dinner. The food was served on a palm leaf and eaten with the fingers: rice, several curries, cucumber and lime pickle, fresh white butter on hot roti, lots of buttermilk. "The food is really very tasty, and I have never found a more gentle or friendly people."

On Boxing Day she followed the ashram program. Up at 4:30 a.m. and at prayers by 5:00. The monotonous chanting almost put Mildred back to sleep again, but she roused herself when they called upon her to make a contribution to the service. She cleared her throat and tried her best to sing "Silent Night." A salutation to the Congress flag at 5:45 was followed by yoga at 6:00. Mildred struggled with the cross-legged lotus position, but she couldn't get it and felt her legs were "unusually exposed" in the attempt. At 7:00 they walked to a nearby village and visited the school, the library and a settlement of Untouchables. They walked back through the ashram fields and orchard. In the afternoon some people set to spinning, while Mildred and others went by bullock cart to a new open-air school run by seven young teachers, all committed Congress Party volunteers. They returned to the ashram for supper, more prayers, raisins and milk, and bed by 9 p.m. Mildred turned down an offer for a "sleeping friend."

The visit to this small ashram was a wonderful preface to Mildred's arrival at Gandhi's home, called *Sevagram*. In Hindi, *seva* broadly means service and *gram* means community. To be considered *seva*, however, the work must be done out of purest love, without any thought to remuneration or recognition.[18] Located in the centre of the sub-continent near the city of Wardha, Sevagram was home to Gandhi and his wife Kasturbai from 1935 until his death. There Bapu and Ba, as they were known, lived with about twenty-five others in a self-sustaining community. It was a shabby village in one of the poorest areas of the country, but after the Mahatma settled there it became known as "the heart of India."

Mildred hired a horse-drawn *tonga*, or cart, for the five-mile trip from Wardha to the ashram. The early morning air was refreshing, the quiet broken only by the driver's incessant haggling at his thin pony. Soon they had to raise the cover over the tonga for shelter from the harsh sun over the barren prairie. Finally arriving in Sevagram, her heart swelled as old friends from London ran out to greet her — first Pyarelal, surprisingly looking somewhat younger. "And then what a joy to see Mahadev — so upright, so gracious, so full of love & goodness."[19]

Mahadev showed Mildred into the thatched hut where the Mahatma sat cross-legged on the dirt floor. The room was bare except for a wooden box upon which sat a typewriter, The Bhagavad Gita and The Bible. Even though the room was so simple, "you didn't feel it was barren because Gandhi was there."

"*Namaste,*" he said warmly, making the traditional Indian greeting — a bow over the palms held together as in prayer. Then with a broad smile and a firm handshake he welcomed her again in the Western way.

Mildred in a sari holding an Indian girl, 1938.

"What a good surprise — you have come two days early. You will be able to lift the burden from my shoulders and help welcome and take care of the guests."

"I hope I'll not be a nuisance," she said.

"We won't let you be a nuisance," he assured her. "You must make yourself at home. Make friends with everybody. Get to know them all." Then he told her: "I'm not going to talk to you now. I must bury myself in these papers. Rest here, and afterwards we will walk."

Then an astonishing thing happened: Mildred actually did "rest here," as he suggested. Like a child, she lay down on the mat at Bapu's feet and slumbered peacefully. She dreamed "of protecting him from the distractions of his grandson." Her trust in Gandhi must have been deep, for Mildred would normally not have allowed herself to be so vulnerable as to sleep in public, and his little hut was a busy place in the middle of the morning: "And then I awake to listen to his interviews. A steady stream of people come with personal and state matters," she wrote.[20]

Gandhi maintained a strict discipline in his schedule for prayer, exercise, work, spinning, eating and sleeping. Twice a day, he would walk out a couple of miles along the dusty country road. Followers would take turns walking beside him, asking questions along the way. "There is continuous discussion, mostly of a serious nature and mostly in Hindi." The destination was always the same — a humble cottage, home of a former ashram-dweller now suffering from "consumption," as people still called tuberculosis. The Mahatma only stopped for the briefest of visits with the man and then would turn right back, but he was there every day, morning and evening.

Mildred tried to share in all the activities of the ashram, rising for prayers at 4:30 and bedding down under the stars a little after sunset. To her, the members of the community seemed very contented. They worked hard, but gladly, and there was a leisurely grace to their work. They believed that silence was correct for meals, which they considered "a sacrament preparing the body as the home for the soul." A good vegetarian diet was served on brass platters, and everyone washed his own plate, bowl and spoon after each meal. Daily spinning was also regarded as sacred, and was usually done in contemplative silence. Many years later, she wrote a report in which she described Gandhi's program for uplifting the poor:

> If ever a man practised what he preached … and before he preached … it was Mohandas Gandhi, and because of the sincerity of his life people believed in him. As he showed his great love for them, they in turn loved him. He held that to have possessions made man fearful, so he gave up all he had and lived as a simple poor villager. All around him he saw people hungry and starving. In the midst of such suffering he could never be content, so he sought a solution. What could be done? The answer must come from the efforts of the people themselves. They must grow their own food and cotton. They must spin and weave their cloth and make their sandals. And so began the plan to build up village crafts and industries. Soon he had millions of people making and wearing their own homespun *khadi* cloth. And what of the children? Surely they must be taught … but what? Again, the practical seemed most important, training in making the things they could use. So Gandhi proposed the Basic Scheme of Education, to start training children in the arts and crafts, so they could use their hands and brains to produce things. Reading and writing were to be correlated with the practical arts. It was the project method really put into action in a full-time program.[21]

In Sevagram, Gandhi tried to show it was possible to reverse the cycle of poverty and misery, and to rebuild the dignity and spirit of the village community. He started with the basics: clean water and simple sanitation measures. The ashram's well was large and deep, and villagers were free to help themselves. He brought better methods of farming and animal husbandry, greater self-reliance among the villagers and new respect for their traditional skills. He said to Mildred, "When this becomes a model village, my work will be complete."

The Maganwadi Institute, a new school and museum for craft industries, was one of Gandhi's latest success stories. The practical education programs were designed to train artisans as teachers to take the lost arts and crafts back to the villages. The museum displayed methods of work, as well as a fine collection of handicrafts ranging from metal and woodwork to paper-making and, of course, spinning and weaving. Mildred and a group from the ashram came out to the opening celebrations. As usual when Gandhi spoke in public, great throngs turned out to hear him and broke into enthusiastic cheers of "Gandhiji, Gandhiji" when they arrived.

As one looked over the great crowd, it was quite evident that the majority were dressed in *khadi*, altho some of the women still wore their more elaborate saris and some of the men were in European dress. The speaking was all in Hindi, but one gathered the interest of the crowd from the attentive faces and the stirring applause. Most attention was given to the quiet voice of the Mahatma as he sat cross legged on a raised form and talked of the interest of the Congress in the village industries, and appealed to the people to support them in the movement to make the people independent … and self reliant by building up their own industries.[22]

Certainly the kind of co-operative cottage and village industries proposed by Gandhi would have offered the ashram workers far greater dignity than the average industrial or agricultural worker. Essentially no formal labour regulations of any kind protected either city or farm workers, and many sweated for as little as three annas a day, a pittance even by Indian standards. A few trade unions had formed and had staged some successful strikes. The propaganda on the picket line was harsh, but true: "Do not scab. Today you will eat, but tomorrow you will starve like us."

Being constantly confronted with people on the verge of starvation put the politics of food forefront in Mildred's mind. Typically, she saw the contradictions between her ideals and her behaviour. One day she "stuffed it in" at a "very posh tea." Then she returned to the ashram, only to find they had kept supper for her. "In starving India I continue to overeat — what a crime!"

On New Year's Eve, Gandhi, Mildred and other members of the ashram slept out all night "so we were right at the place of worship when the bell rang. I could catch something of the fine spirit of devotion even if I couldn't understand the words. For about 45 minutes the prayers continued while the stars seemed to move beyond the horizon."

After prayers were done Gandhi called her and said, "Mildred, I think you had better go in [to Wardha] and meet Muriel and her party. If you can start in fifteen minutes I'll send Munilal with you." So for the next two hours, Mildred and young Munilal walked together across the Indian prairie. She was shod in sandals, his feet were bare. The stars faded and the sun rose, "glorifying the sky." Along the way, Munilal spoke of how he believed that life should be devoted wholly to seeking God and truth. "The artificial wants we have created in the West detract from the real purpose of life," he said. At Wardha station, Mildred and Munilal had a challenge to pack Muriel and sixteen others, along with all their luggage, into various carts.

Once they had gotten settled at the ashram, they all sat down in a circle on the ground and Gandhi gave them a talk on the universal law of non-violence

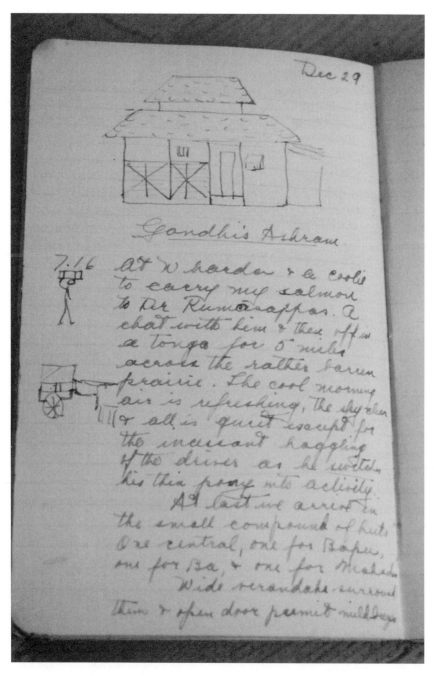

Dec 29.

Gandhi's Ashram.

7.16 At N harder + a coolie to carry my salmon to Dr Rumanappas. A chat with him + then off in a tonga for 5 miles across the rather barren prairie. The cool morning air is refreshing, the sky clear + all is quiet except for the incessant haggling of the driver as he switches his thin pony into activity.

At last we arrive in the small compound of huts. One central, one for Bapu, one for Ba, + one for Mahadev.

Wide verandahs surround them + open doors permit mild breeze

A sketch of Gandhi's ashram from Mildred's trip diary of 1938-1939.

or *ahimsa*, as he called it. "Non-violence begins and ends in humility," he told them. Gandhi believed that non-violence was a comprehensive quality of love, an "attribute of the soul" that everyone must strive to practise every day in all the affairs of life. "[23] It was the active spirit of ahimsa that led Gandhi into the homes and hearts of the lepers and untouchables, the most lowly of India's still-rigid caste system. Gandhi called them *Harijans*, children of God. Mildred had heard him say all these things during their time in London but somehow, here in India, it all made a great deal more sense. Although he was born into the Vaisya caste (second only to the Brahmin), Gandhi considered himself an outcaste. He said:

> I am a "touchable" by birth, but an "untouchable" by choice, and I have endeavoured to qualify myself to represent, not the upper ten even among the "untouchables," because be it said to their shame there are castes and classes among them, but my ambition is to represent and identify myself with, as far as possible, the lowest strata of the "untouchables," namely the "invisibles" and the "unapproachables," whom I have always before my mind's eye wherever I go; for they have indeed drunk deep of the poisoned cup.[24]

The political expression of ahimsa was *satyagraha*, often translated as "soul force." Gandhi wrote that: "Truth {Satya} implies love, and Firmness {Agraha} ... serves as a synonym for force. ... the force which is born of truth and love or non-violence."[25] While many people have mistaken non-violence for passivity, Gandhi's concept of pacifism was always dynamic and active. Independence from Britain was still almost a decade away, but the movement was building and the *satyagrahi*, the warriors of non-violence, included the flower of India's youth, some of her greatest poets and religious leaders, her most influential teachers and wealthiest businessmen. Willing to suffer and even to die in the cause of their country's freedom, nothing would make them kill for that cherished goal. The Mahatma told Muriel's group that a "heroic resolve and willing sacrifice is supreme satyagraha." To Gandhi, the means were all. He often said: "Ahimsa is the means; Truth is the end."

On January 2, 1939, Mildred celebrated her 39th birthday. When the ashram dwellers asked her age, "the awful truth [came] out." Dorothy bought her a brass bowl and jar, but that evening she went to visit a girls' school where she was given the best birthday gift of all — an honorary Indian name. The girls named her *Shanti*, Peace.

All too soon, it was time to leave the ashram. For the rest of her life though, Mildred would cherish the memories of those unforgettable days with Gandhi at Sevagram. She wrote: "In his sincerity and love for truth, one finds the core of the spirit that permeates the ashram and sends one away with a feeling of awe."[26] Half a century later, she looked back on the experience and said, "I felt that it was all very real ... He reminded me so much of Jesus."

Traveling with Muriel, Dorothy and five others, Mildred made her way to Santiniketan, an arts university on the plains of Bengal outside Calcutta. Founded in 1901 by the poet and painter Rabindranath Tagore, Santiniketan was "the abode of peace." Tagore, the 1913 Nobel laureate for literature, was the one who gave Gandhi the name, *Mahatma*, Great Spirit. With his long robes and flowing white beard, his limpid eyes and expressive hands, he looked like a prophet. Mildred's group had half an hour with Tagore, but they had slept little aboard an overnight train and so she was too tired to get much out of the interview. "He is a dear old chap," was all she wrote. "He is now 79 and keeps fairly quiet, but takes an interest in what is going on."[27]

The next day Muriel gave a speech on "The Creative Spirit at Work," in which she praised the ample evidence at Santiniketan of the glorious creative capabilities of the human spirit. But, she cautioned, in countries torn by war, in hearts enslaved by bitterness and hatred, in the evil factory system that enslaved millions of Indian children, in all these ways, the creative spirit has been stifled by the forces of destruction. "Child slaves must be freed or none of us will be free," Muriel declared.

From Santiniketan, the group travelled onto Benares, where they saw thousands of people making pilgrimages to the sacred River Ganges. Mildred found the sights strange and disturbing. "Benares hangs in my mind like a nightmare with its dirty temples and crowds of people washing, bathing, splashing and bowing in the muddy Ganges, and then drinking some of it. Such masses of people tied to superstition and prejudice are very depressing," she wrote. From there they moved on to another inspiring ashram in Lucknow, where Mildred chose not to stay with Muriel's group. "I decided not to keep up with her sketchy pace. I'd rather take two looks at the camels & elephants ... & take time to talk to a few people — & buy another trinket I haven't room for."[28]

Her next stop was Agra, site of the extravagantly beautiful Taj Mahal. More than three decades in the creation, it was built at the behest of the Moghul Emperor Shah Jahan in memory of his beloved wife Mumtaz Mahal, who died in 1629 giving birth to their fourteenth child. Mildred was captivated by the Taj, and went back several times to see it at sunrise, in the noonday glare, and by moonlight. In her trip diary, Mildred drew a careful sketch with her fountain pen. She thought it was:

> Indescribably beautiful, giving one a sense of awe & wonder & seeming more perfect than anything I've ever seen. Completely satisfying. Rhythmical unified chaste. Something of the eternal & infinite makes one tread softly before this structure of ageless beauty.[29]

Taj Mahal, Agra, 1938.

From Agra, Mildred travelled on to Delhi, and then on to Indore, where her head began to ache, then burn and whirl. Luckily she was staying with an English missionary couple, the Taylors. Her hostess treated the fever with aspirin, bromide and quinine, and cared for her tenderly. Mildred was intrigued to hear about their work with a tribal people, the Bhils, among whom were many new Christians. The missionaries would go out on three-week camping expeditions into the villages, where they taught literacy and basic Bible lessons.

Throughout her journey, Mildred was always observing and searching for the best way to make use of her skills, waiting for the call to stay and serve in India. She had considered the possible scenarios and she knew one thing for certain: if she stayed on, she could not live apart from the Indian people, as many of the English and North Americans did. "I wonder about the missionaries," she wrote, "the bungalows, the comforts, the protection & exclusion." However, she also knew herself well enough to question whether she could really live happily in a mud hut.

From Indore, Mildred traveled to Bardoli, a village near Bombay where Gandhi had launched one of the first civil disobedience campaigns back in the early 1920s. There she was welcomed by Mahadev Desai and shown to her lodgings, which were much more comfortable than the huts in Sevagram. The atmosphere was one of contentment. When she asked residents whether they liked it better in Bardoli than in Sevagram, they said, "It does not matter — wherever Bapu is."

That day, Mildred sat down to lunch with Gandhi, Muriel and Dorothy Lester, and a few Indian friends. Over the meal, Mildred took a deep breath and seized the opportunity to speak directly to Gandhi about her growing desire to stay in India. From her diary:

> I confess — "I do not want to go from India, Bapu."
> "Then why go? You are welcome here. There is free board and room as long as you want to stay."
> "If I had something useful to do that would make me feel justified I'd stay."
> "Well, you are a good little washer!"
> "But you have plenty of them already."

> I told him about my visit to Indore and the work that the Taylors are doing with the Bhils. He seemed only just interested. And then the conversation turned Hindi and soon I had to go — at least I went. A warm farewell with Mahadev.[30]

Gandhi's devastating off-handedness in this encounter must have left Mildred feeling crushed. For the second time in her life, she had appealed to him like a supplicant. As she had at Kingsley Hall, she humbly asked him to define her destiny, to justify her yearning to leave her homeland and seek the heroic path. One wonders how Mildred's life would have been different if he had taken her hand, looked her in the eye and appealed for her help. What if he had asked her to start a literacy program in his village, asked her to run a school or an orphanage, or to work with women, or seniors? What if? Her future hung on his reply.

But with regard to Mildred, the Mahatma was no visionary. He quickly dismissed the work of her missionary friends and failed to see her in any role other than that of "a good little washer." The patronizing term must have hurt, and the way he saw so little of her true nature and abilities must have been bitterly disappointing. If Gandhi had suggested anything more challenging or meaningful than offering sacrificial housework, she could have found the "justification" she was seeking to keep her in India. But his words offered no avenue for her best contribution and, besides, she could (and would) be "a good little washer" soon enough back in Vancouver. Mildred's thoughts turned to her Father, and she felt the familiar tug homeward.

She headed into Bombay, the ancient port city on the Arabian Sea. Devadas Gandhi was there, so Mildred phoned him when she arrived and they agreed to meet for lunch. She got hopelessly lost on the way, but finally found the right restaurant. She was surprised and pleased to discover that Devadas had brought a friend along as a chaperone. "How flattered I am," she wrote.

She found Bombay to be a place of sharp contrasts: sublime beauty and utter squalor, great tolerance and deep hatred. One day she heard an inspiring lecture on the shared spiritual and social values of all religions. Another day she went out to "a very swell cricket clubhouse — built upon modern lines and furnished with the latest in upholstered steel. Men in white ducks & women in lovely saris and some in western dress sauntered about in a most sophisticated manner." On the way back to the YWCA, they stopped at a roadside stand for some fresh coconut milk. As she scooped the soft sweet fruit out of the shell, she reflected that although she felt quite at home in a colonial setting, she actually preferred the people of the countryside to the ultra-Westernized Anglo-Indians.[31]

On February 1, 1939, Mildred turned her face towards home. Leaving India, a land striving for peace, she re-entered a world moving inexorably into war. The crew on board her ship were like "Junior Mussolinis in white duck uniforms." What was worse, she wrote:

I have Mr. & Mrs. Hitler & a German friend sitting at my table, so I'm increasing my acquaintance with the Fascist block ...

We have quite a number of Indians in [Economy] class & I am trying to imagine I'm still in India by talking to them. They are more or less segregated at meals ...

We haven't many British officers going home yet but there are a few & I shall probably dump them all overboard before we arrive. It would be easier than to convert them to an understanding of the Indian national point of view, & they shouldn't be allowed to go around without it. Their attitude of superiority just about drives me to forsake non-violence.[32]

The ship sailed westward through the Arabian Sea and into the Red Sea, past the coasts of Ethiopia and Saudi Arabia, bathed in glorious sunshine. At Massawa they stopped to take on new passengers, including the Italian Minister of Colonies, for whom the locals put on a lavish send-off. Row upon row of school children, scouts, policemen, Arab troops and Italian soldiers in black shirts all lined up in front of the *Casa del Fascio*. Mildred was chilled by the display. "These fascist demonstrations freeze my blood rather than stir it — so it was good it was a hot day & I could thaw out."[33]

Mildred disembarked at Port Said, intending to see a bit of Egypt and then visit Riek Liesveld, who was teaching in Palestine. During a week in Cairo she saw the ancient wonders: the Sphinx, the pyramids, the historic mosques and bazaars, the fabulous riches of King Tut's tomb. She also saw poverty worse than anything she had witnessed in India. Despite the discouraging words of the consul who issued her Palestinian visa, Mildred was full of excitement as the minarets of Cairo faded into the distance and the sunset glowed red over the desert.

She was headed for the Holy Land, resonant with its sacred geography: Nazareth and Jerusalem, the River Jordan and the Sea of Galilee. Cradle of three great faiths — Islam, Judaism and Christianity — Palestine then as now was seething with racial and religious strife. Captured from the Turks in 1917, it had been under the British Mandate ever since and the Palestinians naturally rebelled against the English occupation. In Lydda, Mildred was told that no trains, buses or taxis made the forty-mile trip to Jerusalem because the route was too unsafe. At the same time, everyone warned her not to stay overnight because Lydda was in a battle zone. She couldn't get out of town, but she couldn't stay put either. In the end, one of the British Tommies suggested she could get a ride with the mail wagon. The driver agreed to take her, so she squeezed in between him and a policeman, who sat with a loaded revolver in his lap as he told war stories and pointed out the wrecks of bombed cars beside the road.

Finally in Jerusalem, Mildred was eager to see Riek. However, it turned out she was teaching at Bir-Zeit, a Jewish settlement in rebel-held territory twenty-five miles outside of the city, and she couldn't be reached by telephone because the Arabs had cut the lines. Within a few days, a German minister agreed to attempt the drive out to Riek's school. As they approached the settlement, their car was stopped by soldiers, who had surrounded the town in search of "bandits." They were finally persuaded to let the car pass. Mildred found Riek sick in bed with the flu, so they bundled her up and took her back to Jerusalem for some "R and R."

There they stayed with a gracious German couple, friends of Riek. Mildred was amazed to see how they, like all Jerusalem residents, struggled to carry on with their lives despite the terrible violence in the streets. It affected everyone. For example, they were worried about a young Englishman, another former volunteer at Kingsley Hall, who had been shot three times in the back as he went out to mail a letter. He was paralyzed and remained in critical condition in hospital. It went without saying that his assailants had not been arrested, and that no one would ever be brought to justice. Such attacks were an everyday occurrence. For Mildred, the emotional impact of this reality was amplified by the historic setting. She climbed the Mount of Olives to the tranquil Garden of Gethsemane where Judas had betrayed Jesus with a kiss. She walked through the scene of His agony and came back more deeply aware of humanity's ongoing pain.

Later, Mildred wrote an article called "Palestine in Confusion" in which she summed up some of her impressions of the dilemma of the Holy Land:

The life of the city goes on as of old, with its buying and selling in the open markets, the slow procession of men and women, of donkeys and camels through the narrow cobble stone streets. But suddenly there is a sound of shots, a few people scurry by, the crowd scatters to make way for a military car rushing through. A sense of alarm pervades the atmosphere. Someone has been shot. Some hasten to find out the details. Others clutch their purchases and hurry home. For a short time there is a tense, quiet stillness. But in a few moments the street is filled again and business goes on as usual.

Living in the midst of such disturbances many become inured to the danger, and go about their affairs without much interference. Others become so nervously upset that every moment is filled with terror, each shot arouses new alarms, and day and night alike are poignant with fear …

The most unhappy feature of the situation is that with murder and blood-shed running rife, the situation becomes more and more chaotic and no solution appears to the disorder. The Jews and Arabs both claim priority rights. The British have promised to help each nation. The Jews, the more cultured and intelligent group, are rapidly gaining control of the economic and social life of the country. The Arabs are resisting with the only weapon they know, terrorism. The British, unable to check the trouble by ordinary policing, have resorted to concentration camps, and are herding suspects into them in large numbers.

Palestine is just another example of the futility of isolation. To solve her problems without reference to other countries is impossible. As long as refugee Jews cast out from Europe can find no haven elsewhere they will force their way into Palestine. Only a united effort of the nations to redirect the energies of the Fascist powers into constructive expression, and a willingness of all to share in the distribution of land and resources to the deprived nations can bring peace to Palestine or any other country. I left the Holy Land with the question … How long, oh Lord, how long?[34]

Within a couple of days, Muriel Lester arrived in Jerusalem "in more of a flutter than usual even." She was still accompanied by her niece, Dorothy, and her sister, Doris. The three ladies "had got excited about the unsettled state of affairs & had flown in, then taxied a long distance. They had a number of appointments but a meeting had to be cancelled because it was in the curfew area." Seeing Muriel again, this time in the Middle East, provoked some serious doubts in Mildred's mind. It was becoming ever more clear that war was breaking out all over the world, and she wondered how best to respond, on the personal and political levels, to the upcoming conflict. She questioned Muriel's extensive globetrotting on behalf of the Fellowship of Reconciliation. Due to the Lester family's huge fortune, Muriel could afford to go wherever duty called. But was it effective? Mildred, like Riek, seemed to favour the idea of staying put in one place and working for peace at the community level, rather than flitting about the world talking to the like-minded.

> Sometimes I think the sort of thing Muriel is doing travelling about making friendly contacts, is good but at other times I wonder if she is just touching a kindly group of peace-minded people & not causing a ripple on the front of the war mongers. It is so difficult to see any way of being really effective in this appalling situation. Riek & her friends seem to think that just living one's convictions & breathing peace is about all one can do. Well there are enough [people] snorting hate & fear that some counter action is necessary. It seems rather a pious hope that you could get Arabs & Jews together even to talk things over in Palestine now.[35]

This letter signals the first time Mildred articulated the quality for which she would always be remembered: living her convictions, "breathing peace." She was open to people, and they sensed right away they could trust her. A cabin boy, for example, dared to talk frankly about the terrible unemployment and suffering under Mussolini. He even questioned *El Duce's* right to be waging war on the Abyssinians. "No Italians want to live in Abyssinia. Too bad Mussolini didn't know that!" Mildred clung to these hopeful signs. The gondoliers who poled alongside the ship as they docked in Venice harbour were colourful and charming, but she had no intention of lingering in Italy.

"It won't be long now that I'm in British territory — in fact long before you receive this I'll be under the protection of the Great British Navy," she reassured those back home. "With Mussolini reaching out into the Mediterranean one wonders just how long Britain will be able to hold sway there. It is quite evident that Italy has aspirations to control it."[36]

From Venice, to Basel, to Paris, to Boulogne: there she met a German woman fleeing her homeland because "she had some Jewish blood." They had a rough sailing over the Channel and the young refugee was terribly ill, alone and frightened. Mildred cared for her and offered her deep sympathy. On the train from to Folkestone to London, she met another refugee, an elderly man who for twelve years had been the chief rabbi of Berlin. "We gave the Bible to the world and all the world hates us," he told her. She thought "he was a delightful old man with a sparkle in his eye & a zest for living in spite of all the tragedy."[37]

The momentous tragedy that lay in store for the Jews of Europe was as yet unimaginable, but there had been more alarming signals since Hitler marched unopposed into Austria and declared it part of the Third Reich. In September 1938, the British and French met with him in Munich and signed over the

Sudeten region of Czechoslovakia as well. Prime Minister Neville Chamberlain came back to London promising "peace in our time," but Munich soon became a symbol of weakness. Even so, the British maintained their disastrous policy of appeasement. Chamberlain was not the only one taken in by Hitler's false assurances; Canadian Prime Minister Mackenzie King had met him in 1937, and came away convinced he was "a simple peasant" with no plans to fight either France or Britain.

Mildred was relieved and happy to be back in "dear old, dirty old London," especially after March 15, when the news came that Hitler had taken the rest of Czechoslovakia. She went back to the familiar security of Canada House and wrote home:

> Being here in London makes the reality of war so vivid. Parks are still being dug up for air raid shelters. People are being supplied with ... corrugated iron shelters to be set up in their own property, babies are being fitted with gas masks, teachers are receiving instructions about evacuating their classes, and the atmosphere is filled with a fatalistic belief that war must come.
>
> There is ... widespread and growing dissatisfaction with the Chamberlain policy. People seem convinced that Hitler will go on ... and on. The refugees that keep pouring in tell ghastly tales of their own, and their friends' experiences ...
>
> Personally I feel somewhat paralyzed too ... there seems so little the individual can do, but go on in the daily round, and hope.[38]

First thing, she picked up her mail, read and re-read the news from home. Connie was pregnant and everyone was awaiting the birth with great anticipation. A note came from the CCF, requesting her to stand as a candidate in Point Grey in the upcoming federal election. She decided to decline. Instead, she set about re-visiting old haunts. She spent a night with her friends at Kingsley Hall and went to the hospital to see John Morriss, the dear old blind man Gandhi had visited. She joined a big crowd of young people at the Student Christian Movement House to hear T.S. Eliot give a reading (which she found alternately inaudible and incomprehensible.)

With the distinct feeling that she might not have another chance to visit the U.K., Mildred decided to go to Scotland. The problem was how to get there, being just about flat broke. Well, she'd hitch-hike. English friends told her she was mad, that a woman alone might be able to do such a thing in North America, but not here. Others warned she'd get lost or kidnapped.

Mildred ignored all the nay-sayers and set out. It was springtime, and she was charmed by birdsong and deer grazing in the forest glades. She stretched into her long stride between lifts and made good progress by foot as well as thumb. Over the next couple of days, she walked about twenty-five miles and rode about four hundred. Everyone who picked her up cautioned that she ought not to be hitching, but all were friendly and helpful — except one. The details are sketchy, but Mildred did tell of one man who tried to take advantage of her, but she managed to talk him out of it. Her last ride into Glasgow was from a fatherly Scot who was grudgingly impressed to hear of her ramblings around the

Some of Mildred's travel diaries.

world. In his thick brogue, he told her: "If a bairn o' mine tried to do it, I'd take a stick untilt." But anyway, he admitted, "you've a stout heart in yer stummich."[39]

By the end of April she was back in London, and ready to embark upon the SS *President Harding* to New York. Many Jewish refugees from throughout Eastern Europe, accompanied by a few non-Jews also fleeing the Nazis, were on board. One was a psychiatrist who had been in charge of the largest mental hospital in Vienna until he spoke out against the take-over of Austria. In fear for his life, he fled to Switzerland, but he could not persuade his wife to join him in exile. Instead, she divorced him. He was arriving in a new country alone and penniless. "Do you think we'd have room for a few refugees in the attic?" Mildred asked the family. She was outraged at Canada's lack of compassion.

> Whatever is going to happen to them I don't know. Canada is still refusing entree … It seems most selfish and unchristian to keep our great unused areas under lock & key when some of these people might be able to build self-supporting communities & work out a way to a new life.[40]

All was not so sad, however. There was a baby born on the ship, and as they sailed past the Statue of Liberty, his parents gave thanks that he would grow up far from the conflict back home. In New York, Mildred received happy news about another birth — Vic and Connie's first baby was a healthy boy named Donald. Touring New York City again, Mildred remarked upon the luxurious wealth in the shops, the up-to-the-minute fashions and the modern architecture. Strangely, the war fever that seemed to have all of Europe in its fearsome grip was totally absent.

Mildred's focus shifted from the international scene to the Canadian political landscape in Ottawa, where Grace and Angus MacInnis threw a luncheon for her in the Parliamentary dining room. There were thirteen at the table, including M.J. Coldwell and CCF MPs Grant McNeill, Howard Green and Ab Whitely. Her first round-the-world voyage concluded as her bus wound its way past the Great Lakes, across the green prairie and over the Rockies to the West Coast. Perhaps she saw this as her last journey for a long while — indeed, until such time as her father died.

Her world was collapsing once more from the global perspective to the domestic, but Mildred's inner struggle to accept this situation was lightened by her commitment to Gandhi's teachings. *Seva* — pure service to God and man, given out of purest love, without thought of remuneration — was fundamental to her relationship with her father in his final years. Her frustration, insofar as she expressed it, stemmed from her desire to offer service in a broader sense, on a wider stage and for all of humanity. With the world about to go to war, just when she felt most urgently the need to work for peace everywhere, most of her attention would have to be directed to one beloved but increasingly crotchety old man.

She greeted her new nephew with gifts of booties and blankets, good Scottish flannels and woolens. Right away, Mildred loved wee Donnie, a sturdy, curly-haired blonde who brought a welcome spark to the household. His young mother was relieved Mildred had returned and could take over the responsibility for grandfather, leaving Connie free to concentrate on husband and son. The two women shared laughs and chores as they settled into a domestic partnership that would even outlive Vic. Over that summer of 1939, they diapered and gardened and put up preserves as usual, but it was with a growing sense of dread. Like women around the world, they could see that the men and boys they loved would soon be off to war, many never to return. Mildred and Connie prayed for a way to stop the war coming but, as the season turned golden, it only loomed ever larger. By fall, nothing would ever be the same again.

Lucy and J.S. Woodsworth.

Chapter Nine: 1939

WAGING PEACE

August 29, 1939: Mildred knew that a last-minute plea for peace would scarcely be heard above the belligerent crescendo, but she just had to speak out. She wrote to the *Vancouver Daily Province* a "statement on the importance and practise of active *Non-Violence*."

> After the last war, the voices of all nations rose in protest against its barbarities and losses. No nation, looking over its dead and suffering, could claim victory ... Now we are faced with another conflict of the great forces. And what will be the result? Tremendous losses to all participants, great destruction and demoralization to the whole of mankind ... and nothing will be settled. No wrong will be righted. No peace established. Democracy cannot be saved by war, any more than peace can be made by fighting, or love created by hate ... We must recognize ... that the means used determine the end achieved.[1]

In what would have been a heretical suggestion for the times, she cautioned readers not to "be deceived by Empire Builders or by Munitions Mongers," and urged Canada to disarm. "Such action calls for greater courage even than military activity," she asserted.

> It means that with a concern for humanity much wider than that of Nationalism, we must be ready to lay down our lives for our enemies ... Refusing to fight one's enemy, disarms him. Even against aggressive attack, absolute non-cooperation stays the hand of the aggressor, and refusal to accept his dictatorship forestalls his victory, while consideration for him breaks down his antagonism ...

> We must be willing to take the chance of death convinced that in our sacrifice will come victory, convinced that in the heart of the opponent will rise respect and goodwill, completely destroying his hatred. The means of non-violence and love determine the end of peace and friendship.

The *Province* editor returned Mildred's article with an apologetic note saying he had intended to run it in the September 2 edition, "but the swift moving and tragic events of the last week-end so changed the situation that when it came time to publish your letter we felt that in its present form it was out of date."[2]

Clustered around the radio, the Osterhout family heard the terrible news. In the pre-dawn hours of Friday September 1, 1939, the German invasion of Poland began with *blitzkrieg* attacks by air and land. In Britain, the policy of appeasement was immediately abandoned. The army was mobilized and war declared on September 3. The German reply was swift and deadly. It came that very evening, with the sinking of the liner *Athenia* en route from Montreal to Liverpool, killing 112 passengers. Meanwhile the ill-equipped Polish fighters, many of them on horseback, stood no chance against the mechanized German forces, and were rapidly destroyed.

In Ottawa, Prime Minister Mackenzie King summoned Parliament to meet September 7, and declared that "a state of apprehended war exists." The War Measures Act was invoked and any possibility of Canada remaining neutral was quashed. The mood of the Canadian people as they entered this war was sombre and reluctant, in stark contrast to the naive enthusiasm with which many had enlisted in 1914. The horrible memories of that conflict were too fresh, and the Depression had left the nation demoralized. "For the first time many Canadians might even have wondered if the system was worth fighting for."[3]

During the emotional debate in the CCF caucus the next day, J.S. Woodsworth remained steadfast in his pacifist credo, even though he knew he could not carry his party with him. A few others shared Woodsworth's commitment, including the young preacher Stanley Knowles, who would later represent the same Winnipeg riding and carry on Woodsworth's role as "the Conscience of the Commons." However, most of the younger CCF members believed that the defeat of fascism was imperative. Angus MacInnis was not a pacifist and argued persuasively that Canada couldn't remain aloof, that Hitler had to be stopped. Grace had stuck to the pacifist position for a time, and had even gone so far as to disagree with her husband in public, but slowly she had been won over by Angus's views, which were shared by Tommy Douglas and others she respected. It hurt her deeply to vote against her father when the time came.[4]

Although physically frail, Woodsworth's moral strength was evident when he rose to speak for the last time in the House of Commons. "While we are urged to fight for freedom and democracy, it should be remembered that war is the very negation of both," he told fellow Members of Parliament. After Canada officially declared war, Woodsworth made his "last plea," for upholding the rights of Canadians in war-time as well as in peace. He warned that under the War Measures Act, fundamental freedoms could be suspended.

Personally I am not so much afraid of the power of Hitler in this country as I am of the possibility that by entering upon this war we shall be conquered by some of the things which to-day we condemn in Hitler. I would hope that through all the restrictions and privations which necessarily must come in a war, the principles of liberty, the principles of free speech and the principles of a free parliament ... may be upheld to the very end of this war — however long it may last.[5]

"Never was his hold on the respect of Parliament, of opponents as well as of followers, so clearly shown as in the hearing which was given to this last great speech of his," Frank Underhill later wrote.[6] Mildred couldn't have agreed more: Woodsworth's words entered her consciousness with the resonance of prophecy. When the caucus voted to enter the war, she began to question whether she could continue to dedicate her life to the CCF. She felt the members had forsaken their pacifist values and betrayed their founding father. She wanted to remain loyal to the CCF, but her faith was shaken. It was the first fracture in the solid foundation of her commitment to the movement.

It was rather painful I will admit when I found that only J.S. Woodsworth had stayed absolutely true to his conviction that war could bring no solution to international problems and he stood up alone in the House of Commons against Canada entering into the war. And while there were others who were against war ... he was the only one who had the courage to stand alone. I felt that the movement as a whole had let him down very badly and I also felt that I couldn't throw myself into the movement with the enthusiasm I had before. I remained always a member ... but the time had passed when I could make [the CCF] my first and only interest in life.[7]

Mildred's sense of depression was compounded by her constant worry about friends in England and her increasingly difficult role at home. She chafed against the tedium of housekeeping and care-giving, and saw her father as "dependent, possessive, patriarchal, nervous, over-cautious, pessimistic and devoted." She asked herself whether she should try to change her home situation or just get out. But how? "Just returned from 'taking a walk' around the world, which was supposed to build up health and mental poise, but was an escape that was not an escape."[8]

That winter, Grace's brother Charles Woodsworth boarded with the Osterhouts while he was finishing research for his doctorate from the London School of Economics. More than forty years later Charles recalled the experience this way:

Mr. Osterhout ... was at that time somewhere in his seventies. I believe he had had some form of mild stroke; in any event he had a heart condition and during the months I was in his house he did almost nothing but sit in an armchair, one hand constantly trembling — and let himself be waited on hand and foot by Mildred.

I may be too harsh in my judgment of him, but ... I thought he was a selfish old man, taking advantage of a marvelously patient and saint-like daughter ... Of all the people I've known, I think Mildred came closest to being a saint on earth.[9]

Charles Woodsworth was not the only person who saw saintly qualities in Mildred. She was sometimes referred to as "the second saint of the CCF," second only to Charles's father, J.S. Woodsworth himself. Certainly she shared his selflessness, asceticism, discipline, and abiding love for the human family. But Mildred was not always the paragon others believed her to be. She could sometimes be hurtful and, in at least one angry moment, even cruel.

* * *

In the fall of 1939, Mildred obtained a teaching position at Carleton Elementary, a large red brick school located at Kingsway and Joyce in East Vancouver. She was assigned a classroom furnished with straight rows of wooden desks and a Grade 7 class of 28 students. Among them was Pat Hamill, age twelve. Pat considered herself lucky to have Miss Osterhout as her teacher.[10]

"In those days most teachers kept you in the classroom, but not Mildred," Pat recalled. "She took us on lots of field trips. We went out on nature-study walks, and she even took us to the beach. I remember her in a bathing suit — she was very, very thin. We also went to a Sikh temple and a Chinese school."

Mildred often talked to her students about Gandhi and his message of peace and non-violence. In her efforts to make Indian culture come alive for the children, one day she even wore her sari and brought a big pot of homemade curry to school.

"That curry was so hot most of us couldn't eat it, but we loved looking at all the colourful memorabilia she showed us from India," Pat said. "She really cared about the kids, and she was concerned that you absorbed what she was trying to get across to you."

In contrast to the stand-and-deliver style of instruction most teachers then employed, Mildred relied on a more conversational approach that encouraged the children to participate rather than merely listen. Pat was a shy child who normally didn't raise her hand or speak unless called upon, but she began to find her own voice in Mildred's class. "She challenged us to speak out, so the kids weren't afraid to express themselves. She really got the best from us," she said.

Pat's father, a determined Scot, was a proud man, too proud to ever accept charity or government handouts — which is what he believed the CCF was all about. Her dad's opinions mattered a lot to Pat, and she sometimes expressed in class the political opinions she heard around the family table. "My daughters can hardly believe it now," she chuckled, "but as a kid I was actually of the opinion that men should be paid more than women for the same job because the men were supposed to be the breadwinners supporting their families!"

Mildred asked young Pat and her fellow classmates to think about equal pay for equal work and other basic planks in the CCF platform. She encouraged them to question the unemployment and injustice around them,

Carleton Elementary School, Vancouver.

and to envision a more fair method of structuring work and society for both women and men.

"Back then people thought if you weren't working, you were a bum. But Mildred asked us whether if one man was working eight hours and another man not at all, then shouldn't you rearrange things so they each had four hours of work? Wouldn't that be better for everyone?"

Pat thrived on these discussions, testing her ideas — and her dad's — against Mildred's convictions. "Oh yes, we had a few debates!" But despite their different opinions, she always felt Mildred cared about her and wanted to help her learn. Because of the strong bonds she'd forged with her teacher, Pat was shocked speechless when one day her beloved Miss Osterhout suddenly snapped.

"I can't remember exactly what started it," she said, but as it often happened a couple of the boys were "getting out of line" and making mischief in class. Something they said or did must have pushed Mildred into a fury because within a matter of minutes she administered the strap to the open upturned hands of the two boys. Even worse, it didn't stop with them.

"She strapped the two boys ahead of me, and then she hauled me out of my seat and said, 'You might as well get it too!' I was so shocked because I didn't think she was even mad at me. When I was a kid we expected to get the strap if we were cheeky, but I *wasn't!*"

Pat couldn't recall what kind of strap was used, but it was painfully effective. Mildred's aim was poor, or perhaps her own hands were shaking, but in any event she struck the girl on the wrist instead of on her palm. She hit hard enough to raise a welt on the tender skin. After school Pat fled for home, where she struggled to hide her injury and her deep distress from her mother.

"I finally had to tell my mom what had happened because she asked me to go to the store for her and I had to say no because I didn't think I'd be able to carry home whatever it was she had asked me to get."

After Pat tearfully told her parents what had happened, her father was so angry he wanted to go right up to the school to complain. But his daughter pleaded with him, and convinced him not to. Pat didn't understand exactly why she got the strap along with the two boys, but wondered if it was because she had argued about politics with her teacher. Whatever the reason, "I figured if she did it, I must have deserved it." Pat recalled that even without a complaint from her father, the incident caused quite a stir at Carleton Elementary because Mildred did not have another teacher present as a witness to the strapping, which was required under school board rules.

It is easy to imagine Mildred's deep sense of shame as a teacher and as a pacifist at having strapped not just one child, but three. It was a terrible betrayal of the sacred trust that she believed society vested in teachers, and it was a calamitous fall from the path of non-violence. Despite the stress she was under — caring for Father, teaching full time, resisting the war — there could be no excuse for such behaviour from one who claimed to be a peacemaker. Even though Pat readily forgave her, Mildred could not forgive herself. She endured the inevitable feelings of heart-sickness, shame, guilt and remorse — feelings that tormented her all the more because she really did care about Pat. As penance for her sins, she would not allow herself to retreat from the child she had hurt, from the wrong she had done.

After the school year ended, Mildred kept in touch with Pat by mail. Over the summer holidays she sent her former student a letter in which she expressed how fervently she wished she had not given her the strap. After that, the incident was behind them as far as Pat was concerned, but Mildred couldn't let it go as easily. Many years later when Pat was already a grown woman, married and a proud homeowner, Mildred still felt the need to apologize. "She came for a housewarming visit," Pat recalled, "and at the end of the evening, as I was walking her out to the car, she mentioned again how sorry she was she'd done it."

Mildred with her father at home.

The two women remained close over the years, and Pat's five children grew up with the stories of Mom's teacher and the Mahatma.

"When my youngest, Mary Ellen, was in Grade 5 or 6, the teacher asked the class to write about a great leader who had been assassinated. Most of the kids wrote about [President John F.] Kennedy or Martin Luther King, but Mary Ellen was the only student who wrote about Gandhi. The teacher was very impressed when she said her mother had had a teacher who knew him," Pat said.

"Later two of my girls decided to go to India. Before they went, Mildred invited them over to meet an East Indian friend who was visiting and she gave them lots of tips about travelling there."

"She was so concerned with mankind, I just feel lucky to have known her. She was the kind of person that you never felt she was just being tolerant of you. You felt she cared for you. She really did."

* * *

Throughout the spring of 1940, however, Mildred found little joy either in teaching her students or caring for her father. The war preyed on her mind. If things seemed bad on the home front, all she had to do was think about the plight of those overseas. Mildred watched and grieved as the human family made war on itself from one side of the globe to the other.

By May, Hitler had easily conquered Denmark, Norway, Belgium, Luxembourg and Holland, and he had his sights set on France. In Britain, Chamberlain resigned and a coalition government was formed with Winston Churchill as prime minister. In early June, Mussolini declared war on France and Britain, and the conflict expanded into the Mediterranean and North Africa. Within weeks, France had fallen. Britain and the Commonwealth stood alone against Nazi Germany and Fascist Italy. Churchill made his famous "their finest hour" speech to Parliament. Near Cracow in Poland, the Nazis were building Auschwitz concentration camp. Meanwhile, Mildred's father died peacefully at home.

Reverend A.B. Osterhout died on Wednesday July 17, 1940. His obituary was published on page one of the *Vancouver Daily Province* and was headlined: "DEATH TAKES PIONEER CLERIC." In his photo, Mildred's father looked distinguished with a thick head of white hair, a neat goatee, earnest gaze and upright bearing. Reverend Osterhout was praised as one of the "pioneer preachers of the old horse and buggy days on the prairies ... His intimate pastoral work made him beloved by all his congregations while his gracious dignity won him countless friends."

The Reverend Dr. Walter Cooke, an old friend, officiated at the funeral. The two men had first met back in Manitoba, in the good days when Hattie was still alive and strong at Berson's side. Walter remembered the warm hospitality and peaceful atmosphere in their home. He said: "This good man has come to the end of a long and devoted life ... He knew he was coming to the end of the Journey. He knew he was nearing his Heavenly Home. And a week or two ago he asked me, as his friend, to stand in this place in this service, and speak a word for him, that was how he put it, 'speak a word for me.'"

He continued: "I feel with him the great Christian verities shone with such clear light, and the Holy Spirit of truth spoke in his soul with such tones of assurance that there was for him no dubitating [sic] uncertainty ... A.B. Osterhout never failed of the finest, and the highest, and the most generous. His brother ministers trusted him, and honoured him. They gave this token when they elected him President of the Conference.

"His gentle spirit found much happiness in his home and family ... He was proud of his brother, Smith, Dr. S.S. Osterhout, and ... he found great pleasure and satisfaction in the aspirations and achievements of his son and daughter. He welcomed with a warm heart his son's wife, and a new, lovely interest came into his life with the coming of his little grandson."

One wonders if Mildred wept at her father's funeral, or whether she felt it was her duty to suppress her grief in true Osterhout tradition. Perhaps she saved her tears for the privacy of the hearse as the funeral cortege wended its way across town to the Oceanview Cemetery in Burnaby. At the graveside, heads bowed, Mildred stood with Vic as the final benediction was spoken and their father was laid to rest. "The Grace of our Lord Jesus Christ and the Love of God and the Communion of the Holy Spirit be with us all evermore. Amen."

At the end of the day, alone in the house that seemed suddenly so vacant, perhaps that was when Mildred had a good cry. Secretly, though, her tears must have been tinged with guilty feelings of relief that nearly two decades of house-keeping for her father were now over. She must have felt a sense of liberation, but also deep trepidation. She decided to go to Vancouver Island for a rest at Vic and Connie's cabin near Sidney. There, in a moment of introspection, Mildred sat down with pen and paper and took stock of her life.

At the top of the page she wrote *"Facing the Facts."* She was forty years old, five feet seven inches tall, and only 108 pounds. Her ongoing problem of "poor elimination" she attributed to overeating and eating foods in the wrong combinations. Mildred's obsession with diet was partly caused by her awareness of those suffering from hunger, but her writings also show signs of an eating disorder rooted in self-denial and repression. She reported nervous tension, worry, weariness and depression. Her mental and emotional difficulties she listed as restlessness, indecisiveness and self-concern. She criticized herself for dishonesty, "gushing and superficial interest without deep concern for individuals" and accused herself of bluffing, laziness and untidiness.

As to the future, Mildred tried to define her purpose: "To extend the breadth and depth of my love for others. To discover how best to express that love. To have (& show) the peace & poise that passeth understanding." She considered various options, such as working with a community co-operative, volunteering in India and marriage.

It's illustrative that at this juncture Mildred would begin thinking seriously about marriage. Throughout her twenties and thirties she had lots of "political beaux" and a few persistent suitors, but she resisted all proposals saying her first responsibility was to her father. But now, with her father gone, the financial security he provided was also gone. Mildred was facing the fact that her economic position was more vulnerable than it had ever been. Why? Because patriarchs bequeathed their property to their sons.

It seems outrageous that after Mildred spent two decades caring for her father and running his household, her brother was the one to inherit the family home. Vic had long held a steady job as a teacher and, living with Mildred and their father all those years, he had been able to purchase a motorcycle, a boat, and a cabin and hobby farm on Vancouver Island. But even though Vic was already well established, and even though Rev. Osterhout had a rather difficult relationship with his son, he would not have been one to set convention on its ear by leaving the house to his daughter, no matter how deserving. It simply wasn't done. Nothing in Mildred's journals suggests she felt her father's decision was unjust. He evidently left her a cash inheritance, which she put to good personal and political use later on. For the moment though, she urgently needed to find her own place to live and some meaningful work to do.

Perhaps Vic felt guilty about moving his young family into what had been her home. Perhaps Mildred wanted an utterly unconventional home for the start of a new phase in her life. For whatever reason, she ended up living on Vic's boat, *The White Heather*, which was moored in English Bay at the foot of Denman Street. She unpacked her suitcases, hung a couple of flowering plants from the rigging and felt right at home. She hosted tea parties and political gatherings aboard, she swam daily and often threw a crab trap overboard to catch supper. For a time she was technically unemployed, but she got by with characteristic élan.[11]

"She had a lot of men friends and all these CCF people would be turning up on the boat," recalled Elizabeth Keeling, a musician and artist who shared Mildred's interest in progressive education. "They were really exciting times."

Mildred soon became involved with a group of artists and activists who founded the West End Cultural Centre as a creative response to the problems in the neighbourhood. "The West End was chosen as it was seen to be rapidly becoming a slum area, housing an increasing number of young people in crowded tenements with poor district environment," the *Daily Province* reported. Founders included Judge Laura Jamieson, the poet Dorothy Livesay, and the painter Margaret Carter. As a trained social worker, Mildred was appointed director and Elizabeth was put in charge of the pre-school. Their job came with a title but no salary, at least at first.

"All of these people were victims of the Dirty Thirties in some way," Elizabeth recalled. "All of us worked for nothing, but it was a wonderfully democratic set-up." She said they later got a grant from the Community Chest and their salaries were fifty dollars a month for Mildred and thirty-five dollars for Elizabeth. It wasn't a princely sum, but with family money as a cushion they managed very well.

Confident that free cultural and recreational activities would help prevent delinquency and improve morale among unemployed youth, the women convinced the Parks Board to give them free use of the old bath house on English Bay. The site, so near the beach, offered a wonderful natural setting for classes in drama, music, dancing and art. The young painters were proud when

Arthur Lismer, one of the Group of Seven, chose five of their works for an exhibition of children's art to be mounted at the National Gallery in Ottawa. Elizabeth and Mildred saw how the children's art provided a window into their lives. Many youngsters worried about their fathers and uncles who had left for service overseas.

The Blitz of London began in September, 1940. Night after night, bombers pounded the city and valiant Londoners endured. Japan signed the Tripartite Pact with Germany and Italy. In October, the Italians invaded Greece. Under the cold waters of the Atlantic, the submarine war continued ferociously. So far, losses among merchant seamen and civilians had been higher than among the fighting forces.

In the annual Christmas letter she sent to scores of friends at home and abroad, Mildred proclaimed her absolute pacifism, rooted in Christianity and blossoming in international solidarity. The letter has the tone of a pacifist call to arms, a heroic voice crying out, urging everyone to wage the epic struggle of soul-force versus brute-force:

> Gandhi's words still rise above the tumult of bombs and machine-gun fire ...
>
> "*Non-violence is the way of Love.*" Only as I free myself of any ill will, only as I seek to overcome evil with good, can I make any contribution to world peace. Soul-Force repels brute-force.
>
> "*Non-violence is the way of Truth.*" There is no compromise. No one can prove his belief in a God of Love by bombing civilians.
>
> "*Non-violence is the Way of Courage.*" One must cultivate the capacity for sacrifice of the highest type. He must free himself from fear. He must refuse to co-operate with evil ...
>
> "Still propagandizing," you will say. It must be the revivalist heritage my father left me. For this, and his many fine qualities, I am grateful. After 80 years of loving service he walks no more among us, but he has left us vibrant memories that encourage us along the way.[12]

This and other letters indicate clearly that Mildred let her father rest in peace. She didn't worry over old tensions or nurse old grudges. Instead, she retained and celebrated the best of his legacy, and let go of the rest. Now that her father had passed away, Mildred was free in many new ways, even free to marry — especially now that she no longer had her father as an excuse to say no.

Walter Fahrni had asked her to marry him many times, and had shown his love and respect for her in many ways. Now he proposed again, but promised it would be the last time. Ever indecisive, Mildred thought it over some more and went to Lucy Woodsworth for advice. Lucy said Mildred had to make her own decision because only she knew her own heart and her love for Walter, whom everyone knew to be a man of honour and intelligence. But Lucy also pointed out that, as a married woman, Mildred's social standing would rise, she could command more respect, and so marriage would definitely be an asset for a woman called to political life.

In his earlier letter, Walter had made it clear he was not promising to perform the role of chief breadwinner, but Mildred was not looking for a traditional provider. Her needs were simple and two could live almost as cheaply as one. Besides, she wanted and needed to carry on working, not retire into domesticity. In the end she decided to marry him because she loved him and knew him well enough to believe he could be happy in an unconventional relationship, one that would give her the kind of freedom she so badly needed after the duty-bound years.

From the moment they sent out the invitations, it was clear that Walter and Mildred's wedding would not be conducted in the conventional style. As a no-frills alternative to fancy embossed stationary, they simply sat down at her manual typewriter and pounded out the invitations on plain white paper. They closed with, "Yours for a deeper fellowship," and both signed their names with a fountain pen. In another unconventional gesture, they made it clear they didn't want any wedding presents — only donations to their "Good Fellowship Fund," which would be divided equally amongst the Industrial Co-operative Movement of China, the Rural Education Plan of India, the International Student Service Refugee Fund, and the Seamen's Institute.

The party paper reported that Mildred's marriage would be of "special interest in CCF and progressive circles." The article further praised the bride-to-be saying:

Mildred and Walter's wedding, August 1941.

Miss Osterhout has been prominent in the CCF movement ever since its inception ... No one in Vancouver is held in higher esteem. Her whole life has been devoted to promoting the welfare of others, and her kindness and unselfishness are bye-words among those who know her ... The groom is also well known among progressives, but is less well known to the public than his bride.[13]

With Walter's mother, Priscilla Fahrni at wedding.

Almost the entire Osterhout family pitched in for the wedding. It took place on August 1, 1941, in the back yard of the family home, which was now Vic and Connie's home. Flowering vines framed the back porch where the ceremony was performed. Reverend S.S. Osterhout, Mildred's Uncle Smith, officiated. He looked like a heartier version of her dear old father, and she wouldn't have wished for anyone else to perform her wedding ceremony. The rings Mildred and Walter exchanged that day were made from her mother's wedding band. Connie was matron of honour and Vic was master of ceremonies. Cousin Delda Osterhout was there too, along with friends Elizabeth Keeling, who played the wedding march on piano, and Marion and Gertrude Langridge, who helped out

Wedding guests.

with Mildred's dress, hair and flowers. Help also came from fellow CCF women, including Gladys and Frances — "Mrs. Arnold Webster and Mrs. Lyle Telford," as they were identified in the paper.

"In the flower-blooming garden of the bride's brother's home ... about 150 relatives and friends gathered to witness the ceremony," according to the *Vancouver Daily Province*. "The bride wore a simple summer frock of blue sheer with rosebuds and maidenhair fern in her hair. She carried a sheaf of colourful garden flowers."[14]

Walter, tall and slim, his grey-blond hair in a crisp brush cut, looked tanned and handsome in a light summer suit. Except Mildred, all of the women in the crowd wore gloves and hats — mostly broad-brimmed, although turbans and pillboxes were to be seen as well. Two or three of Mildred's erstwhile beaux watched the service rather wistfully from the lane on the other side of the back fence.

The toast to the bride by Arnold Webster was followed by what the society pages reporter called an "unusual feature" of the wedding: Mr. Jerry Hundal proposed the toast to the Rural Education Plan of India; Mr. Frank Mah proposed the toast to the Industrial Co-operative Movement of China; Mr. Angus MacInnis, M.P., proposed the toast to the Seamen's Institute; and Miss Norah Sibley proposed the toast to the International Student Service Refugee Fund.

After cake and tea, the newlyweds said last good-byes, gave the final hugs and came down the front steps into a flurry of confetti. Mildred and Walter grinned as the cameras flashed. They left by car for a honeymoon in the interior of B.C., "the bride travelling in a costume of white silk with a navy redingote and white accessories."

At forty-one, Mildred said she was "quite ancient" by the time she married. Perhaps she felt that if she had married earlier, and thus been able to explore her sexuality more freely in her twenties or thirties, she would have been able to overcome her "inhibitions." Mildred and Walter later developed a loving physical relationship, but she confided to an aunt that her wedding night was a disaster. Miss Osterhout confessed to some difficulty adjusting to her new name but, all in all, Mrs. Fahrni was a happy woman.

In her Christmas letter for 1941 she outlined "the year's chronicle of family events."

Let me introduce Marion Allena Mildred, my 5-month-old niece, and a charming rival to her brother Donnie, nearly 3 years old ...

Next, may I present Walter Fahrni, since August 1, my husband; before that, a respectable engineer ... a man who puts engines in ships and runs them ... but is not above using his talents in the kitchen ... self preservation, you may well say. We've got to know each other better in the last 3 months than in the previous 30 years since we first met ... and it's still fun, but he expects to go to sea before it gets boring.

To those of you who accepted our invitation to share in our "Good Fellowship Wedding Fund," our thanks. We have been able to build it up to $400, which gives us a contribution of $100 to each of the causes. The Secretary of one hopes I'll be a polygamist.[15]

The Fahrnis moved into an apartment just a block from English Bay, and Walter was soon off on another sea voyage. Of his return, Elizabeth Keeling recalled: "She was mighty glad to see that man. She was giggling!" Mildred's diaries from the early years of her marriage contain only one- or two-line entries daily, but some passages offer glimpses into their lives.

Jan. 14 [1942] 2:00 a.m. Thoroughly demoralized ... I guess I do need a husband to come home instead of staying on the boat.
Jan. 15 ... Walter home for dinner. Welcome again! ...
Jan. 25 Gone — a bit too suddenly this time ...
Feb. 6 A lovey day. And all massaged.

Their marriage was misunderstood by many people, but Mildred and Walter built a radical relationship that worked. "We both had long periods of independence and there was no attempt at domination on either side," she said.[16]

The Fahrni family did not approve of the match because their conservative politics were so much at odds with Mildred's. Above all, they couldn't abide their name being attached to what they considered to be her outrageous public statements. Once when a letter of Mildred's was published in the newspaper, Walter's mother wrote in wanting it known publicly that she was emphatically not the Mrs. Fahrni who had previously written in to the paper. The family's need to distance themselves from Mildred partly illustrates how heretical her views were during wartime. Some members of the clan never could believe that Walter shared her political beliefs, preferring to think she had brainwashed him, or that he was quietly in disagreement but overly reluctant to stand up to her.[17]

Still, the family was important to Walter, and the couple maintained cordial relationships with most of its members. Walter especially enjoyed the younger generation, and was always remembered fondly by his many nieces and nephews. "He was everybody's favourite uncle," recalled Jean Fahrni. "He'd come back from Asia with wonderful trinkets for the children."

Despite her new-found happiness, the war was never far from Mildred's mind, especially when she received correspondence from London. In one letter, her friend Flora Bond enclosed a clipping from August 1941 reporting that since the war began 42,257 people had been killed in air raids in the United Kingdom. Still, Flora seemed undaunted, describing for Mildred how putting out incendiary bombs was really "a very simple matter and not dangerous" but "High Explosives, of course, are a different story."

> Politically the country is solidly behind Churchill and there is not the slightest sign of any change in our attitude towards the war, so if you hear anything that points to the contrary you will know that what you are hearing is just another little bit of Dr. Goebbels' propaganda. Of course we are very fed up and sick to death of war, but there is not the remotest likelihood of this country giving in to Hitler or starting any sort of palaver with him, because everyone knows that peace with Hitler would be no peace at all ... We have no illusions about Adolf.[18]

With her cheerful attitude, Flora seemed to personify the irrepressible British character. She signed off: "Cheerio! V for Victory." Within a matter of months, Mildred and other Vancouverites would begin to get an inkling of the difficulties Londoners had been enduring. On December 7, 1941, Japanese pilots bombed the U.S. naval base at Pearl Harbor in Hawaii. Within hours, the United States, Britain and Canada had all formally declared war on the Japanese Empire.

"Vancouver ... has become a war port overnight," the *Sun* reported. "City Rapidly Shifts Onto War Footing." The army, navy and air force were put on the alert. Police and military intelligence went into action only hours after the first bombs fell. "Working in silence and secrecy, authorities are rounding up all suspect Japanese, together with whites whose activities have brought them under observation as possible saboteurs."

Like all other west coast residents, Mildred was obliged to spend time the next day draping and taping her windows to comply with the strict blackout precautions that were immediately imposed. Local retailers struggled to keep up with the rush on flashlights, batteries, tar paper and other supplies. For the first time, the people were deeply afraid. "Tonight, when the city hides under a blanket of darkness, we will be playing for keeps ... The threat of a Japanese attack on the Pacific Northwest ... was grimly and utterly authentic. Blackout restrictions are law, and are supported by the full weight of police and military authority."[19]

The shock waves of fear and disbelief rolled down Vancouver's Powell Street and Alexander Street and out into the Japanese Canadian communities along the Fraser River in New Westminster and Steveston. "Canadian-born Japanese ... professed themselves as stunned and heartbroken when the war-threat became an actuality," a *Sun* reporter wrote. "*Nisei*, second-generation Nipponese born in Canada, promised unwavering allegiance to this country. Spokesmen pointed to the efforts made by young Vancouver Japanese to enlist, said again and again that their loyalty was to Canada alone." The *Nisei* tried to reassure their parents, the *Issei*, that British justice and fair play applied to loyal Canadians of all colours and all cultures. They were soon proved to be tragically wrong.

In January 1942, the federal government issued an order designating the entire B.C. coastline and everywhere one hundred miles inland from it as a "protected area." Japanese males aged eighteen to forty-five were first to be evicted from the coastal zone. Both RCMP and military officers advised against the evacuation, but under the guise of national security, Ottawa exploited the Pacific War to begin the systematic destruction of the Japanese Canadian community on the west coast.[20] By March, the B.C. Security Commission had been established to plan and direct their expulsion. Within six months more than 22,000 men, women and children — three-quarters of them Canadian citizens — had been forcibly uprooted.

Although the government's unjust treatment of its own citizens clearly violated the very principles of democracy that Canadians were fighting and dying to defend in Europe, most British Columbians either openly supported the internment or quietly acquiesced. Not Mildred, however, and not her comrades; the CCF was the only political party to speak out for the Japanese Canadians. Grace and Angus MacInnis were passionate in their opposition to the uprooting. They lost votes as a result, but accepted these losses philosophically. As Woodsworth always said: "We stand by our principles — win or lose." Similarly, Mildred cared less about winning than about doing the right thing, and she wasn't afraid to champion a cause simply because it was unpopular. She attended meetings, wrote letters and collected signatures on petitions.

Mildred also worked with Woodsworth's sister, Mary, helping out at Hastings Park in east Vancouver, where thousands of Japanese Canadians were rounded up before being shipped out to the internment camps in the interior of the province. Mary Woodsworth had served as a missionary in Japan and could speak the language well. Both women were outraged by the conditions in which the Japanese Canadians were held, some of them for months, awaiting "evacuation." Herded into livestock barns that had been hastily converted into living quarters, the internees endured the humiliating reek of manure, the total loss of privacy and dignity. Many were confined there for months; some were driven to undertake a hunger strike in protest.

The Japanese Canadians had so few friends among the mainstream population, that allies like Angus and Grace, her Aunt Mary and Mildred earned great respect and affection in the community. Tom Shoyama, editor of an important bilingual weekly called *The New Canadian*, met Mildred "when she was actively working to help contain the swelling tide of anti-Japanese feeling in B.C." He remembered her as "a particularly gracious and gentle person."[21]

Ironically, the Pearl Harbor bombing indirectly benefited the West End Cultural Centre, where Mildred was still director. Due to fears of an attack or even an invasion by the Japanese, real estate prices near the Vancouver waterfront fell sharply. Mildred and Elizabeth wanted to experiment with co-operative living, and needed some place more welcoming for the community programs. They decided to buy a couple of homes side by side in the 1700 block of Pendrell Street, just across from Lord Roberts School. It is not clear exactly where Mildred got the money for her portion of the houses, but Elizabeth assumed she had inherited it from her father and that seems the most likely explanation. They paid only about five thousand dollars for the smaller of the two houses, which they planned to share with Walter (when he was in port) and a number of unemployed "girls." They rented the larger one to the cultural centre for thirty-five dollars a month.[22] In a sense, Mildred and Elizabeth were building a kind of Kingsley Hall in Vancouver's West End. They scrounged through the thrift shops and rummage sales to furnish the co-op house and run the community centre. It wasn't always easy to have the necessities at hand.

"Rationing becomes the general topic of conversation with particular concern about how to can [fruit] with a 10 lb. sugar allowance (the Japanese get 5 lb.) Our regular sugar ration is 1/2 lb. a week, tea 2 oz., butter 1/2 lb. meat 2 lb. gas 2 gal. That is all but a lot of things e.g. jam, honey, canned goods just disappear off the shelves," she wrote in 1942.

"The shortage of labour is even more astonishing. After the years of seeing 'unwanted' signs in every business window now the cry is for workers. Women are entering every type of work ... street car service being the latest. The streets are full of women in ... overalls but the struttiest ones are those in military uniforms. They certainly look as if they had the whole of B.C. in their pants pockets. I feel like tucking some snuff under their uplifted nostrils."

As she ran her daily rounds, J.S. Woodsworth was never far from Mildred's thoughts that spring. She knew it would be his last. J.S. was being cared for at the MacInnis' West End home, so she visited often in the last days of his life, and offered her support to Lucy and Grace. They knew there would be public tributes, but Woodsworth's primary concern was with what Grace called "the simple leave-taking of the family." To that end, J.S. called Mildred to his bedside.

He said he knew that he didn't have much longer ... and after he was gone he wanted the family to come together in a warm memorial, and he would like me to speak because he felt that I understood his approach more than the ministers with whom he had been in touch. I felt that this was, in a sense, the greatest honour and the greatest challenge that I had had, and I felt very humble. Of course I said that I would try to do what I could, and I would be glad to do so.[23]

March 21, 1942 was a fine day, the first day of spring. With early signs everywhere of God's annual miracle of re-birth, Mildred suggested Lucy take a break from the bedside and come to the park. Lucy said yes, that she'd like to come, but when they returned they got a terrible shock. J.S. Woodsworth had passed away in their absence. Their son Charles was at his side, but Mildred felt heartsick that she had taken Lucy away at the final moments. She expressed her regrets, but Lucy shushed her, saying she was glad to have the memories of new buds and blossoms.[24]

They grieved together, and then set themselves to the task of giving him a worthy tribute. The family met in the dim funeral chapel, "conscious that though he was gone, his spirit would live with us to the end of our lives and beyond, as long as men and women worked for the things he had held so dear." Grace later wrote this account in her loving biography of her father:

> There was little formality to the service. According to his wish, Mildred Fahrni, an ardent pacifist and long-time friend, spoke of the yearning that was nearest his heart, a world where there would be peace and brother-hood among mankind, and of his conviction that such a world could be created only by those who had rejected the instrument of force. She spoke quietly, from deep emotion, concluding with the verses of farewell from the … poet, Kahlil Gibran.[25]

Then the mourners boarded Charles Woodsworth's cabin cruiser and headed out into the Strait of Georgia. The seas were choppy, but the sun shone. Lucy carried James's ashes in a funeral urn.

> In the immensity of sky and sea the launch rode at anchor while Mother carried out his last wish. Slowly she cast his ashes on the waves that they might mingle with the elements that touch all shores and know no boundaries. Then we saw that she held in her hand a few leaves of her shamrock plant, a growing slip from the love-token he had given her before they were married. She looked at the living green for a moment and then very slowly let it drift into the waters.[26]

The following Sunday, a public memorial service was held at the Orpheum Theatre in downtown Vancouver, one of twelve such events across the country. After the opening hymn, "Onward Friends of Freedom," Mildred offered "a tribute of love and respect to James S. Woodsworth."

When a few days ago he asked me to share with his friends in this consideration of the great ideal of his life, his thought was characteristically not of himself. It was of his purpose. His one wish was that even as we take leave of him we might become stirred to some deeper understanding of the meaning of world brotherhood ...

Like Gandhi he understood that brotherhood begins in one's own heart ... and encompasses men of all nations, races and creeds, the highest and the lowliest in all walks of life. He was a friend of the common man everywhere.

Mr. Woodsworth's inspiration came from the carpenter of Galilee. He maintained unswerving loyalty to the principles which Jesus taught and lived ... that love is the greatest thing in the world, that it transcends all barriers ... So sincere was his conviction that he faced criticism and misunderstanding without wavering.

But he was not content to accept a negative attitude. His pacifism was positive ... creative. Loving peace as he hated war, and believing in the constructive power of love as the only deterrent to the destructive force of hate, his whole effort was to teach men how to overcome evil with good ...

Because of him love is more widespread in the world to-day, because of him truth is clearer to us all, because of him justice is more tangible and because of him the brotherhood of man is nearer realization.[27]

Mildred closed her eulogy with a prayer that Woodsworth wrote and often used in the labour church in Winnipeg:

> *We meet together as brothers and sisters of the one big family.*
> *We confess that we have not yet learned to live together in love and unity.*
> *We have thought too much of our own interests and too little of the common welfare ...*
> *We acknowledge we are still divided into alien groups separated from one another by barriers of language, race and nationality, by barriers of class and creed and custom. May we overcome prejudice. May we seek to find common ground ...*
> *May our face be toward the future. May we be children of the brighter and better day which is beginning to dawn. May we not impede, but rather co-operate with the great spiritual forces which, we believe, are impelling the world onward and upward.*

Mildred had suffered two great losses in less than two years. First the death of her own father, and now that of her second father-figure, the one who had first shown her the heroism in non-violent struggle. Woodsworth was her Canadian Mahatma; indeed, she called him one of the "great souls" in her eulogy. Mildred grieved for him, and resolved to keep alive his legacy. But how? How to translate his peaceful ways into a world at war? What would be the most effective form of non-violent resistance?

Through the United Church she heard that teachers were needed in the Japanese Canadian internment camps because both the federal and provincial governments had disavowed any responsibility for educating the thousands of children among the internees. She thought about how Woodsworth refused to see anyone as his enemy, how he defended the "strangers within our gates." In the same way, Gandhi allied himself with the *Harijans*, the untouchables of India's repressive caste system. Upon reflection, it became clear to Mildred that the best way to express her shared commitment to their values was to take a stand with the *Harijans* of her own country — the Japanese Canadians, a whole community unjustly branded "enemy aliens."

Japanese Canadian students and their teachers in front of "Lakeview Collegiate." Stanley Rowe is in the rear with one of the other teachers.

Teachers and friends having a bonfire on the shores of Slocan Lake, 1943. Stanley Rowe is in the centre at the back, beside Walter Fahrni. Mildred is seated at his feet.

Chapter Ten: 1943

WITH THE NISEI IN NEW DENVER

As Mildred's train chugged inland from the Pacific coast past the town of Hope, she left the hundred-mile wide "protected area" that was prohibited to Japanese Canadians. A bit further down the line she passed Tashme, the internment camp named for the three senior men in the B.C. Security Commission: Taylor, Shirras and Mead. In all, the commission established ten internment camps in B.C., eight of them in the rugged mining country between Slocan and Kootenay lakes. More than twelve thousand people were interned at Slocan City, Lemon Creek, Popoff, Bay Farm, Sandon, Kaslo, Roseberry and New Denver.[1]

It was July, 1943, and Mildred was bound first for Zincton, a mining outpost eleven miles from New Denver. Because the war had so disrupted commercial shipping along the west coast, Walter had to look for work ashore. In Zincton, his job was to keep the big diesel engines humming at an old, but still productive, mine called the Lucky Jim. "Walter working hard & greasy!" Mildred wrote. "A good sense of living." She reveled in the mountain air, chummed up to the camp cook, picked wild berries and made lots of jam. Mildred and Walter happily celebrated their second wedding anniversary at the Lucky Jim. From her diary:

Sat. July 31: Sunshine
Huckleberries
Swimming
God Bless Us All

Sun. Aug. 1, 1943: *Zincton* 2 yrs. Is it just! A happy day. Worked in a.m. Roy & Rose ... for dinner. Picnic for supper. Hot in day, cool at night. Yes, it's good to be alive — & married.

The couple who came to share the anniversary dinner were Walter's elder brother, Roy Fahrni, and his wife, Rose. They lived in nearby Kaslo where they published the local weekly newspaper, *The Kootenaian*. They too were involved with the Japanese Canadians interned in their town. Late in 1942, Tom Shoyama and his editorial staff had packed up their banks of Japanese typefaces and moved the internees' newspaper from Vancouver to Kaslo. For the next three years, the columns of *The New Canadian* were set on Roy Fahrni's linotype machine and the papers rolled off his water-powered flat-bed press.[2]

In the fall, Mildred moved from Walter's cabin in the mountains down to New Denver, where the resident population of 300 still seemed somewhat overwhelmed by the arrival of 1,500 traumatized Japanese Canadians. Their most tenacious champion was Gwen Suttie, a United Church missionary who had served in Japan for more than ten years. Indignant that innocent children were being denied an education because of their ancestry, she had appealed to the Women's Missionary Society of the United Church. The Toronto chapter came up with a grant of $4,680 — the total budget for a high school and two kindergartens for 1943. Miss Suttie was happy to recruit Mildred, "a qualified high school teacher with experience and ... a willingness to work for what the budget will bear."[3]

Obviously, with a total budget of less than five thousand dollars, minus the cost of food, housing, school supplies and wages for five teachers, it's evident that once again Mildred was working full-time for very meagre wages, only about twenty-five dollars a month.[4] But the work supported a cause close to her heart, her room and board were covered, and Walter was working nearby, so she was content. Mildred and the other volunteer teachers all shared a co-op house on Josephine Street, which afforded a glorious view across Slocan Lake to the glacier on the Valhalla Mountains. Miss Suttie was the head of the household and principal of the school. Ella Lediard, another missionary who, like Gwen, was fluent in Japanese, supervised the kindergartens and worked with the *Issei*. Here's how Mildred described the rest of the group:

> Helen Lawson, of Hamilton Ontario, specializes in energy and enthusiasm which she credits to carrots and soy beans, and applies to her teaching of English and folk dances.

> Jack Rowe of Alberta ... the best man amongst us, and an ardent member of the C.C.F. (Carrot Chewers' Fellowship) keeps the wood box filled and the cake box empty, and spends the rest of his time teaching Math & Science.

> And as for Mildred ... you can guess, busy with Social Studies at School, and Socialism at home ... two remedies for the one complaint.[5]

In spring 1941, J. Stanley Rowe, a young UBC botany grad, refused military service. The son of a radical social gospel preacher and ardent pacifist, Jack, as he was then called, was staunchly committed to the family's peace tradition. Unfortunately the authorities didn't accept his application for conscientious objector status. Why not? "Basically because I didn't come in to the interview with a Bible in my hand."[6] He was hoeing weeds in the experimental plots at the University of Alberta when the RCMP came to arrest him. He was imprisoned in Fort Saskatchewan for three months before appeals from J.S. Woodsworth and other churchmen were heard. He finally was granted CO status and shipped out to work in forestry camps in B.C. After two years in the bush, he was happy that Gwen Suttie had seconded him to teach in New Denver.

Unfortunately, the civic authorities refused to integrate Japanese Canadian children into the local public school. The teachers were grateful for permission to set up their makeshift school in the Turner Memorial United Church, a one-room wood frame structure built in 1892. From Monday to Friday, Mildred and her colleagues each took one corner of the sanctuary as a classroom. When classes were over for the week, staff and students rearranged the pews for worship. Despite the cramped quarters, "a fine spirit was created amongst those who worked together to build a school in a church," Mildred wrote in *The New Canadian.*

"Inevitably, mathematical formulae sometimes got mixed with French irregular verbs, and the reading of poetry had for background the 'stinks' of the science class opposite ... As we look to the future many difficulties face us, but as we see the distance we have covered we Praise the Lord ... and the W.M.S. [Women's Missionary Society] ... and carry on."[7]

The teens in New Denver had already lost more than a year of school because of the uprooting, and they were eager to get back to their studies. Forty-five students enrolled in Grades 9 to 12 in the fall of 1943, and their numbers soon increased to sixty. The students named their new school Lakeview Collegiate, and Miss Suttie chose their Latin motto: *Per Ardua ad Magna,* "Great things through hard work."

Alice Murakami was one of the students who walked five miles every day from the camp in Roseberry to school in New Denver. Her parents taught her to value education highly and to respect the *sensei,* the teacher. Alice said all the teachers were "devoted" to their *Nisei* students, who returned the affection. She chuckled to recall that quite a few of the girls had crushes on Mr. Rowe, their young science teacher.[8]

"Those teachers really sacrificed to come and teach us," Alice said. "I'll never forget Mrs. Fahrni. She had her hair short and she was very slender. She used to talk about the CCF all the time, and she called it the 'Carrot Chewers' Federation.' She used to explain about Gandhi and the other peacemakers. Deep inside she really believed in all the things she taught."

Classmate George Masuda also remembered the carrot chewers and other jokes and discussions that took place in Mildred's Social Studies 10 class. "Mrs. Fahrni was a vegetarian, which was good because we couldn't get any meat anyway," he said. "She was a staunch CCF'er and that came across clearly in the classroom." Mildred's teaching had quite an influence on young George. "I was not yet politically inclined because I was still so young," he said, "but I found out later through *The New Canadian* that the CCF was helping us out."

Did Mildred discuss with her students the injustices they were living through? "She didn't refrain from putting the facts before us," Alice said. "I was fifteen at that time, and it really got me thinking. A lot of the younger children didn't understand what position we were in vis-à-vis the government."

As early as 1943, Mildred could see that there would be no easy answers in the post-war years. In her annual Christmas letter, she wrote that living in the camp was "an interesting and absorbing experience, but rather hard to see in perspective." She continued:

> The question of what to do with the Japanese after the war is such an integral part of the whole post war problem that it cannot be settled alone. Surely we have a responsibility to open our vast country for the use of those who need it so badly. The placidity with which our government keeps its doors closed against refugees whose plight is so tragic gives one grave concern as to the attitudes that may predominate in any peace settlements. Fortunately some courageous folk are attacking the problem openly. That seems the all-important job, but perhaps too, there is a job to be done in small communities such as this in trying to break down prejudices, and promote better understanding.[9]

Unlike her students and their families, Mildred was free to leave New Denver and come home to the coast for Christmas holidays. It was great to see the family again and astonishing how much Donnie and little Marion had grown. Aunt Mildred celebrated her 44th birthday at Vic and Connie's. There was a heavy snowfall in the Slocan Valley that winter, and the Japanese Canadians shivered in the ill-constructed shacks they were forced to call home. Mildred arrived back in New Denver with a miserable cold, and put herself right to bed "with lemonade, whisky & aspirin!" The next day Walter came "down from the mine with another spell." It's unclear what kind of "spells" Walter had, but some believe they were related to the chronic lung condition he suffered as a result of having been gassed in the First World War. Whatever caused them, they were serious enough to land him in hospital. The Fahrnis were an unhappy, unhealthy pair. From Mildred's diary:

> Sun Jan. 9: A Dead Loss! Full of poison! Felt completely sunk & stayed in bed all day. Slept a lot. Walter in hospital.

Jan. 10: Guess I'll take one more day! Walter out for a week & in for a visit. Static conversation. Must eat to keep my strength up!!

Tues. Jan. 11, 1944: 12:00 My first day back [to the classroom] — after recess. Walter came out of hospital & said if I could work he could too so off he went. Feel my age! ...

Jan. 13: 10:30 p.m. New Denver — thawing & slippery. Walter back in hospital for 3rd bout. Taught all day & fixed up school — 2 meetings. Completely worn out.

On top of her family commitments and school work, Mildred did what she could to build the CCF locally. The movement had an uphill battle in the Slocan Valley, where there were pockets of deep anti-Japanese sentiment. In June 1944, Mildred "made a spiel at the C.C.F. club down in Silverton and had quite an interesting evening with some of the miners there." Like Zincton, Silverton was named for the metal mined in the nearby hills. The town limits were marked by signs reading "No Japs." Not surprisingly, she wrote, "We don't have much success with the C.C.F. here. However there are a few stalwarts." Among those stalwarts who "openly supported the Oriental franchise" was Randolf Harding, who was elected MLA from Kaslo-Slocan in 1945. He said: "By 1949 the Japanese Canadians had the vote, and they voted CCF because they remembered how many CCF'ers went down to defeat because of our pro-franchise stand."[10]

As the end of the school year approached, Mildred longed to be in Saskatchewan, where the CCF was poised to achieve a major victory. "It will be quite exciting watching the results of the Saskatchewan election," she wrote. "I guess a lot of our B.C. people are down there helping in the campaign."

Jack Rowe vividly remembered June 15, 1944, the historic night that brought the dream of a co-operative commonwealth closer to reality. At the co-op house in New Denver, everyone huddled around the radio listening to the CBC for the results coming out of Regina. Such wonderful news! The people of Saskatchewan had overwhelmingly voted in the first CCF government in Canada, giving the party an astonishing 47 of the 52 seats in the Legislature. Their new premier was Reverend T.C. Douglas, the diminutive but dynamic social gospel preacher turned politician, future national leader of the New Democratic Party. Tommy Douglas's unpretentious ways and his fine leadership skills attracted voters across the province. When Tommy's landslide victory was broadcast, Mildred let out a great whoop of joy. She grabbed a red blanket off the bed and tossed it about her shoulders. Then off she went, dancing and cheering down Josephine Street, leading the jubilant teachers in a ragtag parade.[11] She later wrote:

Politically in Canada the C.C.F. has made great progress even in a time of almost universal employment and high wages. Personally, I have not

149

done much to help the movement this year apart from making speeches which sometimes aroused embarrassment as I sponsored the Canadian Japanese cause. The C.C.F. is probably more aware of racial discrimination than any other political group and is prepared to protect the rights of all loyal Canadians.[12]

By contrast, some Conservatives and Liberals campaigned on a platform that was overtly racist. Take, for example, Ian Alistair Mackenzie, Liberal MP for Vancouver Centre, and one of the instigators of the uprooting and internment. In a nomination speech in September 1944, he said: "Let our slogan be for British Columbia: No Japs from the Rockies to the seas."

Per Ardua Ad Magna. Mildred's students felt the impact of such hatred, and still they persevered. Despite all the obstacles to their education, the *Nisei* students excelled. When Lakeview Collegiate opened in the fall of '43, the school supplies consisted of a box of chalk and a rolled blackboard. When it closed four years later, 97 per cent of its candidates had passed the department of education examinations. George Masuda graduated from the little school-within-a-church, even though he had to leave for the camp at Tashme before the end of his last term. He studied for his final exams on the train going to Hamilton, Ontario, where the family eventually settled.

Mildred cared deeply about those young people, but felt that she had to be more directly involved in the peace movement and the political process. In late July, she said emotional good-byes to her fellow teachers and, especially, her students. "Give our love to Vancouver," the kids shouted. "We wish we could go too." There was a wistfulness in their voices that broke Mildred's heart. She knew how it felt to be homesick, and she understood that Vancouver was the only hometown they'd ever known. She waved and promised to remember them to friends back in the city. No one mentioned it, but the question was on everyone's mind and the injustice was clear for all to see. When would George or Alice or any of the young *Nisei* be able to hop on the train and go home? No one knew.

Alice Murakami's time at Lakeview Collegiate ended when, in order to be reunited with her father, the family agreed to go and work on a sugar beet farm in McGrath, Alberta. There, conditions were infinitely worse than in New Denver. "We were treated like animals," she said, "like slaves."

Looking back, Alice always felt grateful to Mildred and the others who "stepped out from the shadows and helped, despite what other people would say. There were very few of them."

If people like Mildred were few and far between, it's because they knew they would pay a certain price for supporting the Japanese Canadians: "We were more or less looked upon as people who were not very loyal to their country," Mildred said in a classic understatement. "Sometimes I felt a bit alone."[13]

Alone, but uncompromised — unlike the Prime Minister, who finally admitted in the House of Commons what Mildred and her comrades knew all along: that Japanese Canadians were loyal citizens. Mackenzie King said: "It is a fact no person of Japanese race born in Canada has been charged with any act of sabotage or disloyalty during the years of war." Nonetheless, his government embarked upon a double-edged plan to solve "the Japanese problem."

In the spring of 1945, Japanese Canadians were offered two options: "dispersal" east of the Rockies, or "repatriation" to Japan. "Dispersal" was intended to prevent Japanese Canadians from returning to the coast and from congregating anywhere else in numbers that might arouse hostility in white society. As a result, any possibility of rebuilding a cultural community was destroyed for a generation. "Repatriation" was a cynical misnomer; the *patria*, or homeland, of most interned Japanese was Canada. Repatriation meant exile. Still, having lost their faith in Canadian democracy, some 10,000 felt compelled to sign for what amounted to a deportation order.

Gradually, Canadians began to awaken to these injustices on the home front. A national coalition called the Co-operative Committee on Japanese Canadians was formed in opposition. Together with a *Nisei* group called the Japanese Canadian Committee for Democracy, they challenged the repatriation scheme and called for the lifting of all restrictions on Japanese Canadians. They took their challenge all the way to the Supreme Court of Canada and the United Nations, and they turned the tide of public opinion. By the time they were successful, however, 4,000 Canadians had already been sent to Japan where they were also treated as aliens.

Sometimes Mildred, too, felt like an alien in her homeland. The big news that summer was D-Day, the Allies' massive invasion of Nazi-occupied Europe. It began on June 6, 1944 on the beaches of Normandy. By the end of the day, more than 145,000 British, Canadian and American soldiers were ashore; within a week their ranks had grown to 325,000 strong. They advanced rapidly, and by summer's end the German occupiers of Paris had surrendered. Charles de Gaulle and the Allied liberators led a triumphal march down the Champs Élysées.

Mildred tried to take heart that the war seemed closer to an end, but she was still gloomy. "The absolute necessity of having peace made me go on," she said, but it was difficult work for a widely-despised cause. Socialists and pacifists were shunned by regular people and considered subversive by the Canadian government. Some were locked up under the War Measures Act. Asked many years later if she had been among those arrested during the war years, Mildred said: "That never happened to me — unfortunately."[14] She always regretted not being called to make that kind of sacrifice; indeed, she would have welcomed imprisonment as an opportunity to demonstrate the absolute nature of her commitment. Like Gandhi, Mildred would have felt at peace in prison.

As it was, she left Walter toiling at the Lucky Jim, and headed out with Elizabeth Keeling to CCF Summer School at the new camp on Gabriola Island. She had "good sleeps under the stars," and renewed her connection with the movement. Later she visited Vic and Connie at their little cabin near Sidney on Vancouver Island. There she swam, made jam and "took on the kids." The Osterhout brood by this time had grown to three, with the birth of Bobbie after Marion and Don.

It was not until April 1, 1949, almost four years after the end of the war, that Japanese Canadians were granted equal rights with other Canadians, including the right to vote. They were free to go west again, but what was left?

The Murakamis never gave up the dream of returning to Saltspring Island, but weren't able to make it home until 1954. They tried to buy back their own farm but the new owner, a war veteran who bought the 17-acre property at a firesale price from the Custodian of Enemy Alien Property, refused to sell. With all their savings, the family managed to buy five acres of raw land and once again set about clearing it by hand.

"I will always carry a deep sense of injustice for what my parents suffered." Long after the bitter years were over, Alice (Murakami) Tanaka reflected upon Mildred's teaching and witness. "I think it's ironic how years go by and you finally really understand what your mentors have meant to you. For me, I feel deeply indebted to her," she said. "Mildred Fahrni made me become a free thinker."

Chapter Eleven: 1945

NOT UNDER A STAR, BUT A SWORD

"Once again December breaks, not under a star, but a sword, but surely by this time next year the swords will be sheathed, and men and women will give their thoughts to Peace."[1]

This was Mildred's Christmas wish, 1944. By the New Year, the Third Reich began to disintegrate rapidly, and the world began to glimpse the truly atrocious scale of the Holocaust. The Russians swept through Poland and liberated Auschwitz concentration camp, where millions perished. In February, Allied bombers destroyed the city of Dresden, killing 140,000, mostly civilians and refugees. In March, the Allies crossed the Rhine. In the Pacific theatre, the Japanese suffered defeat in Burma and faced the Americans' assault on Iwo Jima. On April 12, U.S. President Roosevelt died from a cerebral hemorrhage. While the death tolls still mounted on all sides, people everywhere could see that the tide of the war had turned.[2]

Having learned hard lessons through the failure of the League of Nations, world leaders were ready to try again to create an international body that would be more effective in preventing future wars. The Dumbarton Oaks Plan was to become a blueprint for the new United Nations. Named for the Washington, D.C. mansion where it was hammered out by American, British, Russian and Chinese officials, the plan gave those four nations and France the strongest position. The "Big Five" were to hold veto power and would be the only permanent members of the proposed eleven-member Security Council. The General Assembly would consist of representatives of the member nations, each with one vote.

To Mildred's way of thinking, Dumbarton Oaks was flawed from the start, mainly because of the veto power. She said: "If the destiny of the peoples of the world is to hang upon such a precarious thread as the veto of Churchill, Roosevelt or Stalin, we might as well admit that we have lost every semblance of democracy and have returned to a big power dictatorship."[3] She raised her concerns in a "Citizen's Forum" broadcast nation-wide over CBC Radio in February 1945. The other panelists were *Vancouver Sun* columnist Elmore Philpott and Dr. Norman McKenzie, president of UBC. The show was moderated by writer Morley Callaghan, who opened the discussion by asking:

"Would you, madam, or would either of you gentlemen, care to give an explanatory endorsement of the Dumbarton Oaks proposals so we can see where we stand?"

"Not me, Mr. Callaghan," Mildred jumped in right away. "In the first place, its purpose is to provide a police force. What people want today is a plan for peace." She advocated electing delegates to the United Nations, thus giving the people of the world more direct representation. The men asked whether she really thought any government would consent to a delegate it could not control. Philpott urged her to be more realistic, to "start from where we are with what we've got." He then set up a remarkable series of exchanges by explaining geopolitics to her in these terms:

"We're at a stage of history something like the Wild West movies we see on Saturday afternoon, where the robber gangs shoot up the town and rob the banks, then what they call the good cowboys turn out all mounted on magnificent steeds and they have a wonderful chase ... "

"And the big powers are riding at the head of this posse of good cowboys," interjected Callaghan.

"Exactly," cried Philpott. "And if they don't ride ... "

"Dead Eye Dick escapes," McKenzie concluded the scenario.

"You boys have been going to too many movies or else you are incurable romantics," Mildred said.

"I believe the people of the United Nations have arrived at the stage where they are ready to participate democratically in an international organization. Dumbarton Oaks is unreal to most of them because its proposals have all been made by diplomats and government officials far removed from the people. It's high time the people themselves, and by the people, Dr. McKenzie, I mean the people of defeated and occupied as well as victorious countries — and the people in the Colonies too — it's time they had a chance to express their own desires. They want peace and security above all else, even national sovereignty."

As she had done so often before, Mildred articulated her belief that war is the inevitable consequence of capitalism and the economic injustices it creates. "People will not starve peacefully. My whole point is that true peace must be founded on economic rather than military security."

Dr. McKenzie told her she was "still chasing rainbows." Her radical concept of a world-wide body based on internationalist values and true reconciliation sounded like pie in the sky to these men, who prided themselves on their rational, realistic assessment of power politics on the world scene.

Mildred's style of debate — energetic, but always friendly — could be persuasive as well. "So you have come around to my point of view, Mr. Philpott," she said at one point. "If I can only convince Dr. McKenzie," she added, with mischief in her smile. The learned gentleman responded with a patronizing: "Don't give up hoping, dear." That smarted, but Mildred was heartened by a letter from CBC's Supervisor of Talks and Public Affairs in Toronto, who had been "delighted" with the "provocative and entertaining" discussion.[4] A friend in Ottawa also wrote:

> Hearing your voice last Tuesday night over the Forum was the next best thing to seeing you in the flesh. You were just splendid and I have heard a lot of comment since then about the courageous stand that you refused to relinquish ... I did want you to know that ... you left the seeds of courage in the minds of a great many here who heard you on Tuesday.[5]

In this period, Mildred wrote for the *CCF News*, a weekly tabloid published by the B.C. branch of the movement. She occasionally reported from the Legislature in Victoria and covered peace and women's issues at large. When news came that the founding conference of the United Nations was to be held in San Francisco — tantalizingly close to Vancouver — Mildred decided she had to see it. "I'm pulling all the ropes I can to get to San Francisco as a reporter," she wrote from the CCF convention that spring.[6]

As ever, when Mildred set her sights on a destination, she managed to cobble together the necessary funding. She arranged to cover events for the Co-operative Press Association, a collective news service for the CCF movement. With the press credentials that would bring, the problem of access to the events was solved. She further cut costs by riding the overnight bus to San Francisco and by inviting herself to stay with a friend named Margaret who lived in the hills overlooking the city.

Monday morning, April 23, 1945: Mildred's first task was to obtain a press pass. Security was tight for the opening ceremony at the San Francisco Opera House. The stage was draped in rose velvet, and set with a massive golden arch framed by flags of the 46 nations represented. Only those countries which had declared war on the Axis powers were invited to the conference, thus excluding neutral states such as Sweden and Switzerland, and "enemy" states Germany and Japan, and their satellites.

"Yes, hurrah my press ticket," she wrote in her journal. "No place for a gate crasher. I show it 8 times to get in. But I get a place in the balcony & see the great procession of great & small."

As Mildred looked down from the press gallery, she remarked upon Britain's representative, the elegant Anthony Eden; General Jan Christian Smuts, the South African statesman and friend of Mahatma Gandhi who drafted the preamble to the UN Charter; and the enigmatic Vyacheslav Molotov, "the most talked-of man at this conference ... Stalin's mouthpiece here."[7] Onto the stage strode the American Secretary of State, Edward Stettinius, chairman of the conference and "glamour boy" of the diplomatic world. He welcomed the delegates and called for a minute of silence to reflect upon the great challenges before them. Despite her reservations, in that moment Mildred was deeply moved.

"Dedicated to the cause of world peace, the conference opened with ... a moment of silent and solemn meditation," she wrote. "A hush fell on the audience as men and women of all ranks, colours and creeds in this great democratic gathering, faced the solemn tasks ahead. For a moment at least, differences were forgotten and representatives of the United Nations were bound in a common brotherhood."[8]

Next Stettinius introduced the President of the United States. Over radio waves from Washington, the voice of Harry Truman flooded the loudspeakers. He welcomed the delegates, and told them: "You members of this conference are to be the architects of a better world. In your hands rests our future. By your labours we shall know if suffering humanity is to achieve a just and lasting peace."

As a "middle power," Canada was "adopting a policy of maximum helpfulness." The Canadian delegation included Prime Minister Mackenzie King, Justice Minister and future prime minister Louis St. Laurent, and several MPs, including M.J. Coldwell, the CCF leader. Among their advisors was a young Lester Pearson, then ambassador to the United States, another future prime minister and Nobel Peace laureate. Mildred reported that in his speech "Prime Minister W.L. Mackenzie King ... expressed the hope that social security would come to be regarded as the natural inheritance of humanity. He said, 'Justice is the common concern of mankind.'"

Over the weekend came the first news that Nazi Germany had fallen. Then those reports were contradicted, and no one really knew for sure. Mildred went on a wonderful outing with some friends, but the beauty of the day was underscored by her deep yearning for the war to be over, for the killing to stop and the suffering to end.

A great blue stretch of gleaming sea with the sun dazzling the eyes — &
miles of sandy beach ... And bombs still falling in Germany & people
dying ... [We drove] Miles & miles through the hills glowing with
poppies, lupines & buttercups ... Pick calla lilies by the roadside ...

Mon. May 7 PEACE! Or is it? For days they say hostilities are over — &
then they say it's true.[9]

Mildred enjoyed working as a journalist because it gave her the opportunity
to be at the centre of events and to meet so many remarkable people. In San
Francisco she interviewed Elsie Robeson, chemist, anthropologist and "wife of
the noted Negro singer, Paul Robeson." She wrote about Elsie's work for equal
employment practices and the vote for southern blacks. She interviewed the
Friends of the Spanish Republic, and reported on their efforts to keep Franco's
Spain out of the United Nations because of his support for the Nazis. She talked
to the stateless people, Jewish refugees struggling "to restore, rehabilitate and
resettle the remnants of European Jewry."[10]

Indian *swaraj*, and the larger question of the future independence of all
colonized nations, was another key issue facing the fledgling United Nations.
An enormous crowd turned out to an "India Freedom Meeting" to hear Mrs.
Vijaya Pandit, sister of Jawaharlal Pandit Nehru, future prime minister of India.
Mrs. Pandit stated that "without an independent India, there could be no peace
for the world."[11] She said little had been accomplished at the United Nations
conference because delegates were "playing around with words." She criticized
the British Labour Party for making hollow promises when thousands of
Indians remained in prison without trial. "Justice, honour and freedom are
denied" under the colonial system, she concluded. Mildred was fascinated and
inspired by these strong women of the Free India movement. With her formidable intellect and articulate expression, wearing a graceful sari and her long
white hair pulled back, Mrs. Pandit was a striking person.

Even Molotov was impressed by her and listened intently as she described
conditions in her struggling homeland. At the next plenary session he spoke out
in support of independence for all colonies, especially India.[12] Without doubt,
Molotov was the sensation of the conference. He represented a new Russia, the
strongest military power in Europe, a Stalinist Russia. "Steel keynote of Stalin,"
Mildred noted. The press corps was kept on the alert, trying to get the scoop on
the Communist side of the story. Here's how Del Finlay of *The Vancouver Sun*
chronicled his pain-in-the-arches assignment of dogging the elusive Molotov:

Meantime the lobby was buzzing with conversation.

The high, medium and low-priced correspondents were peddling their
own rumors to each other, on the theory that if you repeat a thing often
enough it might begin to sound reasonable enough to print.

We heard that Molotov and his car simply passed through a stone wall of the Fairmont Hotel on Wednesday without even denting a fender, and disappeared from the view of the frustrated and frantic newsmen.

Somebody else volunteered the information that when 'Molly' came to town the Russians cleared out the tenth floor of the Fairmont, shooed out the chambermaids, took up all the rugs and tore down the plaster looking for dictaphones …

By this time we weren't sure whether we were talking to ourselves or hearing voices … Anyway that's the atmosphere the Russians have created here.[13]

Even as the Second World War was ending, the suspicious attitudes and rigid stereotypes of the Cold War were already emerging. Before the world entered that next stage of history, though, there was the cataclysmic milestone of August 6, 1945.

At seven o'clock that morning the air raid siren wailed in Hiroshima. No one took much notice because it often sounded at that time. There was no warning at 8:15, though, when an American B-52 bomber called the *Enola Gay* dropped the world's first atomic bomb onto the 245,000 people of Hiroshima. It exploded 2,000 feet above ground, and about seven square miles of the city were instantly reduced to rubble. Nearly 100,000 were killed by the blast; 100,000 more were injured. Some of the victims, their lives vapourized, cast shadows that were instantly seared into nearby walls. As the toxic mushroom cloud rose to the heavens, fires flared up in the high winds. The day grew darker. Half an hour after the searing flash and massive concussion, a black rain fell from a cloudless sky.[14]

Three days later, on the morning of August 9, the people of Nagasaki met the same awful fate: as many as 75,000 more perished. Estimates vary widely because so many died later from burns, injuries or radiation. On September 2, Emperor Hirohito of Japan surrendered before U.S. General Douglas MacArthur. In the last eight years, Japan's ambitions in Asia and the Pacific had taken the lives of about 16 million people, mostly Chinese soldiers and civilians.[15]

The war was over, but at what a price! Few of Mildred's personal writings remain from those first post-atomic days, but it's not hard to imagine her reaction to this terrifying new weapon. In September 1945, the *CCF News* published an article headlined "Atomic Bomb and World Peace Organization." It asked the question that was preying on everyone's mind.

What does it mean for mankind?

Here we have a bomb, small enough to be carried by the fastest planes, yet with enough destructive force to wipe out half a dozen square miles of any city — level every building and kill every living thing.

Against such a weapon there can be no safe defense. A combination of the atomic bomb with the V-2 rocket, hurtling down out of the stratosphere, would create a weapon of almost irresistible power.

Yet if we neither take steps to control the use of atomic energy nor to end war itself, we must face the prospect that another war will see every important city in the world blasted into nothingness. Our industrial civilization will perish under a new barbarism, as the Roman civilization did in its day. A remnant of survivors may be left — orphans of a murdered world, ushering in a new Dark Age of Man.[16]

As Mildred had predicted at the outset, nothing was solved by the war. "No principles were saved, no ideals maintained ... No peace established."[17] On the contrary, the Cold War had begun, and the very evils the Allies fought against — fascism, race prejudice, genocide — continued to flourish. Vague fears of "the Commies" became a reality on the night of September 5, 1945, when a young cipher clerk named Igor Gouzenko defected from the Russian Embassy in Ottawa. He carried documents revealing that a Soviet espionage ring was operating in Canada. Twenty-one people were charged under the Official Secrets Act; nine Canadians and two British were convicted.

The Gouzenko affair was only one symptom of a profound suspicion permeating world politics. The technology of spying and killing had made diabolical progress during the war, and the forces of evil took on new, and more sinister forms. As the long-term effects of the atomic bomb began to emerge, Mildred's sense of urgency grew. Surely now, she thought, people would see that if only the vast resources and human ingenuity wasted on warfare could be re-directed to peaceful uses, what a wonderful world it would be! She always kept a faded newsprint flyer headlined "What Price Glory" which states that, apart from the incalculable loss of at least 55 million human lives, the Second World War cost an estimated 400 billion dollars.

> With that money we could have built a $2500 house, furnished it with $1000 worth of furniture, placed it on five acres of land worth $100 an acre and given this home to each and every family in the United States, Canada, Australia, England, Wales, Ireland, Scotland, France, Belgium, Germany and Russia.

> We could have given to each city of 20,000 inhabitants and over, in each country named, a five million dollar library and a ten million dollar university.

> Out of what was left we could have set aside a sum at five per cent that would provide a $1000 yearly salary for an army of 125,000 teachers and a like salary for another army of 125,000 nurses ... Join the Peace ways Movement.[18]

Mildred believed ever more strongly in education for peace, so she ran a second time for the Vancouver school board in the election of December 12, 1945 — a contest which turned out to be disastrous for the CCF. The conservative forces in town, allied under the banner of the Non-Partisan Association (NPA), took almost every seat. The CCF managed to win only one seat on the parks board, none on city council. Mildred got 9,424 votes and stood seventh in the race for four seats on school board. She lagged far behind Ada Crump of the NPA. With 17,568 votes, Mrs. Crump was the only successful woman in any race.

Mildred and other members of the CCF knew that their support for the Japanese Canadian franchise had cost them dearly. It was an unpopular position, but it was the right one and so they stuck by it. They had one small success when CCF members of the park board successfully fought to lift the colour ban at Vancouver's Crystal Pool. The *CCF News* reported: "By a vote of four to three, it was decided to open the swimming pool to the public regardless of race or colour. CCF commissioners have always opposed racial discrimination in the use of this public facility."[19]

Mildred worked with the Co-operative Committee on Japanese Canadians to try to prevent the federal government's heinous "repatriation" plan, which would have exiled thousands of Canadians to post-nuclear Japan. "The Orders in Council passed for their deportation are now before the Supreme Court, and we are anxiously waiting results ... It seems so horrible to think of sending 23,000 people from this well-stocked country to starving Japan."[20]

Grace and Angus MacInnis led the anti-racist activism in Ottawa. In the House of Commons, Angus denounced repatriation as a "violation of every democratic tradition and every Christian principle." Grace appealed to "fair-minded Canadian citizens" to save Canada "from one of the blackest and most dangerous deeds possible to a modern country. If not, the race-haters will win." She urged them to "make our united determination shout across the Dominion. This national crime must not be."[21] At times like this, when Grace's eloquence and passion moved people to take action for justice, Mildred felt proud to be her comrade and friend. In the face of growing sympathy and support for Japanese Canadians, Prime Minister Mackenzie King called off the deportation orders.[22] For their courageous stand, Angus and Grace MacInnis would be loved and honoured in the Japanese Canadian community for the rest of their lives.

Although the fighting was officially over, the war was still claiming its victims by the thousands. An ocean away from the bombed-out cities and teeming refugee camps, Mildred did as much as one person could to ease the suffering of so many others. Perhaps it helped her to deal with the immense grief she felt for the human family. She volunteered for the Save the Children Fund, making stirring fundraising appeals that played upon the heart-strings of her audiences.

"It is difficult for us who have never been seriously hungry to realize that starvation faces 500 million people in the world to-day," Mildred told students and teachers assembled in the auditorium of King Edward High School. She remarked upon the poignant photos honouring alumni who had died in "defense of their homeland and the principles of democracy that they were taught in this school." The best way to keep faith with them, she said, is to help alleviate the suffering of the survivors. In the immediate post-war period, more than 140 million Europeans were homeless and hungry, most of them orphaned children, she said. "Three times more people will die of starvation this year than were killed in all the years of the war." She cautioned her listeners not to be paralyzed by the staggering numbers and the sheer enormity of need.

We dare not say that because we cannot do everything, we should do nothing, that because we cannot save all, we should save none. Is there any one in this room that does not think his own life would be worth saving? Surely then it would be worth our effort to save one child in Europe, and we can do much more than that. If we accept the challenge we here in this room can save the lives of as many boys and girls as are enrolled in this school, and we shall be doing so not only for Europe but for ourselves, for the building of a better world.[23]

Mildred urged young people to save their summer earnings and the spare change they would normally spend on chocolate or soda pop. Only twenty-five dollars could feed a destitute child for six months. Clothing and medical supplies were also urgently needed. The motto was "Save And Send." She said: "They have been called nobody's children, these half-starved homeless waifs … but in a very real sense they are our children, and we must accept responsibility for them."

Mildred and Walter Fahrni accepted responsibility for at least five of them through the Save the Children Fund in London and the Unitarian Service Committee of Canada. Mildred always kept the little black and white photos that came with their registration cards from France and Czechoslovakia and Belgium, and she often pondered their beautiful, serious young faces. From eleven-year-old Michelle's case history: "Completely bombed out. Living with another woman and her little son in three small rooms and tiny kitchen." Yet the social worker in France described her as "very frank, full of life, very obliging, well-balanced character." In Czechoslovakia, young Josef and his brother had been taken to a "preventorium" where they would receive special care and diet to allay the tuberculosis that had already stricken other family members. "JOSEF and JIRI are very weak owing to undernourishment. They are, however, recovering slowly. They are both gay and playful, and it is to be hoped they will be spared from becoming tubercular," the card read. The Fahrnis also sponsored Maria and Antoine, two of a set of triplets in Belgium. Their father

Mildred, Connie, an unidentified man and Vic, mid-1940s.

was a factory worker but could not support his eight children on his meager salary. When she could, Mildred also sent parcels overseas. She received heart-rending letters of thanks; some from total strangers, this one from Riek Liesveld in Bethlehem:

> Mildred dear, …
>
> I received a letter from mother, telling me all about your wonderful parcel … about her "abundance" and being able to let other people share! It was not just the food, but when things became almost unbearable, they just meant the little something that enabled them to carry on more hopefully and to realize how much love and kindness there still is in the world.[24]

To Mildred, however, it often seemed there was not near enough love and kindness in the hearts of Canadian policy-makers, who continued to keep the nation's doors closed to refugees. In 1947, Canada's immigration policy gave preferential treatment to migrants from Great Britain. In 1949, the same preferential treatment was extended to those from France, and by 1951 it included persons from Northwest Europe. In a radio broadcast Mildred pointed out how all Canadians (except the "North American Indians and the Esquimos") are products of the immigrant experience. The pioneers, she said, "were people of exceptional courage and initiative who refused to accept the political, economic and religious restrictions that were imposed upon them in the old world." For Canada to turn away the next generation of nation-builders "would be a strange denial of our heritage," she said.[25]

She believed that Canada should open her doors for both economic and moral reasons. "First," she said, "Canada can absorb and needs more people for her development, and secondly because starving homeless people are knocking at our doors and we cannot in decency or Christian brotherliness leave them on the outside to starve while we could very well provide them with opportunities to feed, house and clothe themselves." Mildred advocated a scheme of "planned immigration" which involved settlement services for the new Canadians and education for the native-born. Immigrants need to understand our laws and institutions so they can achieve citizenship with its full rights and responsibilities, she said. At the same time, Canadians must be educated against racial discrimination if newcomers are to be successfully integrated. As an immediate measure, she urged the government to encourage Canadians to adopt destitute orphans and to help bring the children over promptly. The other most pressing need was to find sanctuary for the homeless Jews of Europe:

"The war left only one and one-quarter million of the seven million Jews formerly in Europe. Surely these could be given an immediate asylum in Canada, New Zealand, Australia, United States and Latin America. If Canada would open her doors to a certain number, her example might well be followed by other countries and the lives and suffering of these unhappy people saved, and the tragedy that is going on in Palestine brought to an end."

Unfortunately for the Holocaust survivors, few Canadians shared Mildred's views. Scholars have summed up the national attitude in the words of an anonymous civil servant who was asked by reporters how many Jews Canada would accept after the war. "None is too many," he replied. Between 1933 and 1945, Canada admitted fewer than 5,000 Jews. After the war until the founding of the state of Israel in 1948, only 8,000 more were granted refuge in Canada. "That record is arguably the worst of all possible refugee-receiving states."[26]

***

The year after the war ended Walter's mother, Priscilla Fahrni, marked her 85th birthday. At that time her children realized she was getting on, and really

163

shouldn't be living alone anymore because she needed daily care and companionship. As the youngest of the five children, Walter was the one who had lived with their parents the longest. He seemed emotionally closest to their mother and he already lived nearby. For all these reasons, it was logical for his brothers to simply assume Walter would be the one to care for her at the end. So, after five years in the West End, Walter and Mildred moved into his mother's home on West Second Avenue in Kitsilano.

Mildred must have approached this change with some quiet misgivings. After nursing her own father for so long, she had no illusions as to how much work was entailed. She might well have questioned whether it was fair for the Fahrni sons to expect her to accept such a large responsibility for their mother's daily care, but she seemed to have accepted it without complaint. Friends recall that she always spoke affectionately of Mother Fahrni, but the affection was not returned. In fact, Mother Fahrni was quite frank about her dislike of her daughter-in-law and her politics.

"It must have been difficult for Mildred to live in that household with a matriarch who didn't approve," said Dorothy MacDonald, a friend and later co-op house mate.[27]

Walter's eldest brother, Gordon, also made no bones about the fact that he had never liked Mildred, just as he had never liked her father before her. Gordon never forgave Rev. Osterhout for the "ghastly incident" back on the farm in Gladstone when the preacher lectured the boy for using his horse at harvest. And then along comes his daughter, preaching socialism at him. "She'd get talking about the goddamn CCF," Gordon recalled. "Looked like she was trying to convert me. She was tied right up in it." Gordon never accepted that Walter was "tied right up in it" too, an indication that he didn't know his youngest brother all that well. Anyway, he certainly didn't understand what Walter saw in that Osterhout woman. "I could never understand Walter's marriage to Mildred. I never saw any love between them," he said.

To be fair, though, Gordon never saw them at all for years at a time because he was living in Winnipeg, and busy building a distinguished career in medicine. However, given his previous feelings, it came as no surprise to receive a pitiful letter from his mother, saying she had felt miserable ever since Walter and Mildred had moved in and taken over the house with their political meetings and people she didn't know coming and going all the time. "For the love of God, save me from this woman!" she begged.[28]

Gordon immediately flew to Vancouver and on arrival found his worst fears realized. The living room was full of women drinking tea and having a meeting, while his mother was all alone in her bedroom, lying on urine-soaked sheets. Furious and indignant, Dr. Fahrni called an ambulance and had his mother admitted to Vancouver General Hospital. He got her settled in, called upon colleagues to ensure the best care for her, and then returned to Winnipeg. Mother Fahrni died "of old age" a couple of weeks later. After that, Gordon said, he wanted no further dealings with Mildred because he would always believe she neglected his mother in her dying days. True to the prejudices of his profession, Dr. Fahrni did not hold his brother accountable for their mother's unhappy situation, only his brother's wife — after all, nursing was always women's work.

But the question remains: Did Mildred neglect a vulnerable old lady in her care? Certainly the condition in which Gordon found Mother Fahrni was appalling. However, anyone who has cared for an infant or an incontinent elder knows that a person can go from dry to sopping in a minute. The timing of Gordon's arrival could have been simply a matter of hideously bad luck for Mildred. It's impossible to know for sure. However, it is quite probable that while she carried on as usual with her fast-paced political work, she didn't take time to notice that her mother-in-law found all the activity in her home distressing. After all, Mildred kept up the same work while she was looking after her own father and he hadn't minded. The difference, of course, was that Father loved her and respected her calling, while Mother Fahrni did not.

After the death of his mother, Walter and Mildred moved into a co-operative house which they shared with three other families. Altogether there were ten adults, two teenagers and four children in the household, including Mary and Watson Thomson, with their three-year-old son, Colin. Mary Thomson described how to all of them, co-op housing was much more than a roof over one's head: it was a way of life.

"The idea was it would be a microcosm of the international community, of what the world might be like if we lived co-operatively. It meant a lot of individual change, and helping each other. It was pretty exciting," she said.[29]

The house often rang with the music of piano, guitar, and enthusiastic voices raised in song. For the children, they started a play school which was run by a Jewish doctor from Vienna. Men and women shared in all the chores and, on the whole, it was a happy household. "We were all very fond of Walter," Mary said. "I adored him. He was a wonderful person."

Walter had always been very inventive, but had never tried to earn a living from his tinkering. Finally, in his fifties, he decided to try to market the best of his many inventions. "In the business world we are adventuring too, with Walter putting up shop and putting his new indicators on the market," Mildred wrote.[30] Walter incorporated his business under the name of Precise Engineering Limited and set up an office down on Main Street north of Hastings, near the industrial area and the harbour. Walter invented one of the early power tools, which he dubbed "Fahrni's RECIPROCUT." An advertising flyer read: "FAST HANDY RUGGED VERSATILE The All Purpose Power-Tool for Heavy Work ... Most particularly those time-killing Hard-to-get-at knuckle-barking jobs that so often crop up."

Walter's other major invention, a gauge for measuring compression or combustion pressure, was called "Fahrni's Diesel Pressometer." It was "PRECISE STURDY SIMPLE and LOW IN PRICE" at seventy-six dollars, but unfortunately Walter failed to patent his invention promptly. Inevitably someone else snapped up the idea and made himself a lot of money. Mildred was often frustrated by Walter's inattention to practical details. His elder brother was too, and later lamented that a large tool manufacturer was reaping the profits from Walter's fertile imagination. "He was a bit slipshod, a dreamy sort of a guy," Gordon said.

The Fahrnis were known to sleep separately ("supposedly because of his snoring") and this fact led some of the co-op residents to wonder whether there was any "passion in the marriage," Mary Thomson recalled. Yet Dorothy MacDonald clearly recalled "a visual picture of her putting her arms around his shoulders, being close to him ... I think they had a sexual relationship," she said. Years later, when Mildred's niece Marion asked herself similar questions, she pictured Walter as a man who could be happy in a caring, companionable, but chaste marriage. He was quiet and self-contained, Marion recalled, a favourite with the children and famous for his artistry and skill at carving marvelous Halloween pumpkins.[31]

Among the co-op dwellers there was great interest in the kibbutz movement, and the house became a centre for Jewish refugees as well as a meeting place for various pacifists, socialists and communists. Their many political activities included helping to found a new group called the Vancouver Peace Assembly. Mildred Fahrni and Watson Thomson were involved, and so was Dr. Norman Black, future president of UBC, and Sheila Young of the Women's International League for Peace and Freedom.

It was a time that demanded the courage of one's convictions. Society was so hostile to their views that the peacemakers were often chased off the streets by the police, Sheila Young recalled. "They branded us as Communists, and the clergymen started dropping out," she said. "They wouldn't let us march, and if we handed out leaflets, we would be charged with littering. When I went door-to-door, the housewives would call the police on me."[32]

Despite all these obstacles, "they were very enthusiastic about it," Mary Thomson recalled. "The notable thing was that it included the Communist Party, although it was not called the Communist Party then, it was the LPP — the Labour Progressive Party. They worked with the Communists because they

Mildred with Vic's family, 1949. From left to right: Connie, Bobby, Mildred, Vic, Marion and Don.

believed that because they had been our allies during the war we should go on being allies."

The Thomsons were more aware than most people of the difficulties then faced by Communists — in Canada as well as in the United States, where the witch-hunts of the McCarthy era were about to begin. Although he was not a Communist, Watson had been smeared as one and subsequently fired from his job as director of adult education for the CCF government in Saskatchewan. "When he was fired his career was ruined. Nobody would hire him," Mary said. "And Tommy Douglas didn't raise a finger to defend him," even though Douglas himself had "begged" Watson to take the job. Mary attributed this terrible breach to an extremely "paranoid" attitude within the CCF. The Thomsons moved from the prairies to the west coast in the wake of this fiasco, and Mary went to work in an office to support the family. "It was a very depressing time for us," she said.

The other families in the house were farther to the left politically than either the Thomsons or the Fahrnis. "Maybe one of the families were card-carrying Communists, but I don't know for sure," Mary said. Both she and Watson could see that Mildred didn't feel totally comfortable in this milieu. They felt she was "more defensive about Communists" than she ought to be.

It was sometimes difficult to talk about these issues, though, because "you didn't get intimate with Mildred easily," Mary recalled.

Indeed, Mildred was very restrained in her emotional life, but she was still passionate about politics, peace and especially India. Gandhi had been arrested, along with his wife and closest followers, within days of launching his historic "Quit India" campaign. In prison, Mahadev Desai, the Mahatma's beloved companion and secretary, suddenly collapsed and died of heart failure. Mildred grieved for Mahadev, whom she too had loved from the moment they first met at Kingsley Hall. Miraben inscribed the word *Om* and the cross upon his grave. Within months, Kasturba, Gandhi's wife of 62 years, also died in prison.

With the post-war defeat of Winston Churchill and the election of Labour Prime Minister Clement Atlee in England, the Indian independence movement entered its final phase. Battered by the war with Germany, the English people had no desire to go to war for India. As Krishna Kripalani wrote, "the brightest jewel in the British crown was turning into a rankling thorn."[33] Having decided to quit India, the British wanted to act promptly, but they could not bring together the two major forces for self-rule: the Indian National Congress and the Muslim League. The Muslims, led by Mohammed Ali Jinnah, insisted upon a separate state of Pakistan. Utterly frustrated in their negotiations with Jinnah, in August 1946 the British Viceroy invited Pandit Nehru to form the government. The outraged Muslims of Calcutta responded with a massacre of Hindus, including women and children. Then Hindus retaliated with equal fury.

> And so began a chain reaction of violence and horror which set the country ablaze from east to west. What India was spared during the War she now had with a vengeance and in manifestation vastly more ugly — carnage without courage, hatred without heroism, savagery without sacrifice. The pride of non-violence was humbled in shame, the voice of sanity drowned in a howl of hatred, and the sweet fruit of freedom turned sour and snapped into halves before it could ripen. This great sin of Indian history, who will expiate?[34]

Gandhi, of course. Freed from prison, he travelled to Calcutta, Noakhali, Bihar and hundreds of villages in between, where Hindus and Muslims had once lived in harmony but now were mortal enemies. But his anguished words fell on deaf ears. "The Gandhi way, infallible earlier, had somehow, somewhere, gone awry. It was alienating the Hindus, without winning over the Muslims."[35]

Prime Minister Atlee appointed Lord Louis Mountbatten as the last Viceroy of India and gave him a sweeping mandate to dismantle the British Empire in India. Although Gandhi and Mountbatten developed a relationship of mutual trust and respect, the Mahatma's pleas for a united India could not be answered.

At the stroke of midnight, on the 15th of August 1947, the independent nations of India and Pakistan were born. Mountbatten later called it the most remarkable and inspiring day of his life. Great hordes of joyful celebrants from all castes and all faiths embraced each other and called out, "*Azad Sahib!*" "We are free, sir!" Prison doors were flung wide, pardons were issued, death sentences commuted. Everywhere the day was characterized by good will towards the English and, for their part, great dignity in the transfer of power ceremonies.[36]

Mourning what he called "the vivisection of India," Gandhi refused to be in Delhi to participate in the independence celebrations. He had a terrible foreboding that "rivers of blood" would flow in the aftermath of Partition. His fears were realized all too soon as fearful Hindus fled south into India and Muslims north into Pakistan. In Punjab, North-West Frontier and Sind, nearly ten million people were on the move.

On her next trip to India, Mildred would learn first-hand about those brutal days, and would speak to survivors of this largest refugee migration in human history. But first, she was bound on a different journey, the first of many trips to Latin America, especially to Mexico, which became in many ways like her India.

Mildred in Antigua, Guatemala, 1947.

Chapter Twelve: 1947

BROADENING HORIZONS

In 1947 Mildred was elected president of the local branch of the Women's International League for Peace and Freedom. Founded in 1914 in The Hague, the league's B.C. branch was started by Lucy Woodsworth and Laura Jamieson. One year earlier Emily Greene Balch, WILPF's current international secretary, was awarded the Nobel Peace Prize.[1] With the aim of building closer links between peace-minded women throughout the Americas, the League planned its first Inter-American Congress of Women to be held in Guatemala City. Mildred couldn't wait to get on the bus. She departed for Mexico City in April. When she got there, as in India, she was struck by the stark disparity between rich and poor.

"The beautiful Spanish homes with their colourful gardens look out on the miserable adobe huts of the penniless squatters," she noted. "As the graceful fountain sheds its sparkling spray into the lovely tiled pool, a ragged urchin comes up to drink ... But perhaps the strangest contrasts are between the noble words of governmental officials and their corrupt practices."[2]

After a couple of weeks, Mildred was becoming disheartened by the lack of rigour in the Mexicans' approach to peace work, and dismayed to discover that the conference had been postponed until August; in fact prospects didn't look all that good for a successful meeting. She wrote home:

Frankly I'm feeling disillusioned because of the lack of co-operation or community spirit of any noticeable amount. I have been waiting for days to meet some of the W.I.L. women and finally the president invited me to her home and had 3 others there, but the talk was all trivial and none of them seemed to think it possible to build up a sizable or effective group. They are all too busy ... with their manicurist and hairdresser. They don't turn up even when they promise to do so. They are hours late for any appointment they keep ... and think nothing of it. I was given a written invitation to a meeting of a coordinating committee to bring the various women's organizations together ... and I was the only one who turned up. I am further advised that most of these organizations exist in name only, although they have high sounding titles.[3]

Never one to sit around waiting, Mildred took off to Puebla. It was a gorgeous drive past the famous volcanoes whose rhythmical Aztec names she loved to say, and for which she developed her own pronunciation clues: "The two great volcanoes Popcatepatl (Poppy Caterpillar) and Ixstacewatl (Eyes to see Walter) reared up magnificently amongst the clouds." Mildred delighted in Puebla, its narrow streets and chaotic open markets redolent with the scents of wood smoke and corn tortillas, burros and bougainvillea. The balloon man and the toy peddler caught her eye, as did the colourful baskets, woven *serapes* and carvings in onyx. Mildred always loved the folk arts and crafts of Mexico, especially their use of brilliant colour. But in Latin America, as in many parts of Asia, she abhorred the flamboyance when it came to religious expression.

> The cathedral and churches in Puebla are ornate and lavish in their display of gold, marble, carving and statues. I find them most depressing. The garish figures of Mary and the gruesome ones of Jesus, with blood dripping from wounds are horrible and almost as unpleasant as the idols in Hindu Temples ... The contrast of these elaborate display of trappings and the thin little mother with her undernourished baby kneeling before some ornate images makes one feel how barbaric men are in their interpretation of religion. I had no idea of what was meant by the power of the church in Catholic countries before coming and seeing.[4]

After her disappointing meetings with the WIL members, Mildred was overjoyed to meet Herberto and Suzanne Sein, Mexican Quakers whose depth of commitment stood in sharp contrast to the superficial interest of others. Herberto Sein was coordinating rural development work reminiscent of Gandhi's efforts. "Herberto is Spanish and English with a good mixture of Indian somewhere," Mildred wrote. "He is able and sincere, a committed well-balanced character and a glowing personality ... To-day he leaves for Washington with [then-President] Aleman to act as interpreter and then in a couple of weeks they go to Geneva for two years with the I.L.O. [International Labour Organization]."[5]

Through Herberto, Mildred visited a village about one hundred miles from Mexico City to see the work being done by volunteers from the American Friends Service Committee. She first spent a weekend, and was so impressed that she later returned for a couple of weeks to Tetelcingo, "an old Aztec village where the people are living in a primitive culture not far removed from that of their ancestors." At first, the whole village looked just like one big squalid farm yard. Everywhere was littered with corn husks and straw, while dogs, pigs, chickens and children all wandered freely in and out of the mud huts. Everyone was barefoot. The women wore long skirts and their hair plaited in long braids. Although they had little, the people were kind and hospitable. Mildred stayed with the young volunteers who were living co-operatively in part of a school building. She helped at the health clinic where they dispensed cod liver oil and castor oil, treated infections and gave injections for syphilis.

"Before winning the friendship of the Mexican people they had to break down the widespread antagonism to the 'Gringos' which the Americans have won by their officious interference in Mexican affairs, by their exploitation of labour, and their overbearing attitude as tourists."[6]

One day the Friends opened their door to find local villagers carrying a man who was clearly feverish and very ill after being bitten by a scorpion. One of the young women rushed to the fridge for the antidote, and quickly gave him an injection. Later in the day, Mildred and the others went to check up on the poor fellow who they found lying on a straw mat on the mud floor of his adobe hut, his worried family members squatting all around. They beseeched the North Americans to promise them he would not die, and the man did indeed recover in a few days.

Mildred loved the warmth of the tropics, but it took some getting used to the *cucarachas* and other many-legged *amigos* that were so numerous.

The typical experiences of Mexico soon started to move in on me and I had to get out the DDT to chase them from my bed …

The boys work in a village about 6 miles away where they make friends with the people, and are starting on a DDT project to clear out the bedbugs and insects. Where it was done in one village the people said they had the first undisturbed sleep of their lives.[7]

Mildred later travelled with Carolyn Threlkeld, a WIL member from Berkeley, California. They ventured to Queretaro, San Miguel de Allende, Guanajuato, Guadalajara, Manzanillo and back to Mexico City, and south to Guatemala City. Fortunately for Mildred, Carolyn spoke good Spanish and so she was able to get closer to the people and understand them in a way she could not have done on her own. They found "obvious and definite" differences between Mexico and Guatemala. She attributed the relatively healthier situation in Guatemala to the fact that the indigenous people, descendants of the great Maya civilization, had been able to retain "their local characteristics, their costumes and *costumbres* to a greater extent" than their Mexican brothers. Although Mildred thought the Mayan languages sounded "just like guttural mumbling," she recognized they were at the foundation of an entirely different, more peaceful culture. From Santiago Atitlan to Chichicastenango and Huehuetenango, everywhere she travelled she saw a way of life based on co-operation instead of competition. The sophisticated North American, she thought, could learn from the simple Mayan.

I am continually amazed at his gentleness and his courtesy. I have never seen a quarrel, and seldom hear loud words, except from the occasional *borracho* who has had too much fire water. Men and women help each other off and on buses with their heavy loads, and bus drivers patiently wait while bundles are packed away and friends shake hands and say their *adios*. One seldom sees or feels the hurry of the life of the *Norte Americano*.

The effect of this patient attitude on children is interesting too for they are not shoved about, not hurried here and there, not rushed into a routine, and one seldom sees a child showing any sense of pressure. I have seen very few unhappy children, practically no quarrels and little tears or fretting.[8]

However, Guatemala's children, although beloved and cherished, grew up in poverty and worked hard from an early age. In nearly every country home one heard the chug of pedals and the clack of shuttles as children worked at looms.

In one cottage in which we stopped, a young boy of 11 was working so hard at a loom that he would not even stop to talk with us, but he flashed his big eyes at us ... and they were enough to melt the hardest icicle. We found on enquiry that he did not live there but was hired out at 3 cents an hour. The fact that he was supposed to be at school meant nothing. Such laws are not enforced in the country. I'll not forget him easily ... especially when I am bargaining for a cheaper price on textiles![9]

Once in Guatemala City, Mildred right away "started running messages for the [Women's] Congress" and began to see how profoundly Washington and its policies influenced events in Latin America.

The government here is criticized by many as being 'Communistic,' by others it is condemned as totalitarian, and by some is lauded as democratic. Whatever their attitude, all seem anxious not to do anything to win disfavour in government circles. It seems that many have directly or indirectly felt the loss of position, prestige or life by opposing the government in the past. On the other hand, it does not do to be too openly in favour of the government, because one does not know when it will change, and then one is just as likely to be thrown out by the new party coming in. Therefore many people try to keep clear of 'politics' altogether.

U.S.A. towers over these Latin American countries like a great menacing power that can bring them good or ill, and they are very anxious not to do anything that will run counter to her policies. Perhaps that is why at the present time the attitude towards Russia is very critical, and there is a great fear everywhere of Communism. On the whole I think people here are not very well informed about International affairs ... that is, they don't see the whole picture, and their attitude is quite biased.

Women have not taken a very active part in politics or public affairs, and are still largely interested in getting and keeping ... their men, and raising their families ...

Perhaps with this background you can get the picture of what happened, when a few alarmists started spreading the rumor that the W.I.L. was a Communist organization and that the Congress would be Communist controlled. Others heard it was not likely to be a very large Congress and thought there would be little prestige gained through having it ... in fact they began to think they might lose face altogether. A couple of rabid anti-Communists took it upon themselves to write to the [Guatemalan] Minister of External Affairs and tip him off as to their suspicions.[10]

Unaware of these behind-the-scenes events, the conference organizers were rudely awakened when they received a telegram from the Guatemalan chapter of the WILPF announcing they were no longer willing to sponsor the meeting. Several influential women immediately flew in from Washington, D.C. and attempted to convince the *Latinas* that the League was not a Communist front organization, but to no avail.

A few women got up and in the usual Latin American oratorical manner presented very emotional statements, calling on the women not to forget their patria, advising them of the strategic position in which this small country was, and how dependent they were on the good will of the U.S. etc.

Actually their minds had been thoroughly poisoned in private sessions by a few of the rabid members and nothing could change them. I had tried previously to clarify the position but my lack of their language ... and knowledge of their emotional background ... made it impossible.[11]

The remaining women "took up the challenge valiantly" and immediately formed a new organization, The Union of Democratic Women of Guatemala, which undertook to sponsor the conference as its first project. When it finally opened, the first Inter-American Congress of Women welcomed 69 delegates from 18 countries, all of them committed to finding new ways to build peace in the nuclear age. In a world still ignorant of the perils of atomic power, the women's faith in new technology and in humanity's ability to use it wisely was perhaps not as naive as it would later seem.

Facing the threat of the atomic bomb, the Congress felt its first responsibility was to disabuse the minds of the public of the fear surrounding it and to instill into them an appreciation of the constructive use of atomic energy ...

Convinced that control of the atomic bomb should be invested in the U.N. they recommended further investigation of trusts controlling factories that produce material for atomic and other armaments. Such trusts should be broken and all atomic research carefully supervised.[12]

Pledging support to the United Nations, the Congress made a plea for better representation of women at the UN. They also urged governments to enact laws to protect fundamental freedoms and minority rights. They agreed on the importance of combatting alcoholism, tobacco use, social diseases and prostitution, and they advocated compulsory pre-nuptial health certificates and sex education. Literacy programs needed to be expanded throughout the Americas. The women noted that neutral Costa Rica, without the enormous expenses of arming and equipping an army, was able to provide free primary and elementary schooling for its citizens.

After the conference Mildred travelled north by train through the tropical countryside, stopping at every little gathering of shacks along the way. Naked and ragged children waved from the stoops. "*Cafe, leche, coco, agua, tamales.* Coffee, milk, coconuts, water," the vendors cried.

> People came and went with a great variety of baggage, bundles and bags, baskets and *bolsas* [sacks] and what was left over they just carried whether cabbages or bananas and hung them up on every hook. All I hoped was that a coco would not fall on my head, and fortunately none did. However the chickens under the seat did startle me when they started picking at my bare legs ... turn about so to speak.[13]

A derailment on the line ahead delayed their train most of the night, but in the morning she boarded a fine, clean new train which carried her through the mountains "as smooth as a waltz." The tropical growth was luxuriant and the vendors who came to the windows now had exquisite gardenias and orchids, as well as huge bunches of fruit. She sped down into the valley and through fields brilliant with purple and yellow flowers. The landscape was "enchantingly lovely."

> I went to collect my various bundles and baskets ... and found them making merry in the second class car. A mariachi player was singing loud plaintive songs and around my seat *pulque* was being passed around, so I joined in and could hardly keep them from refilling my mug. Then somebody pulled out a bottle of wine, so we came in quite hilarious ...

Hasta Lo Visto, Carniosamente, Mildred.[14]

She took classes in Guatemala City at San Carlos University's *Escuela de Verano*, but Mildred's Spanish would always remain rudimentary. Here, for example, she used the wrong gender for *la vista* and confused the word *cariño* for *carne*, so that while she meant "affectionately" she actually signed off with something like "meatily, Mildred" — a funny farewell for a vegetarian!

She travelled north through Mexico to San Antonio and New Orleans. In the Deep South she was shocked to see that "the buses, street cars, etc. are divided into 'Colored' and 'White' and even the restaurants and lunch rooms are completely apart. Some of the tenements I saw in the big cities, and the miserable shacks in the country certainly indicate a condition of poverty that doesn't have much to boast over Mexico." She was relieved to leave the south and head to Philadelphia and New York where she met with others from the Fellowship of Reconciliation, including Nevin Sayre. She stayed with friends who lived in Greenwich Village, "perhaps the most exciting of all with its medley of artists and crack pots and varied Bohemian life."

Mildred looked forward to getting "back where I can wave the CCF flag again." In Ottawa, she met with David Lewis at CCF House and with Dr. Lotta Hitschmanova of the Unitarian Service Committee. She also found time for visits with her dear friends, Islay Johnston and Marion Langridge. In Toronto she visited Rev. James Finlay and Lavell Smith, two of the founders of the Fellowship of Reconciliation in Canada, and had a good talk with Ab Watson, then national secretary of the Canadian FOR. She also saw Hide Hyodo, a friend from the days in the camp at New Denver. She made a few speeches on behalf of the Women's International League on the way home, and arrived back in B.C. late in the fall. She wrote up her experiences in an article for the *Canadian Forum*, a leading socialist journal. Besides Mildred's article on the Inter-American Women's Congress, there was in the same issue a report by Dorothy Livesay on China's Co-operatives.

* * *

Almost half a year after independence, there was no end in sight to the "rivers of blood" Gandhi had foreseen before Partition. It was the massacre of the dream of a free India born without violence, and it was agony to witness. On his 78th birthday, the Mahatma told his followers he had no wish to mark another birthday "in an India still in flames." He began to speak of his own death as already having occurred. "Don't you see I am mounted on my funeral pyre?" His inability to stop the killing and bring his compatriots together as brothers and sisters gnawed at him. Finally, he decided to put his life on the line in the cause of Hindu-Muslim unity.

On January 13, 1948 he began his last, greatest fast. Indians across the land watched and waited over the next few days as he grew weaker in body but more resolved in spirit to die if necessary to expiate the violent sins of his people. Mountbatten's press attaché later wrote: "You have to live in the vicinity of a Gandhi fast to understand its pulling power ... He has a genius for acting through symbols which all can understand."[15]

The fast lasted five days, and evoked different responses ranging from awe to irritation, but among some Hindus it bred deep resentment and a sense that the Mahatma was expecting much more of his own people than of the Muslims. His sublime penance seemed to them just emotional coercion, and they were in no mood for reconciliation. "Violent passions had been aroused and hatred was in the air. Muslim fanaticism in Pakistan had provoked its counterpart in India, and the militant spearhead of this reaction looked upon Gandhi as the main stumbling block to their lust for vengeance for the atrocities committed on Hindus and Sikhs in the name of Islam."[16]

Gandhi and his disciples were staying at Birla House, a mansion owned by one of his wealthy supporters in New Delhi. Every day, thousands of pilgrims came to his prayer meetings, which were held in the garden. Faced with such enormous numbers of people the security police wanted to mount an armed guard to protect Gandhi, but he refused all such offers. On January 20, as he spoke to the crowd, a bomb exploded just a few yards away from where he sat cross-legged on a wooden platform. Mistaking the blast for the sound of routine target practise by the military, Gandhi was unperturbed and simply continued preaching. His faith was fearless, but he continued to muse upon the bomb attack during the next ten days. Several times he mused aloud to his grand-daughter, Manu, about "assassin's bullets" and "a shower of bullets." The night before he died, he told her:

> If I were to die of disease, be it even a pimple, you must shout to the world from the house-tops that I was a false mahatma, even though people may swear at you for saying so. Then my soul, wherever it be, will rest in peace. If, on the other hand, someone were to put a bullet through me, as someone tried to throw a bomb at me the other day, and I met this bullet on my bare chest, without a groan and with Rama's name on my lips, only then you should say that I was a true mahatma.[17]

Although Gandhi never claimed the gift of prophecy, his words were borne out the very next day, January 30, 1948. All morning he was busy as usual with interviews, correspondence and meetings. He completed a blueprint for the future of the Indian National Congress, his legacy for the leaders of free India. Hating to be late for his five o'clock prayers, he hurried through the throng of devotees, leaning on the strong shoulders of Manu and Abha, his grand-niece. All of a sudden, a young man pushed his way out of the crowd and knelt before

Gandhi as if in reverence. Explaining they were late, Manu tried to stop him but the man sprang up, aimed and shot three times point blank at Gandhi's chest. As he had longed to do, Mahatma Gandhi died crying, "*He Ram!*" Oh God!

The bleeding body of India's "apostle of non-violence" was carried inside where family members offered prayers through their tears. At his bedside, Prime Minister Jawaharlal Nehru, Home Minister Sardar Patel and other Congress leaders wept together. In the gardens of Birla House, meanwhile, worshippers grabbed the assassin and beat him severely before the police apprehended him. That evening, Nehru went on radio to break the devastating news to the nation. In a voice quivering with emotion, he said:

> Friends and comrades, the light has gone out of our lives and there is darkness everywhere. I do not know what to tell you and how to say it. Our beloved leader, Bapu as we called him, the father of the nation, is no more ... The light has gone out, I said, and yet I was wrong ... For that light represented something more than the immediate present; it represented the living truth, the eternal truths, reminding us of the right path, drawing us from error, taking this ancient country to freedom.[18]

Mildred clipped out the eloquent editorial in *The Vancouver Sun*, which she read and re-read through her tears. It said:

> The assassination of Mahatma Gandhi is an epochal event. It is likely, as years go by, to rank with the crucifixion of Jesus in the annals of redemptive sacrifice. Both Gandhi and Jesus were valiant warriors against evil; both loved all mankind and prayed for their enemies; both were put to death by their own people.[19]

For Mildred, the light of Gandhi's love and truth burned on. As she grieved, she wrote:

> To-day, Gandhi the man is dead, but Gandhi, the Mahatma, the Great Soul, the spirit of love, lives on and men everywhere bow in recognition of the truth that shone in him. It is this acknowledgment that brings a sense of brotherhood, and of the eternal. Each one of us knows in his heart that Gandhi is right, that love and truth must supersede hatred and violence. And this awareness links us with Gandhi, with Jesus, and with all who have sought and are seeking to bring peace upon the earth ...
>
> By the perfection of our instruments of destruction we to-day face the possibility of our own self-extermination. But Gandhi shows the way out. He demonstrates the practical reality of the way of love ... Men do not need to act like fiends. Men can act like God.[20]

After Gandhi's death, Mildred did as Nehru urged and dedicated herself ever more fervently to the cause for which Bapu was martyred. That summer the opportunity arose for her to take the post of National Secretary of the Fellowship of Reconciliation. Although it meant moving to Toronto, she took up the challenge and headed east in August, 1948. Ever after, Walter's relatives would criticize Mildred for "abandoning" him to her peace work. She wrote that the move came thanks to "the patient endurance of a much-too-nice-to-protest husband."[21] With his new business to tend, Walter decided to stay in Vancouver and agreed they would maintain the relationship by mail and with the occasional visit when Mildred was on a speaking tour.

Working from a tiny office at 108 Charles Street, she wrote: " ... now I'm glad to be able to concentrate on the F.O.R. for I'm convinced that the way of love and non-violent action is the way to creative living, and the way to a solution of our individual and group problems." Never one to take herself too seriously, she added parenthetically: "(Anyone wishing to be exposed to the full blast of propaganda please send a self-addressed stamped envelope.)"

Mildred did not have an easy time settling in Toronto, however. She had pulled back from the CCF mainly because of the party's support for Canada's entry into the war. From that moment, she felt that the CCF had lost its way, by veering off of the path of absolute pacifism. She remained a life-long supporter, but couldn't any longer devote her life to the movement. But, having shifted her energies from the CCF for the FOR, many people doubted her motives and some even had their suspicions she was a Communist.

"One makes new friends ... but slowly here, for it takes the East a long time to tolerate, much less accept, the stranger. Once they realize you haven't any horns, sickles or hammers under your hat they open the door. They aren't quite sure of me yet, but there is a crack in the door. Of course the size of the city makes it difficult to be chummy."[22]

Over the years, some of the luminaries of the post-war pacifist movement in the U.S. and Europe came to speak and meet with the FOR in eastern Canada. They included Nevin Sayre, A.J. Muste, Bayard Rustin, John Swomley Jr., Andre Trocme, and Stanley Jones. Plainclothes policemen often attended these meetings. The founding of the Canadian Peace Congress in 1948 intensified peace activism. "To organize the congress on a national basis the committee enlisted Dr. James G. Endicott, the radical United Church missionary who resigned from his missionary post and from the ministry because of the church's disapproval of his outspoken support for the Chinese Communists."[23] In the spring of 1949, Mildred made a cross-Canada trip to promote the FOR and found herself travelling in the wake of James Endicott, who was also on a speaking tour at the time. On her way back east she reflected upon the state of the peace movement and the impact of Cold War ideology on people's understanding. From Swift Current, Saskatchewan, she wrote:

Everywhere I have been I found great confusion re: the relation of our movement to the National Peace Councils. Dr. Endicott preceded me across the country and on the whole made a very favourable impression. People everywhere believe in his sincerity and appreciate the facts he has made public. Many church people and others are in the Councils without any recognition of any political implications. However there is also a widespread fear from the outside that the Councils are Communist controlled and in one case at least I found evidence of meetings being watched by Plain Clothes men and members being under surveillance. Most church people are afraid there is some connection between our movement and the Councils. I keep thinking what a tragedy that the church did not give the leadership in a peace movement that would have rallied great numbers to the cause of peace ... and have been above suspicion ... or would it?[24]

It's doubtful that anyone espousing Mildred's point of view could have been above suspicion in those days. But there were bright spots in the dismal picture. One of the highlights of Mildred's time with the FOR in Toronto was a visit by Gandhi's friends, Dr. and Mrs. Chakravarty and Shimanti, their eighteen-year-old daughter.

You can imagine how I have enjoyed it too ... for Dr. Chakravarty was a close friend of Gandhi and interprets him better than anyone I have heard. He was with Tagore for 6 years and knows Nehru and other leaders well too ... Like Bapu his sincerity wins people immediately. It has been an inspiration to know him and now more than ever I feel I must hitch hike to the World Pacifist Conference in India ... If anyone knows any planes or canoes going my way ask them to watch out for the crooked thumb.[25]

Mildred's salary from the FOR was minimal, so how did she manage to hitch-hike to a conference on the other side of the world? It seems likely that significant help came from Franc Joubin, who she met in 1933 as a hungry and threadbare UBC student. At the urging of a kindly lady in her father's congregation, Mildred had invited Franc for Sunday dinner. When he complimented her on the delicious meal she hastened to pass on the praise to the real cook, an unemployed teacher named Mary Torvinen, who was then living with the family and working for room and board.

Thus Franc met Mary, the love of his life, in Mildred's kitchen. When they were married four years later, the ceremony took place in the Osterhout's living room with Mildred's father officiating. For young Franc, who suffered in orphanages throughout his early childhood, being welcomed into the Osterhout family was a real blessing, one he repaid many times over. He became one of Canada's foremost geologists and mining prospectors and built a huge personal fortune, which he put towards many good causes. Franc and Mary Joubin remained life-long friends of Mildred and generous patrons of her peace and development projects. Asked whether he helped Mildred financially, his reply was, "Yes, almost continuously."

"She was very charming, and a very practical woman," Franc said. "She was talking bread and food and school books. If you listened carefully and asked an intelligent question or two, she had all the facts. When she had a particular request to make, it was always in such a modest range ... When there was a need, she had a reason."[26]

So, with Franc's assistance and other funds from the FOR, Mildred set off for the World Pacifist Conference. The concept had been suggested years earlier, first by a group of British Quakers who wanted to work with Gandhi on a global gathering. In consultation with Albert Einstein and others, they agreed that Gandhi would invite fifty men and women from the western world to meet with him and fifty from the eastern hemisphere. The conference was postponed after Gandhi's assassination, but it was never called off. On the contrary, everyone involved agreed that it was ever more important to understand Gandhi's vision and its implications for peace work in the atomic age. "The recent pronouncement of the bomb explosion in Russia makes the conference especially significant at the present time," Mildred noted. Still, at 49, she was not unrealistic.

> While great hope is held for a renewed spiritual impetus from the conference, it is not suggested that it will lead to immediate tangible results in the political world, but rather than it may generate new spiritual power in the world and spread new faith and assurance in man's capacity and destiny to live as one family under heaven.[27]

Mildred's second trip to India was as much a spiritual journey as her first. She sailed from Montreal and arrived in London eager to revisit old haunts. The Blitz had forever changed the London she had known. In Bow, only Kingsley Hall remained standing, "alone unshaken in the midst of destruction all around." Mildred met up with a dozen other pacifists also bound for India. All together, they set sail October 21 aboard an Indian ship, the *Jal Azad*. They sailed through the Mediterranean to Suez, where military camps could be seen among the camels and palm trees along the canal. From the Red Sea into the Arabian, the heat was intense and Mildred was among the second class passengers who dragged their mattresses outside to sleep on deck most nights.

As the miles slipped by, the little band of pilgrims explored their common ground. Mildred was quickly and profoundly impressed by Magda Trocme who, with her husband André, was joint secretary of the French Fellowship of Reconciliation. Together they founded an international school called

Mildred loved elephants and made sure she saw some each time she visitied India, 1949.

Le Chambon. "Their experiences sheltering Jews during the war, and later his period in a concentration camp, make a dramatic story," she wrote.

They arrived in Bombay after 22 days at sea. The conference organizers had graciously arranged for them to receive VIP treatment in the homes of Indian supporters. Mildred and Magda were quietly dismayed to discover they were to stay in "a mansion with a Guest Suite and a servant of our own. 'Twas not for this I came to India," Mildred wrote home.[28] It was quite difficult because whenever she or anybody in their party tried to carry something, their Indian hosts would insist, "Leave it. He will take it." Mildred felt awful as "the coolies struggled under terrific loads." After many rounds of lavish refreshments, she felt out of touch with the people who were most beloved by Gandhi, so she sought them out.

> Tonight I went to the "Chawls," the terrible slums, and I cannot forget the scenes of wretched misery I saw with children lying on rags on the streets ...

> Across the bay the lights of the waterfront make the Necklace of Pearls famed round the world ... But their beauty is blurred by the pictures I have in my mind.[29]

The conference delegates were invited to a reception at Government House hosted by Prime Minister Jawaharlal Pandit Nehru. After the words of welcome, conversation turned to Gandhi, his death and the trial of his assassins. After six months in court, the case of Nathuram Godse had ended in a guilty verdict and the death sentence. Mildred and her friends believed that nothing would have pained the Mahatma more than other deaths claimed as vengeance for his own. Two of Gandhi's sons and other close followers shared this view and had appealed to Nehru to commute the sentences, but their petition was denied. Although they knew it would be futile, the pacifists made a last-minute appeal to the Governor General.

"The Prime Minister approves of hanging," Mildred wrote. "At least we shall voice our protest but there hardly seems a dissenting voice in India. Everywhere people tell us India is not following Gandhi ... but actually she never did."[30]

The executions took place as scheduled — at dawn on November 15, 1949. Of the eight conspirators in Gandhi's murder, only Godse and Narayan Apte, the "brains" behind the plot, were hanged. Three others were sentenced to life imprisonment, two were acquitted and one was released after turning state's witness.

On this trip to India, Mildred met a remarkable Christian named Reverend K.K. Chandy, who with his wife, Mary, was totally committed to Bapu's way of simplicity and service. Together, the Chandys had founded the *Kerala Balagram*, a community for homeless boys in the state of Kerala, on the Malabar coast in southern India. Mildred gladly accepted an invitation to visit, and was so moved by what she witnessed there that she became a life-long supporter. She saw K.K. Chandy as a kind of Gandhian "Father Flanagan," with the Kerala Balagram as the Indian equivalent of "Boys' Town." Here's how she told their story:

> It really started one day [in 1935] when K.K. Chandy saw a couple of boys digging in a pile of garbage. He went over and talked to them, and said, "What are you doing? What are you looking for?"
>
> And they said, "For some food."
>
> He asked them where they lived, where their home was, and they said they didn't have any. He said, "Well, where do you sleep at night?"
>
> They said, "Well, anywhere, under some steps or wherever we can find."
>
> And they were very poorly dressed, [with] scabs on their legs and so on. So K.K. Chandy brought those little boys home.[31]

There he and Mary cleaned them up, healed their wounds, and fed their malnourished bodies and souls with simple food and abundant love. The boys began to lose their defensive, fearful ways and to open up, to smile and play, to learn and work. The Chandys began taking in other street urchins, and gradually they founded a whole community, the *Christavashram*.

When Mildred visited, the Chandys and other volunteer teachers were caring for about twenty boys, but their number would later grow to one hundred. Some of the boys were abandoned there, some were rescued from the city slums, others arrived voluntarily, seeking a home. The ashram was situated on a hill, surrounded by palms and rice fields, with the blue hills of Travancore rising in the distance. The facilities were very simple: three cottages named Mercy, Peace and Friendship each housed fourteen boys and two staff members. Everyone worked in the vegetable garden and the barn, where they eventually had a cow for milk and hens for eggs. The boys went to public school and received training in trades such as paper-making, printing, leather-tooling, spinning and weaving. Especially bright boys were both encouraged to go to university and helped to find scholarships.

Balagram boys "helping."

The Balagram was directed by an advisory committee of Christians, Hindus and Muslims. Although it was partly supported by government and social welfare grants, it depended largely upon private donors. Back home, Mildred organized a sponsorship program through the FOR whereby donors could "adopt" a boy for five dollars a month, and receive his photograph and story. By the mid-fifties, they had donations sufficient to care for twenty-five boys. The adoption scheme was later abandoned, though, because it gave special attention to a few boys and wasn't fair to the rest. Instead, FOR donations to the Balagram were then directed to be used where most needed to benefit the greatest number of children. Mildred had no doubt that their contributions were making a critical difference in the boys' lives.

Mildred returned to Bapu's ashram for Christmas, full of the memories of her first visit when Gandhi was still alive.

This time as I went back, I felt Sevagram would be very empty without him, and I went somewhat sadly to the little hut which is kept just as he left it. I shook off my sandals and went in. There was the bedroll, the shelf of books, the spinning wheel, the 'see- think- and speak-no-evil' monkeys and an incense burner. Everything was in place, neat and simple, and so suggestive. I didn't feel lonely any more, for it seemed as if he were still there and again his voice was saying 'welcome.' Perhaps that is why so many people go, just to visit the hut and feel his blessing or, as they say, his *Darshan*.[32]

Sevagram had changed a lot in the eleven years since she was last there. The original centre was still standing and the little huts were still the same, but so many other buildings had been constructed and such improvements had been made to the barnyard and fields that Mildred was amazed. About three hundred children, students and staff lived there, at a cost of about eight annas a day each, then the equivalent of twelve or thirteen cents.

To see the members of the ashram fulfilling their humble tasks is an inspiration, for they go about their work quietly and devoutly, never complaining about the most irksome or arduous labour. Long before dawn they are at their places in the kitchen, at the well, with the animals … They move silently in their bare feet, carrying heavy baskets or jars on their heads, walking always with dignity and grace, never tense, never hurried …

They make us feel very selfish about our high standard of living in the West. One boy said, "I think America has much food, why does she not send some to the hungry in India." I said, "How can India pay for it. She has no money." All he said was "Oh" in a very puzzled way as if he could not understand how any country that had more than it needed would not be willing to share freely with those in need.[33]

Mildred experienced an inspirational Christmas at Sevagram. Including all the teachers, workers, craftsmen and their families, they numbered about five hundred people for a vegetarian Christmas dinner.

At dusk … we went to the *Goshala* [barnyard] again. The cows were all in their stalls, nice gentle white animals which we could see quite plainly as lanterns were lit … We sat on straw mats in the centre and listened to the chanting of Hindu songs. Then the Nativity Play was put on by members of the ashram. Never could there be a more appropriate setting. No properties were necessary … they were all there naturally. Practically no costuming was needed as the long flowing garments and shawls of the men seemed the appropriate apparel. Off to one side a choir of the Christian delegates sang carols while the members acted their parts. One of the cows especially sensitive to the situation gave birth to a calf just before the performance. The stars shone brightly in the open sky above and the bright glow from Jupiter added the extra gleam as the shepherds watched their flocks.[34]

New Years Eve, 1949: the end of the bloody decade of the forties also marked the end of the World Pacifist Conference. Prime Minister Pandit Nehru spoke on the last day, and stayed to take his turn at washing the dishes. In Sevagram, above all, Nehru was vulnerable to criticism that his government had strayed from the Mahatma's path.

There is a great disappointment amongst the Gandhi workers that the government is not following his principles. They say that 52% of the budget goes for military expenditures, that the Ministers are all receiving very high salaries and are living at a luxurious level. Everywhere lip service is paid to Gandhi ... but only in a few places is the work consistent with his teaching. However, in such centres as [Sevagram] the loyal devotion is remarkable.[35]

Nehru believed that, as a worker for peace and a servant of the people, he was subject to their will. Unfortunately, that sometimes meant he had to act in ways contrary to Bapu's teachings. "I have to compromise, for not compromising means standing alone and not accepting the democratic process," he said. Meanwhile, his job was to feed the starving, nurse the sick and clothe the naked.

Conscious of the great economic need of India, he stated that he felt meeting the primary needs of the people was the government's first obligation. Without that, political democracy meant little to them. Because of India's significant position in the world to-day, he hoped that she might be a bridge between East and West, without allying herself with either power bloc ...

Dr. Rajendra Prasad ... was also conscious of the inconsistency of his position. As president of the constituent assembly of India, he found himself part of a government now building up a large military force. He said, "If Gandhiji were alive, he would have shown us how we could exist without an army. We who are left behind are weak instruments.[36]

Mildred celebrated her fiftieth birthday the next day and was presented with a lovely *khadi* sari, which she wore with delight. She stayed on at the ashram for two weeks after the end of the conference.

It was good to have that extra time in India, to stay at Sevagram and watch it come back to its normal routine and share in the happy activity of the students and teachers there ...

I felt very much at home as I sat with the spinners and tried to learn to twirl a *takli*, as I squatted before an open fire and rolled out chapattis or went out to help bring in the harvest ...

I'll long remember the quiet times in Bapu's hut, the evening worship under the stars and everywhere the friendly folk of the ashram.

Chapter Thirteen: 1950

HOPE IN THE COLD

"*God of our life, these are days when the burdens we carry chafe our shoulders and weigh us down; when the road seems dreary and endless, the skies grey and threatening; when our lives have no music in them and our hearts are lonely, and our souls have lost their courage. Flood the path with light, we beseech thee; Turn our eyes to where the skies are full of promise; Tune our hearts to brave music; give us the sense of comradeship with heroes and saints of every age; and so quicken our spirits that we may be able to encourage the souls of all who journey with us on the road to life, to thine honour and glory.*"

Typed neatly on a three-by-five-inch recipe card, this was Mildred's prayer for the 1950s, a time when west and east waged such bitter ideological warfare that the atomic apocalypse felt like an imminent threat. The A-bomb spawned the even more terrifying H-bomb. The cold warriors squared off in dead earnest over their negotiating tables, talking insanely of a balance of power through mutual assured destruction, MAD. The world was suspicious, paranoid and still making war, this time in east Asia.

A tiny peninsula nation between the Yellow Sea and the Sea of Japan, Korea had been occupied since before the turn of the century by the Japanese. When they were defeated in 1945, the Russians and the Americans moved into Korea and split the country along the 38th parallel. The Korean War began on 25 June 1950, when troops from the communist North invaded the capitalist South. The United Nations denounced the North Koreans for invading and demanded that they withdraw from the south, which they refused to do. US President Harry Truman and General Douglas MacArthur immediately vowed to help South Korea defend itself against communism. It would be an American fight but, instead of the Stars and Stripes, they would wave the blue and white flag of the United Nations.

Most Canadians accepted or even applauded American leadership in resistance to Communist expansion. Lester Pearson, Canada's secretary of state for external affairs, commended Washington and believed Ottawa had to respond as well. Canadians of all political stripes agreed; even the CCF was urging the government to commit ground forces. A month after the war started, Prime Minister Mackenzie King died. After the state funeral, his successor, Louis St. Laurent, met with Pearson and other colleagues to decide Canada's future policy on Korea. They agreed to send in Canadian troops — not so much for Korea, but for the United Nations and the principle of collective security. Sixteen UN members committed men to fight alongside the South Koreans, but the Americans supplied more than ninety per cent of the manpower and firepower.

Under General MacArthur, UN forces quickly drove the North Koreans back behind the border. Everyone expected him to stop there, but he didn't. To Pearson's shock and disappointment, MacArthur carried the war on into the north. Although the Canadians tried to restrain the massive American military action, it predictably provoked the Chinese Communists into joining the battle on the side of the North Koreans. The Soviet Union soon began supplying them with military equipment. Within six months, all the major protagonists in Cold War geopolitics had been drawn into the fray. Pearson and other Canadians became increasingly troubled by the quality of American leadership. First, President Truman made careless remarks about General MacArthur's right to decide alone on the use of atomic weapons. Then, MacArthur clearly indicated he wanted to expand the war into China, an action that could have ignited a Third World War.

As the awful events unfolded, Mildred drafted a statement that was issued just before Christmas 1950 entitled "CANADIAN F.O.R. and the INTERNATIONAL SITUATION." It warned that "the nations of the world stand precariously poised on the very brink of disaster."

> The proposal made by some to drop Atom bombs on Chinese troops, or elsewhere, is a council of utter despair, ruthless, hopeless, uncivilized. We believe that the use of the Atom bomb at any time or in any place would be an act of utter desperation. It is difficult for us to understand how men of Christian ideals would seriously consider such a course for the decision then made would mean the abandonment of all decency and the deliberate choice of death or ruination for millions.

> We commend Britain's Prime Minister, Clement Atlee, and the Canadian Foreign Secretary, Lester Pearson, for their policy of caution and restraint, and their unwillingness to consent to the use of the Atom bomb. We urge the complete outlawry of Atomic and other weapons of violence. We oppose and shall continue to oppose through non-violent resistance, any

form of totalitarianism. We believe that nothing could be worse than blundering into the use of the Atomic bomb and the Third World War ...

We submit that peace demands sacrifices equal to those made in [war]. We believe that such sacrifices willingly made would be more effective in achieving lasting peace than dependence on military force.

We believe that a continuation of the method of war constitutes high treason to the welfare of mankind, and denial of the sovereignty of God.

We believe peace can be secured by governments genuinely desiring it, but the price will include ...
(a) freedom for all Colonial peoples
(b) food, machinery and technical aid for needy areas
(c) rehabilitation of exploited and war torn areas
(d) a willingness to undergo loss for peace, even as now great loss is suffered for war.

THE PRICE MUST BE PAID OR DARKNESS WILL ENVELOP US AND OUR CHILDREN'S CHILDREN.[1]

There is a sense of doom here that is not felt in any of Mildred's earlier writings. The final lines, pounded out in full capitals on her old manual typewriter, reflected her anger, which was not often expressed, and despair, which she fought off through sheer force of will. When things are really bad, she said, we have to *will* hope.[2] This seems to be one of the times, though, when willing hope was just too difficult. She had long been super-sensitive to the sufferings of humanity, but now her sensitivity seems tinged with grief on a global scale. Still, it was crucial to carry on, she wrote at Christmas 1950.

Never have we faced a more ominous New Year. Never has the task of making peace been more difficult ... but never more imperative. As we enter into the second half of the century, it is important to remember that each one of us has a responsibility and an opportunity to help bring peace into some part of the world. May each of us face the New Year prayerfully, with courage and faith, determined to do all we can to "overcome evil with good" and help to establish the Kingdom of Love and Peace.[3]

Unlike Mildred, most people chose not to face up to the possibility of nuclear annihilation and thus to try to prevent it. Instead, they retreated into fearful conformity and meaningless consumerism. Instead of building peace they built bomb shelters. Canada's first "backyard" A-bomb shelter was constructed on the side lawn of a home in Vancouver's posh Shaughnessy Heights district in the summer of 1950. Economic activity in Canada hit new highs. Jobs were plentiful and the dollars were flowing. It was easy come, easy go. An automobile was no longer considered a luxury by most families. The baby boom generation was growing up in suburbia. For Mildred, the Cold War was just as bad as the fighting war. In some ways, it was worse because people were still dying around the world but most North Americans now were too apathetic to take a stand and do anything about it.

As much as Mildred believed absolutely in her cause and would never have been swayed by mere public disapproval, it still hurt to be snubbed and rejected socially. Sometimes she felt utterly out of synch with wider society, which heaped derision upon her and all like-minded souls. She began to better understand Gandhi's writings on the loneliness of the *satyagrahi*. As national secretary of the FOR, she crossed Canada twice a year by bus, train and on her thumb. The FOR was small in numbers, and members were often isolated in small communities. In all the cities and towns across the land she spoke in public and met with these tiny peace groups — "cells," as they then called them. The idea of a peace army came up again and they talked of building *satyagraha* units, teams of trained peacemakers who could go into conflict zones to help protagonists find non-violent solutions to their disputes. Mildred brought literature and ideas into those small towns, as well as much-needed moral support for pacifists who clung to their ideals despite their neighbours' sneers and their community's scorn.

"Do you agree that PEACE is a good Christian word?" she wrote. "To-day when many are lost, frightened, despairing, we, who have heard the *Good News*, must share it, even if we are misunderstood, mocked, abused. We must live it as completely as we can; we must tell it as convincingly as we can."[4]

In all her public speaking, Mildred warned her audiences that the role of peacemaker demanded sacrifice, and the way was risky. "Living the life of peace means striving to replace all the ugliness, bitterness, pessimism, gloom, hate and fear and letting the love of God live in and through us, shedding life all around. It involves accepting responsibility in our homes, communities and in the world. And not waiting for others, being the courageous ones willing to take the stand, willing to risk being called a queer, perhaps a pacifist, perhaps even the dreaded label of Communist."[5]

Absurdly but predictably enough, the "dreaded label" was used against Mildred, who most decidedly was not a Communist. Although Mildred was not afraid of the epithet, she understood that fear inhibited many peace-minded people from active participation in the movement. In a time when the slogan "Better Dead Than Red" was common, Mildred always refused to demonize Communists. Instead, she challenged others to see beyond the propaganda and envision their brothers and sisters behind the Iron Curtain. She also was not afraid to point out that the Communists were doing some things right, like struggling to meet the basic needs of their people. With four-fifths of the world's population in dire need, how can we claim to be Christians and still do nothing? she asked. "Any enlightened mass consciousness would turn its energies to the meeting of those needs. Is it any wonder that Communism is making great strides in the Orient as its leaders promise land reform, food, medicine, education and machinery while we build up defenses and proceed to hold what we have?"

She often quoted Lester Pearson, who warned it would be futile to wage a military crusade against Communism. He said: "Because Communism is an idea it cannot be destroyed by force. It must be resisted by intellectual and spiritual weapons and also by removing the economic and social conditions of poverty and misery and injustice in which it finds such favourable grounds."[6]

North Americans understood that Russians were subjected to systematic propaganda that gave a distorted picture of life in the West. However, they were quick to reject the galling notion that their own governments might be perpetrating some of the same tricks. In 1953, Mildred was fascinated to read a study by the American pacifist John Swomley Jr. called "Press Agents of the Pentagon," in which he revealed the rapid growth of military influence and control over American life and institutions since the Second World War. "With millions of dollars available each year, the Pentagon and its branches throughout the world have been able to employ thousands of skilled publicity personnel to sell their ideas to the people." In other words, Swomley warned, the government is practising "thought control."

In those suspicious days, Senator Joseph McCarthy was orchestrating "witch hunts" for Communists in the State Department, in Hollywood, and throughout American society. In Canada, the RCMP was keeping a close eye on pacifists, who were all suspected of being "Reds." In 1953, Mildred wrote in an FOR newsletter: "The Mounties have been visiting some FOR members and offering to help us purge the Communists. Anybody seen any?"[7]

The name of the FOR came from the words of Paul in II Corinthians (5:18): "And all things are of God, who hath reconciled us to himself by Jesus Christ, and hath given to us the ministry of reconciliation." Reconciling east and west, communist and capitalist, was not so difficult for Mildred with her inclusive vision of God's family. At the same time, she never let her pride in Canada's more peaceful ways swell into nationalistic fervor. "It's good to be a Canadian … although I just live here. At heart I'm an Indian and a Mexican, a Japanese and a German … yes, and a Russian too. For as 'I am a part of all I have met,' they too are a part of me."[8]

In her fifties, Mildred began to see herself as a revolutionary, and to speak of the message of Jesus that way too. She reminded people that His "unorthodox, revolutionary, startling statement" urges his followers to "love your enemies and do good unto them that hate you and despitefully use you."

So why does 20th Century man fail to live by this creed?

We are ready to accept that it was right for him ... that he showed the *truth* ... but we think what was true for him was not true for us. We must be practical ... we must save our own precious lives not by giving them up as he did ... not by taking the cross, not by loving our enemies ... but by hating them and killing them.

Can we do this and call ourselves Christians? His followers? Could we put Him in a uniform today? To drop atomic bombs? ...

We are not pawns of the devil, forced to take this suicidal murderous path ... We as Christians have a new way to proclaim, a new message. How feebly we have whispered it from the housetops. How inadequately our lives have demonstrated it ... and yet we know it to be right ... and there is yet time.[9]

In Mildred's personal life, though, there was suddenly not nearly enough time, not enough with her brother nor her husband. The fifties were a decade of great personal loss. In the summer of 1952, Vic Osterhout fell ill when the family was at their cabin in Sidney on Vancouver Island. In September he tried to return to the classroom, but it soon became impossible for him carry on teaching. Vic was always skeptical about conventional medicine, so by the time he actually consulted a doctor his disease was quite advanced. He was diagnosed with what people then called "galloping cancer," and his condition deteriorated rapidly. As the frightful days passed, Mildred stayed at his bedside or with Connie and the children. She wrote constantly, keeping friends and family informed. One friend replied:

My darling Mildred, I am simply dumbfounded over dear Victor's serious condition and I can assure you I am praying earnestly and fervently for his recovery and shedding tears over him ... probably he will sense the atmosphere of prayer around his bed ... I am so glad you are with Connie. You and she will be given the strength you both require from day to day, for underneath are His everlasting arms.[10]

But all the prayers were not enough. Vic's death was so unexpected and so sudden that she was shaken to the core. He was her only brother, her closest family, her friend. She loved him deeply and had counted on growing old with him, never imagining their parting would be like this. "It was just agony to see him go down, down, down," Mildred said.[11] He was only fifty, a vigorous man in the prime of his life. Helplessly watching him suffer an anguishing death too soon, Mildred struggled to see God through her pain.

He died on October 6, 1952 in Vancouver General Hospital. It was evening when he passed away, and as the darkness fell Mildred and Connie grieved together at his bedside. They wept for Vic, and for themselves, and for the children: Don was thirteen, Marion was eleven, and Bobby was only seven. Fatherless children, a woman without her man, a sister without a brother; the Osterhout women were hurting but they didn't let it show. In those days, children were to be protected from death, shielded from its imminence until it was too late. To young Marion, both her mother and Mildred seemed distant in their grief. She never saw her Auntie Mildred crying.

Instead, Mildred got busy with the necessary arrangements at the church and she wrote an obituary to send to editors of the local papers. In lieu of flowers, friends and relatives were asked to donate to a scholarship fund in his name. Vic's memorial service was held at West Point Grey United. The eulogy was offered by an old friend, Harold Fullerton. Harold told the mourners it was Vic's wish that the service should be "one of Thanksgiving and praise for the fullness of life." He said Vic wanted people to remember him with laughter, "even at this hour."

> I remember when Vic started teaching he bought a cabin cruiser, and it was big enough — as his heart was big enough — to take many a boy of those he taught, on trips up the beautiful waters of Howe Sound. The beauty of the forested islands and the snow-capped mountains became more real when in Vic's company …

> He sharpened our awareness of beauty. All of us now reflect on "that best portion of a good man's life: his little, nameless, unremembered acts of kindness and of love."[12]

After losing Victor, Mildred's awareness was heightened as to the precious-ness of each human life, each soul a spark of God. Her intense grief deepened her sense of empathy with the those in war-torn regions, the Koreans who had also lost their beloved ones, and she felt her pain echoed around the world. Her compassion grew as the ever-increasing death tolls seared the spirit.

During the Korean War, more than 25,000 Canadians served; 312 of them died and more than 1,200 were wounded. At the same time, many other Canadians worked with exceptional zeal and skill at the UN to advance a negotiated peace. It finally was achieved on July 27, 1953, when the United Nations and North Korea signed an armistice agreement to end one of the bloodiest wars ever. In just over three years, one million South Korean civilians had been killed, and several million more had been rendered homeless. About 580,000 UN and South Korean troops perished, and as many as 1,600,000 North Korean soldiers were killed or wounded.

During this period, Mildred and other pacifists began calling upon the government of Canada to disarm unilaterally. Their position was outlined in a remarkable document called "A CALL FOR A MORE DISCIPLINED AND REVOLUTIONARY PACIFIST ACTIVITY." It began:

> The world faces today the most serious crisis since the beginning of time. We are moving rapidly toward a third world war. Events may develop in the next few months which will alter the lives of the common people the world over.
>
> The Communist coup in Czechoslovakia is part of the expansionist policy of the USSR. The United States of America is rushing its preparations for war at a feverish rate and the re-enactment of the selective service measure is indicative of this mood. Canada's foreign policy seems to be in substantial agreement with that of the United States ...
>
> At this crucial period in the world's history, it is time that some nation decided to stop talking, thinking and planning for war and to begin talking, thinking and planning for peace. We believe that Canada, because of its geographic and strategic position, should take the lead. If war should break out between Russia and the United States, it has been said many times that Canada may well become the Belgium of World War Three.
>
> Now that the situation has become so serious, the only solution is for some nation to accept a drastic alternative course of action. The issue before the world today is not war or peace, but *total war or total renunciation of war*. There is no easy or middle way out of the dilemma we face. Therefore, the one hope for preventing a war and the complete catastrophe it will bring, is for Canada to accept total renunciation of war as a national policy. Specifically, it means that the Canadian Government should renounce the act of war-making for all time and use its influence to get other nations, notably the United States of America, to do the same. There is, of course, no guarantee that if some nations accepted such a policy they would not be destroyed, but there is some hope in such a policy, however remote, and none at all in the present one of war preparations. The nation that would accept such a policy could literally lead the masses of the people all over the world to peace.[13]

Mildred outlined a radical political program for peace: embargo the mining and export of uranium, ban arms exports everywhere, dismantle the military establishment, demilitarize the northern border, cancel all joint defense agreements with the United States, work with other nations towards limited world government in an unarmed Federal Union, change immigration policy to admit large numbers of displaced persons, repeal all discriminatory laws, provide for equal opportunity regardless of race religion or national origin, and develop natural resources for the good of the people.

In promoting this plan, Mildred worked with Reverend James Finlay, then chairman of the Canadian FOR and minister at the Carleton Street United Church in Toronto. A courageous pacifist, Jim Finlay preached that, "Peace is not an end result; peace is a present practice. Peace is not simply a fruit, it is the nature of the tree." A.J. Muste of the American FOR had a similar saying. "There is no way to peace. Peace is the way." These were expressions of the same truth taught by Gandhi and by Jesus: the means are both the way and the end. It was a message Mildred repeated time and again: you can never make peace by making war.

FOR members in central Canada expressed their ideals by creating a rural peace centre called Winterbrook. Located on a co-op farm twenty-five miles west of Toronto, the big old barn was cleaned, restored, painted and furnished by FOR volunteers. By February 1953, the central Canada office moved to the Winterbrook Community. "We hope that ... next summer we may have some study-work projects and use it as a training center for peace action. In time we hope a family can be brought from Europe to live in the center," Mildred wrote.

The FOR's move to Winterbrook signalled Mildred's return to western Canada. In 1953, she and Walter bought their first home at 2350 West 2nd Avenue in the neighbourhood of Kitsilano. She was happy to be back home with Walter; they got busy in the garden and enjoyed walking with Frisky, a dog inherited from friends who had gone to Asia as missionaries. She carried on as the Western Secretary, working full-time from her home office. They called it Fellowship House, and FOR meetings were regularly held there as well as social gatherings and political fundraisers.

As well as for the many causes she supported, Mildred had to fundraise for her own salary. In 1955 a FOR pamphlet urged supporters to donate funds to provide "a modest salary to Mildred Fahrni and Mary Needler, our devoted hard-working secretaries." Mildred and Mary, the eastern secretary, couldn't have been paid much more than six hundred dollars annually, according to the finance committee's subsequent report. An unrepentant fundraiser, Mildred always gave more than she asked of others. Every month she would add up the donations she had collected and then throw in her own best amount to round off the total. Often hers was the largest for the month. From November 1954 to December 1955, total donations to the FOR in the west were $869. Mildred gave $127.90 of that, far more than any other single donor.

FEBRUARY 18, 1957 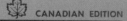 CANADIAN EDITION

TIME

THE WEEKLY NEWSMAGAZINE

Montgomery, Alabama's
REV. MARTIN LUTHER KING

$6.50 A YEAR   VOL. LXIX NO. 7   TWENTY CENTS

Chapter Fourteen: 1956

SATYAGRAHA IN THE DEEP SOUTH

Mildred had always believed that active non-violence, as Gandhi had exercised it in India, could bring about social change in other parts of the world. She got a chance to see it in action in 1956, about twenty-five years after that first transformative meeting with the Mahatma. That summer she went to Chicago for the national conference of the American Fellowship of Reconciliation. There she met Bayard Rustin, an African-American pacifist and radical intellectual who had worked with the FOR for many years. Rustin had already been at the vanguard of the civil rights movement for more than a decade, in a time when black activists risked everything for their dream of equality and citizenship with dignity in a desegregated South.

In 1946, after the U.S. Supreme Court decision outlawing segregation of passengers on interstate buses, the FOR and the Congress of Racial Equality sent members on a "Journey of Reconciliation" through fifteen cities in Virginia, North Carolina, Tennessee and Kentucky. Bayard Rustin was among those imprisoned because they refused to ride "Jim Crow" — that is, to ride in the blacks-only section at the back of the bus. He was sentenced to hard labour on a chain gang, but his resolve and friendliness won over guards and convicts alike.

In 1947, the Indian National Congress invited Rustin to visit India, where he was introduced to Gandhian non-violence. In *satyagraha* he found the philosophical and practical blueprint for change. He was convinced it could be made to work not only in India, but everywhere. He thought the Mahatma's concept of "soul force" would translate just fine in the southern states. By the mid-fifties, Rustin and other FOR workers were full-time organizers of non-violent direct action campaigns against the laws of segregation — in the schools, at the lunch counters, in parks and public beaches, and on the buses.

Rustin's role at the FOR conference that summer was to report back from Montgomery, Alabama on the progress of the now-famous bus boycott. It was already more than six months long and, as it turned out, there were still six more months yet to go. The Montgomery bus boycott started on December 1, 1955, after a black seamstress named Rosa Parks quietly but firmly refused to give up her seat on a city bus to a white man. Mrs. Parks was arrested on charges of violating state segregation laws and briefly jailed. When asked why she wouldn't budge, she said it was because her feet hurt and because of the principle involved. "It was a matter of dignity," she said. "I could not have faced myself and my people if I had moved."[1]

Rosa Parks was well respected in Montgomery, and black leaders believed her arrest could spark enough indignation to fuel mass action. At first they only called for a one-day boycott, but it was so successful they carried on. It got off to a great start largely because one of the organizers did some skillful advance work with the press. He leaked the story to a friendly reporter, who wrote an "expose" that was published on page one the next day. That way, while warning white citizens about the boycott, the story helped to inform thousands more blacks as well. The next day, and the next, the black population of Montgomery — about 42,000 people in all — stayed off the buses. Instead, they walked. And for the next year they kept on walking together towards a more just future.

At the outset many blacks did not expect the boycott to succeed because they had no faith in their own people's ability to work together. Their resolve was strengthened, though, after the police began to arrest and harass black motorists and taxi drivers. They set up their own car pool and volunteer drivers stepped forward. The car pool system they developed was a model of efficiency. When the judge found Mrs. Parks guilty and fined her fourteen dollars, support for the boycott grew even stronger. A once-compliant black populace was transformed by a dawning sense of their own destiny and a powerful new tool: non-violence.

The leading proponent of the non-violent action was a 26-year-old Baptist minister from Georgia named Reverend Dr. Martin Luther King, Jr. Like Bayard Rustin, Martin Luther King was a student of Gandhian philosophy and a member of the FOR. Mildred called him "the second Gandhi." Along with Reverend Ralph Abernathy and other black ministers, King led the Montgomery Improvement Association which had as its motto, "Justice Without Violence." They helped their congregations see that racism was fundamentally un-Christian, and that its violent grip on their lives could be defeated only through Christian means, non-violent means.

To the blacks of the South and to all the oppressed peoples of the world, the message of Jesus was one of freedom, said Martin Luther King. And, although Jesus gave the world the message, it was Gandhi who demonstrated the method. King applied Gandhi's analysis and began accurately describing southern society as a caste system. The police and the Klan used brutality and violence, often with impunity, to "keep the niggers in their place" and their place had always been in the lowest caste. But no longer, King declared. All that is changing now. With the Lord's help, we are standing up. He gave voice to the dream of equality with such poignancy and conviction that people were full of hope in the movement. One of King's many gifts was that he could channel faith into action. At the same time, he didn't want to ask too much of the people, especially the elderly and the ill.

Martin asked this old lady, he said, "Now listen … you have been with us all along, so now you go on and start back to ridin' the bus 'cause you are too old to keep walking … "
She said, "Oh no." She said, "Oh no." Said, "I'm gonna walk just as long as everybody else walks. I'm gonna walk till it's over."
So he said, "But aren't your feet tired?"
She said, "Yes, my feets is tired, but my soul is rested."[2]

Rustin wrote of how King preached the gospel of *satyagraha*. He told his congregation:

We are concerned not merely to win justice in the buses but rather to behave in a new and different way — to be non-violent so that we may remove injustice itself, both from society and from ourselves. This is a struggle which we cannot lose, no matter what the apparent outcome, if we ourselves succeed in becoming better and more loving people.[3]

Active non-violent resistance was something the southern authorities hadn't ever figured on, and they didn't know how to react to it. The police began arresting the leaders, including twenty-four ministers of the church. All promptly made bail, thanks to donations from the local community and from across the country. Each one of the ministers went back to his church and preached about the experience, and affirmed publicly that he stood prepared to be arrested again if necessary. Typically, the authoritarian minds responded with intimidation. The bus companies invited white supremacists to negotiation meetings, and disturbing pamphlets calling for "the annihilation of Negroes" were widely distributed.

When in the course of human events it becomes necessary to abolish the Negro race, proper methods should be used. Among these are guns, bow and arrows, sling shots and knives.

We hold these truths to be self evident that all whites are created equal with certain rights, among these are life, liberty and the pursuit of dead niggers …

My friends it is time we wised up to these black devils. I tell you they are a group of two legged agitators who persists [sic] in walking up and down our streets protruding their black lips. If we don't stop helping these African flesh eaters, we will soon wake up and find Reverend King in the white house.

LET'S GET ON THE BALL WHITE CITIZENS[4]

In response to this volley of hatred, Bayard Rustin gave the benefit of the doubt to the majority of the white community: "I cannot believe that this leaflet reflects the thinking of all white people in Montgomery. Thousands of them would no doubt be nauseated by it. Yet I report its distribution because such hate literature, against both Negroes and Jews, is being circulated in Alabama and unfortunately is an aspect of the emotional climate in which grave problems must be solved."[5] Despite the threats and intimidation, perhaps in part because of them, the black community remained strong, unified and non-violent. Then came the night when a stick of dynamite was thrown at the King's home, the first of several bomb attacks on black homes and churches.

Within minutes hundreds of Negroes flocked to King's home; also the police. It was at this moment that non-violent resistance almost faded. Many Negroes wanted to launch a counter-offensive. Rev. King, standing on the front porch of his "bombed" home, pleaded with the angry Negroes: "We are not harmed. Do not get your weapons. Let us not answer hate with hate, violence with violence. But we will continue to stay off the buses." Probably this saved the city from a race riot.[6]

Hearing these stories first hand from Rustin, who himself was tremendously eloquent, Mildred began to see Martin Luther King as a young Mahatma Gandhi. She recalled how as a young man Gandhi had struggled against racism in South Africa. Now, half a century later and half a world away, here was another remarkable man who also returned hatred with love, violence with an olive branch. Here once again was powerful evidence that Bapu was right, that his ideas and his love lived on in different hearts all over the world. Everything told her King was another Great Soul. She badly wanted to meet him, and see how the Indian experiment in truth would translate to the American scene. Even in India she hadn't had a chance to see *satyagraha* in action. The idea gave her a potent sense of hope, a spiritual shot in the arm.

"Could I, as a white Northerner, a Canadian, offer any worthwhile support in Montgomery?" Mildred asked Rustin.[7]

"Definitely," came the reply. "The only way you can really understand is to come down South and see for yourself."

The two boarded the train together in Chicago and headed south through Nashville and Birmingham to Montgomery. En route, Mildred and Rustin shared stories of their experiences in India and thoroughly enjoyed their conversation. Just before they arrived in Tennessee, though, he abruptly excused himself.

"But why?" she asked.

"Because we're coming up to the border and it would be too dangerous for me to be seen talking with a white woman," he answered.

Mildred was shocked. She had travelled through the South before, but never stayed long enough to learn anything about life there. This was only the first of many shocks she experienced on entering a segregated society. Arriving in Montgomery, she looked for a taxi to take her to King's church, Dexter Avenue Baptist. A black cabbie was nearby, but as she approached he just shook his head and looked away. She had to hire a white driver who wasn't at all happy about taking her over to the black part of town.

While she was waiting to see King, Mildred was fascinated to watch the constant stream of people coming in and out, doing the work of the boycott. The church was an incredibly busy place, and Mildred wasn't sure she ought to be taking up Dr. King's time, "but he made the appointment, and kept it." Her first impression: "He was very pleasant, very sincere, very deeply concerned." In her diary she recounted his answer to her question about whether he was risking his life.

> He realized that he was taking chances in what he was doing, but he wasn't afraid. He showed me in his way of life that he was prepared to talk with white people, to make some attempt, actually, to help them under-stand what they were doing to other members of the human race.

> He talked very openly and clearly and helped me find an understanding of the situation in which people for all their lives were looked upon as second-class. He made me understand that the struggle was continuing and suggested that I come to some of the services that they were holding, although … I would be the only white person, or maybe there might be one or two others that were there.[8]

Mildred resolved to defy the segregation laws in all ways possible, so she asked King if it would be possible to stay in the black part of town as she couldn't imagine staying in a whites-only establishment. It was a calculated risk, but his secretary was able to arrange a room in a blacks-only boarding house next door to King's home. The proprietor agreed to the arrangement only because Rev. King had asked, and on the condition that Mildred not appear at the table at meal times. This meant that she didn't get much of a chance to meet any residents other than the landlady but, nonetheless, she "felt that [she] was there with them, that [she] was in the movement too."

It was a simple establishment, with a shared bathroom down the hall. One evening, Mildred went in to wash up and found a few black curls in the sink. It was funny, she thought, the contrast of those curls with her straight brown strands, and all the meaning that the racists attached to such meaningless things as hair type or skin colour.[9] Another night, lying on her bed in the boarding house, Mildred heard hymns floating in through her window on the balmy southern air. The voice seemed to be coming from the King's house, and indeed it was. Next day the Kings invited Mildred to tea, and during the visit she asked about who had been singing so sweetly. It turned out to be Martin's wife, Coretta, who had the heavenly voice. Mildred was about thirty years older, but the two women still found much in common.

Mildred also went to see Rosa Parks, whose arrest had sparked the boycott. "She lived in a very, very simple place," she wrote. "I found her a very open and strong-minded person." Some accounts unfairly portrayed Rosa as a drudge who momentarily stood up to the bus driver, but who lacked understanding of the larger struggle for racial justice. In fact, Rosa Parks was proud of her "life history of being rebellious against being mistreated because of my colour." She was on staff with the National Association for the Advancement of Colored People (NAACP) for a dozen years and she spent time at the Highlander Folk School, an integrated retreat in the Tennessee hills. After the experience of living in harmony with people both white and black, Rosa began to act on her vision of a desegregated America.[10]

In her rambles, Mildred picked up a tourist pamphlet published by the Montgomery Chamber of Commerce. "Alabama is truly the 'Industrial Heart of Dixie,'" it boasted, and marked the birth of Alabama by the arrival of the white man in 1540. As for Montgomery? "It is a real Southern city of gracious and friendly people … and the history of Montgomery has had much to do with creating the ability of its people to live together in harmony as a pillow of strength." Reading the rather ungrammatical publication, Mildred raised an eyebrow and chuckled to imagine pillars and pillows of strength. In a sense, though, that's what was happening in Montgomery. The black community was coming together into one amazing non-violent pillow of strength. They held mass meetings of the Montgomery Improvement Association twice a week. She wrote:

> Coloured churches are used for the gatherings and are crowded long before the time set. People talk, sing and pray with a sense of community and joint purpose that has brought a new vitality into the church. Enthusiastic speakers stir the audience to renewed effort and one feels that the morale is high and people are determined to carry on until their demands are met. These are simple, only asking for courteous treatment by the bus drivers, first come first served in seating and some coloured bus drivers. They have been walking for six months and show very little sign of weakening.[11]

Mildred also noted that "the protest cuts through all social barriers and brings the educated, the well-to-do and the illiterate labourer together." The meetings attracted thousands of boycotters, who all impressed Mildred as being "organized, disciplined, non-violent, democratic and determined." They began with songs and prayer, moved on to the latest news and plans, followed by a "pep talk" during collection. The atmosphere was informal, with a lot of genial humour from the pulpit. Many people in the congregation spontaneously cried out "Hallelujah!" or "Amen!" in response. The singing and clapping were loud, passionate and totally unlike anything Mildred had ever seen in a church before. It was a whole new experience from the gentle silence of a Quaker meeting, or the restrained hymnary of Methodism.

During her time in Montgomery, Mildred was intensely aware of the hatred among white people, who were openly racist and suspicious of her motives. Although the meetings were open to all, very few whites ever attended. Certainly the white church didn't encourage it. "Aside from a Lutheran minister who has a Negro congregation, no local white preacher has publicly identified himself with the Negro cause. Many, of course, give assurances privately. A few are in 'hot water' for real or suspected sympathies with the boycotters."[12] Mildred wrote:

> The situation is quite tense but in some areas it is fairly quiet. Some say bloodshed will come, but most realize it does not have to come. If it does come it will probably be provoked by the whites. The Ku Klux Klan walks again, spreading terror as much amongst whites as the coloured ...

> In some areas half or more of the population is coloured and the white man holds on to his sense of superiority and privilege. Undoubtedly he fears that he will lose it. So he tries to guard it by every means possible, legal and illegal. He is building White Citizens Councils, which claim to be for the protection of the White man but in reality are often for the humiliation and degradation of the coloured man.

> The white folk ... are determined and many of them say, "Let the niggers walk. We don't care." ... Others say, "We'll never give in to the niggers. We like it the way it is and we are going to keep it this way."

> Some say, "I hate all niggers except one — my nigger." Many say, "Niggers are all right but you've got to keep them in their place." Others say, "We were getting along all right until agitators came in from the North and started stirring up trouble. What right have outsiders to come and tell us how we ought to live? If they'd leave us alone we'd get along all right."

> Few whites take part in the movement, partly because of the traditional sense of superiority which refuses to recognize the rights or the abilities of the Negroes, and partly because of their inability to break from their own social group. The lot of the liberal white man in the South is a very lonely one and may be a very dangerous one, physically as well as economically.

Whites who try to be friendly are criticized as "Nigger-lovers, Communists, Agitators," etc. One soon loses any opportunity to even talk with the traditional Southerner if one is known to be on the side of "equality" — which poses a great problem. For after all it is the white Southerner who must change and we must seek the way of reconciliation. The white church is silent ... the minister a prisoner in his own pulpit, afraid to identify himself with the freedom movement ... too conscious that he is in the wrong to speak openly against it.[13]

When she came back to Vancouver, Mildred wanted to tell as many people as possible about all she had witnessed down south. She proposed to CBC Radio that she do a series of broadcasts on the struggle for desegregation, but it was rejected. She resolved that if she couldn't get the word out over the CBC, she'd do it in person. Her talks had such titles as "The Two Gandhis" and "Non-Violence Walks in the South." She spoke at the national FOR conference in Toronto, and at gatherings in Montreal and Ottawa. All the way home she stopped from town to town to bring the message of Montgomery. She always emphasized that the black people in the South were walking for all humanity, not just for themselves. Walking away from a history of slavery and towards a future of freedom, they were showing the way for us all to take our legitimate power and use it peacefully to shape our world for the better. Mildred also tried to show people that racism can be expressed in many ways, and that it was a serious issue north of the border as well as down south.

"What about us?" she asked. "Are we prejudiced? Do we feel superior to the Americans?" She challenged her Canadian audiences to ask themselves how often they had heard someone say, "I'm not prejudiced, but ... " And then she named some of the typical lies told in white society. "I'm not prejudiced but ... I just don't like niggers. Or I don't want to work with Japs, I don't want Jews next door. I just don't think Indians have brains. I wouldn't trust those Russians." She named the stereotypes and thereby, in a sense, disarmed them.

On December 21, 1956, more than a year after they began walking, the black community, the bus company and the city fathers reached an agreement. Montgomery's buses were integrated and the 381-day boycott was called off. Satyagraha had won. From the Montgomery buses, the action soon shifted to the student sit-ins, the freedom rides and the great protest marches of the 1960s. In Birmingham and Selma, in Atlanta and Raleigh, the civil rights movement washed a tidal wave of dissent over the South, changing it fundamentally and forever.

To the end of her days, Mildred always cherished a song she learned in King's church: "Black and white together, we shall overcome some day."

Chapter Fifteen: 1958

REBUILDING IN WIDOWHOOD

A s they grew into middle age, Mildred and Walter enjoyed their home and garden in Kitsilano. They walked their little dog, Frisky, on Kits beach daily. Walter continued working on his inventions and read widely. Mildred carried on with the FOR, and volunteered at the YWCA, teaching English to Hungarians thrown into exile by the Soviet invasion. Life was full and happy, their marriage an easy partnership of like minds and hearts. Walter was quiet and reserved but affectionate, the sort of man who would give his wife a personal gift for no particular reason at all. In the spring of 1958, Mildred expressed surprise and delight noted in her diary: "Walter gave me a lovely new watch!"

Not long after that, she was scheduled to give a presentation on socialism to the Society of Friends meeting, over in Victoria. She bid Walter a quick farewell and hopped on a ferry. Quite a few turned out at the Friends' House for Mildred's talk. Towards the end, she became aware of quite a disturbance at the back of the room. Several people were fussing around and "getting all stirred up."[1]

As soon as the meeting was over, a couple of people came up to Mildred and asked her to sit down because they had to talk to her. Something in their manner must have hinted at the bad news, because she right away asked: "Is it Walter? Is there anything wrong with Walter?"

"He's dead," came the awful reply.

Mildred was stunned. She couldn't believe that Walter, still so strong in body and mind, could suddenly be dead. No, it couldn't be true! He was only sixty-six — too young! Through a fog of disbelief, she understood that someone had already phoned and made a reservation for her to fly back to Vancouver. Walter's elder brother, Gordon, picked her up at the airport. On the drive home he told her that Walter had been working in the garden and then had come inside, apparently to lie down and rest with the newspaper. While he dozed there on

the couch, Walter suffered a massive heart attack and died immediately.[2]

Besides Gordon, the other Fahrni brothers came for the memorial service on April 21: Roy from Kaslo and Stanley from Portage la Prairie. The next day, Mildred wrote to friends and family:

This is to let you know that Walter had a heart attack and slipped away in his sleep on April 17th. He had been well and active until that time.

We had a lovely spring and Walter had taken over the garden, giving a great deal of time to developing and beauti-

Walter in the garden, undated.

fying it, and enjoying nature's responsiveness. He had also been doing some carpentry as a hobby, and continued his extensive reading. All this was in addition to his work on his inventions and machines ...

One feels especially at a time like this the preciousness of each moment of life, and the importance of living it significantly. To be aware ... to feel ... to share ... to relate to that which is real and eternal ... this is life.

I pray therefore to live the day well.[3]

In response came a flood of mail from across Canada and from India, letters full of love and praise for Walter's fine qualities and prayers for Mildred's strength to bear the pain of his loss. Lucy Woodsworth wrote:

Dear Mildred,

This morning word has come of the sudden passing of your husband. My heart goes out in sympathy — in what this means in one's life. Strength will I know be yours to bear the loss of the steady support and sympathy of your husband and all else that is a part of the wonderful life with a husband of similar ideals ...

I remember, Mildred, your loving sympathy with me and mine — I can never forget that spring day upon which your thought was of me. May your work bear much fruit.

Very lovingly, Lucy L. Woodsworth.[4]

Watson Thomson wrote: " ... we had some rare moments of fellow-feeling and the memory of his big granite-like figure and his fine, sensitive ethical quality stays alive and is a source of inspiration. So much a man, so much a child — a living protest against the tawdriness of our pecuniary culture ... to me he was, I think, the perfect elder brother that I had always wanted."[5]

From a friend in India: "I am just shocked to hear about Walter. He was a man whom nobody can forget. I [have] never seen such a nice man before ... God give him peace to his good soul. You are doing good for the world, so naturally God will help you too. Love from us all, Ranjit."

It turned out to be more difficult "to live the day well" than Mildred had expected. One friend, also recently widowed, gave her this advice: "You will probably be more aware than ever how successfully you two managed to intertwine your lives together and these months ahead will be really tough. Don't be too brave. Let the tears fall where they will."[6]

Mildred worked out her grief as she tended Walter's garden through summer and fall, cutting the flowers he planted and canning the vegetables. The garden is likely where she let her tears fall for the big-hearted, soft-spoken man who had always loved her best of all. Without him, her world seemed out of kilter. Ten days after Walter died, Mildred went to a Friends Meeting, but she felt totally out of place. "I 'belong' — and yet I don't," she wrote in her diary.

There were some in the Fahrni family who would have preferred it if Mildred had observed a longer period of private mourning after Walter's death. Only six weeks later, she was once again making headlines with her peace work. Anyone who knew Mildred would never have expected her to stop working — Walter least of all. She kept up the familiar round of political meetings and visits with friends, but she felt horrible. Her head was always buzzing, her left eye was swollen for no apparent reason, and she was eating too many suppers alone, standing up at the kitchen counter.[7]

As she struggled to accept Walter's death, Mildred also had to cope with the physical and emotional impact of menopause. She had mood swings and was "haunted by bad dreams of illness." She wrote: "Every a.m. I awake from troubled dreams feeling heavy & disturbed, guilty & depressed. Force myself to get up & into action but feel conscious of all the malfunction of my body — my head, my intestines, my back — the aches, the flushes, the heaviness."[8] Mildred had already faced the fact that she would never have children of her own. Now, she had a terrible nightmare about losing some friends' children overboard off a boat, and sacrificing something precious to keep the only remaining child safe.[9]

At fifty-eight, Mildred found herself profoundly alone. For the first time in her life, she had no close relative: no father, no brother, no husband, no child. She read and reread the cards about Walter, and wrote back faithfully to every one. As she did so, she began the process of saying goodbye. Walter had always loved the life at sea, so it was natural that water should be his final resting place. She chose a beautiful May evening to scatter his ashes on the waters of Burrard Inlet. Mildred and Connie, Walter's nephew, Brock Fahrni, and a few other close friends went down to the harbour line at dusk. They said a prayer together and read aloud some of the tributes sent by friends. Mildred had brought an armful of flowers from their garden. She let the blooms slip from her fingers and watched them float away on the last rays of the setting sun.

"Peace & beauty & gratitude for memories," she later wrote in her diary. "In a sense, I couldn't feel that he was gone." And at Christmas she wrote: "This has been a year fraught with sadness and loss as well as with joy. It hardly seems possible that Walter slipped over the border six months ago, for he was so well up to that time and seems so alive still, as I feel his quiet presence around. Now, his older brother Roy has just passed on after a heart attack."[10]

In the New Year, she faced the question of how to carry on without Walter. Her family circle was small: just Connie and the three kids, who were almost grown. Mildred knew she had to re-build her life now on her own. She began with a decision to try to stay in the house they had shared. She would manage it by renting out rooms to boarders and students. Over the subsequent decades, Mildred generated income and spread the gospel of peace by keeping her house full of young people, who she always treated as family. The international family that took shape under her roof included citizens of all the enemy states in the war. German, Russian, and Japanese soon came together in a harmonious Canadian household, with Mildred as the spark of reconciliation.

When Ursula Mueller-Schade decided to leave her homeland, she wrote to the German Fellowship of Reconciliation and was given Mildred's name as a contact in Canada.[11] Ursula wrote that she was a social worker and single mother of a seventeen-year-old son, Einar. Mildred invited them to stay until they got settled, so Ursula came "from West Berlin to Mildred" in July 1958. Even without much English, Ursula got right to work. She was proud that she could begin paying Mildred some rent almost right away. Soon after, with help from Mildred's contacts, she got a job as a social worker at Vancouver General Hospital, a position she held for twenty-four years.

Ursula loved living at Mildred's place. Coming from the ruins of Germany, where only remnants of her family were scattered about, she felt grateful to be welcomed into a homey circle. "I lost a lot of material things, but the hardest was missing my friends and family," she said. "I felt I became part of Mildred's family." Perhaps both women understood one another through their shared sense of loss. Certainly Ursula could see right away that Mildred was still suffering. Walter's death had come so quickly after Vic's, and she still missed her father, even after all these years. She used to tell Ursula about her father and her childhood on the prairies.

"They had to grow their own food because he was paid so little. They were very poor, but when there was food in the house, if someone came to the door hungry, he got to eat first," said Ursula. "And so it was in Mildred's home. It was the house of the open doors. She'd always invite people to stay and eat. It was amazing. That's one of the reasons her friends are so mixed. Everybody's welcome. At dinner there could be a famous person from India sitting beside a totally unknown person. There were no class distinctions. We were all brothers and sisters."

English Bay, Vancouver, undated. Mildred often walked on the local beaches when she needed to reflect or grieve.

Ursula had grown up in a devout Christian home — "my father was a very strict, proud Lutheran" — but she never knew anybody to express her faith so comprehensively as Mildred. Living in her home "was the first time in my life I experienced Christianity in action." She recalled another young refugee woman who also lived with Mildred for a couple of years. She was a Czech Jew who was the only member of her family to survive the Holocaust. "Mentally she was very unstable, and she really clung onto Mildred," Ursula said. Mildred gave her a home, a loving atmosphere and a steady sense of support. Gradually, she seemed to be able to heal herself and, later on, she married and had children of her own.

"This was something very good that Mildred did," Ursula said. "She was a very deserving woman."

A young UBC engineering graduate named Noboru Omoto also joined the household just after Walter's death. He saw a "Room For Rent" sign in the window of Mildred's house, knocked, and "a very cultured and soft-spoken person answered the door," he recalled. He felt instantly befriended. Mildred always called him "Nobby" and he enjoyed the nickname. In 1959, Nobby's application to sponsor his fiancee from Japan wound its way through the immigration department bureaucracy. Finally Teruko, his future wife, arrived in Vancouver. She was all alone, and couldn't speak the language. "Both my parents were dead by that time," Teruko said. "Mildred was so special, like a mother or an aunt to me, always gentle." Mildred taught Teruko "some English, and about Canadian ways."[12] On February 28, 1960, Noboru and Teruko Omoto were wed in a candlelight service at Mildred's house. The bride wore a traditional wedding kimono, the groom a dark suit. In their wedding portrait, from left to right, were Mildred, the newlyweds and Xenia, another member of Mildred's international family.

Mildred's relationship with Xenia, a Russian exile, perhaps most fully exemplifies how she put love into action. One day, Xenia simply arrived at the door. Mildred invited her in, and offered her a meal and a bed. The woman ended up staying for years. As time passed, and Mildred learned more of how Xenia suffered in the war, she came to care more deeply for her, to the point where she loved Xenia more than anyone outside of her immediate family.

"Xenia considered Mildred a mother substitute," recalled Ursula Mueller. "She expected everything from Mildred." Years later she moved out of the house, but continued to rely heavily upon Mildred, who didn't seem to mind that a much younger woman expected her to perform chores and care for her needs. As her health failed, Xenia became more and more demanding. Many friends withdrew because she didn't try to help herself, but Mildred remained loyal.

"Mildred was an angel to that woman," said Carolyn Kline, a friend through the WILPF. "She was an impossible woman — constantly complaining. Yet Mildred was so kind to her. I really think Mildred thought God had dumped Xenia on her doorstep for a reason."[13]

Mildred lived her radical vision at home, and didn't hesitate to articulate it abroad either. Our collective responsibility to care for all God's creatures, young and old, was her theme. Nuclear bomb testing, which was still being done above-ground, was of prime concern. At a CCF public forum, Mildred outlined her plan for the Fellowship of Reconciliation in Canada. She said future peace action could include marches, public burning of war toys, and pickets of warships visiting the port of Vancouver during the city's centennial celebrations.

"We hope we shall stir up people to express themselves publicly in demonstrations and outdoor meetings against testing of bombs and bomb manufacturing," she told reporters. In response came an indignant letter to the editor criticizing "a certain pacifist 'fellowship'," and scoffing at its methods: "The problems of peace, war and international security are too serious for such childishly silly antics ... " The letter was signed "ADULT" in North Vancouver.

For the times, Mildred's methods were indeed audacious and dramatic, but they had a serious intent: "The objective was to educate and inspire. Startling methods such as toy burning might hasten the shift in consciousness needed to stimulate mass opposition to nuclear weapons."[14]

Vancouver's first peace walk was scheduled for the afternoon of Sunday June 8, 1958 in Stanley Park. Mildred typed up a list of the committed participants — all twenty-eight of them. There was Sheila Young, another veteran activist and then leader of the Women's International League for Peace and Freedom. There were also Quakers and other church people, socialists and members of the CCF among them. Mildred followed Gandhi's example of always informing opponents of one's plans well ahead of time. Accordingly, she sent press releases to the local paper, which published a four-line announcement in advance of the walk.

Mildred and the other peacemakers knew they ought to be ready for the possibility of a confrontation, either with the authorities or with people hostile to their point of view. To help prepare the walkers to remain calm and peaceful, she wrote a handout on nonviolent self-discipline.

Nonviolent action for peace, or any other humanitarian cause, derives its power from the degree to which those who act are able to express truth and love in imaginative, dynamic ways ... We ask all participants on this walk to accept this discipline.

DISCIPLINE

1. Our attitude towards officials and others who may oppose us will be one of sympathetic understanding of the burdens and responsibilities they carry.

2. No matter what the circumstances or provocation, we will not respond with physical violence to acts directed against us.

3. We will not call names or make hostile remarks.

4. We will adhere as closely as we are able to the letter and spirit of the truth in our spoken and written statements.

5. We will always try to speak to the best in man, rather than seeking to exploit their weaknesses to what we may believe is our advantage.[15]

The walkers assembled at Lost Lagoon in Stanley Park and passed out the placards amongst themselves. "Stop Testing Now," they urged. "For Peace and Disarmament" and "For True Christian Government." Under the banner of the Fellowship of Reconciliation, the little band of peace pilgrims set out. Perhaps Mildred convinced a couple of dozen other people to come along after she made up her original list, because it was reported that fifty persons took part in the walk, including a mother pushing her baby in a buggy. They didn't get far, though. About half way along their intended route, Vancouver city police officers stopped them and informed them they would have to leave the park. Evidently, the pacifists did not put up any resistance to this blatant denial of their right to free expression and Mildred apparently didn't waste any time worrying about the aborted walk.

"We were told it was against a bylaw to carry the posters," she was quoted as saying. "We tucked them under our arms and took them to a car we had parked at Lumberman's Arch."[16]

Mildred's other major focus in this period was reconciliation with the people of Japan. For August 6, 1958, the thirteenth anniversary of the day the A-bomb was dropped on Hiroshima, Mildred planned a pilgrimage, a solemn cavalcade from Vancouver east into the Fraser Valley, stopping at Coquitlam, Haney, Mission, Abbotsford, Langley and New Westminster, with a brief service at the cenotaph in each of the communities.

> We hope that this will be a sincere act of contrition for the tragedy of Hiroshima, and a commitment to the way of peace through non-violence … Any banners on the cars etc. will also be carefully chosen. The purpose is to stir people to think of the Christian way to peace, through under-standing and love, but not to arouse antagonism.[17]

By the end of the fifties, the Canadian Fellowship of Reconciliation had about eight hundred members in four centres: Toronto, Calgary, Edmonton, and Vancouver. Responsibilities were split. As Eastern Secretary, Edna Barnett and later Margaret Boos coordinated events in Toronto. Peter Gorrie did the books and accounting from his home in Downsview, Ontario. As Western Secretary, Mildred worked from her study. Among other things, she wrote for the month-ly newsletter that Isabel Showler put out for many years from her home in London. Mildred reported on peace activities in Vancouver and encouraged members to keep working. Students on a protest fast, the first crocus of spring — she seized upon the small signs of hope, and held them up like a talisman. Don't lose heart, she urged them.

The absolutenesss of their pacifism set Mildred and the FOR members apart from others socialist and CCF activists. As Marcia Toms notes: "Fellowship activists insisted on absolute pacifism, and while this gave them moral authority it did little either to swell their numbers or to influence government policy."[18]

On a cross-Canada trip, Mildred reflected upon how the nation seemed to be growing rapidly, yet the Fellowship of Reconciliation was moribund. "I try to evaluate our work in the F.O.R. and ask if we show a proportionate development. While appreciating the loyal support and concern of our members I must admit that as an organization we are not suffering from growing pains. We are glad to welcome a couple of new groups and hope for more."[19]

Delegates at War Resistors International Conference, Gandhigram, India, 1960.

Detail of the photograph above showing Mildred in the centre of the group, in the third row.

Chapter Sixteen: 1960

MEXICO, MY INDIA

"Why am I going to India? I must go. (Perhaps I'll know why when I return.)"[1]

At the age of sixty, Mildred embarked upon her third, and last, passage to India. Mildred had learned to trust her spirit's yearnings, and she didn't always need to understand all the reasons before she acted upon them. In practical terms, she was going to a conference of the War Resisters International. For that purpose, she was given five hundred dollars by the Canadian FOR towards her India ticket. To finance the rest of the trip, she sold her Kitsilano home to her friend and benefactor, Franc Joubin. (Years later, when Franc sold the house at a tidy profit, he sent Mildred two thousand dollars to give "to projects you consider worthwhile in India.")

Mildred's other main goal was to walk with Vinoba Bhave, Gandhi's spiritual heir. Most of all, though, she was going back to India simply to "soak in *darshan*," to immerse herself in the mysterious blessings that abounded there. She bought a plane ticket for October 1960.[2] The first time she made the Pacific Crossing by sea, it took two weeks. This time, by air, the transition from Occident to Orient was radically accelerated, and Tokyo was suddenly upon her. First stop in this pilgrim's progress was post-nuclear Hiroshima.

In Hiroshima, Mildred saw despair deeper than she had witnessed in all her travels. She saw the graveyard behind the cancer hospital where casualties of the A-bomb lay dying of leukemia, lung tumors, aplastic aenemia and liver disorders. She saw their paralyzed faces and looked into their bloodshot eyes. At the hospital Mildred was told that research by American government scientists revealed "no hereditary results of the bomb" and, within one month of the attack, "no measurable radiation in Hiroshima."[3]

At the Peace Museum she joined the hushed crowds, stunned into speechlessness by the evidence of atomic devastation. Everywhere were photos of bodies, torn and broken beyond imagining. Some people had essentially been vapourized. Their shadows remained, though, seared into the walls of nearby buildings, eerie visions of the souls that flew up and away from the vast suffering below. "In the distance, the skeleton of the one remaining building stands up starkly," Mildred wrote that night.[4]

As she tossed in her sleep, haunted by atomic nightmares, John F. Kennedy was being elected the 35th president of the United States. Mildred welcomed his election over the Republican, Richard Nixon. In the years to come, both men would loom large in her political work and in her prayers, as she resisted the war they waged in Vietnam and sheltered those who refused to fight it.

Meanwhile, dramatic events were unfolding in Mildred's next destination — Saigon. Then president of South Vietnam was Ngo Dinh Diem, a despot who one American official described as "a puppet who pulls his own strings."[5] Faced with rising Communist insurgency, Diem used arbitrary arrest, torture and murder to silence dissidents. Thousands were seized. No one was safe. The people petitioned for reforms, and even the Americans urged him to be more moderate, but Diem wouldn't listen. His own men began to plot against him. Near dawn on November 11, 1960, rebel soldiers launched an ill-planned attack. They surrounded Diem's palace, but loyalist troops soon marched in to his defense and the revolt was quickly crushed. By the end of the day more than four hundred people were dead, including many civilians.[6]

Mildred was tense when she arrived in Saigon just five days after the coup attempt. Thanks to the influence of Charles Woodsworth, who was working with the Canadian delegation, she sailed through customs with an official who simply called out *"Diplomatique!"* at every juncture. She was whisked into the official car and delivered to a lovely big room at the Continental Hotel, which itself had not escaped the recent violence. There were bullet holes in the walls, and bloody punctuation marks on many nearby buildings. She walked down by the river and found it congested with gun boats at anchor. Heavily-armed soldiers patrolled everywhere, taut and jumpy in the muggy afternoon.

To Mildred's eyes, the people looked weary and overworked. Their clothes were like pyjamas, and old ragged ones at that. Their homes, too, were squalid. Flies buzzed over the slimy ditches. Young and old simply squatted in the streets to relieve themselves. Everywhere smoke rose from the street-side cooking fires, where people ate standing up, concentrating on the rice or noodles in their bowls. "Grim, drab, unhappy. I hope I'll get out of here before there's another revolution. The situation is not stable and not likely to be, for the president is very autocratic and exacts heavy taxes … from the very poor people."[7]

Still, there was tremendous beauty to be found in Vietnam as well. In a downpour of tropical rain Mildred walked, feasting her senses on the herbs and spices, fruit and flowers, baskets of fish, shrimp and eels. A boy ran past carrying a dozen fragrant baguettes. A vendor offered her elegant Chinese miniatures. Teeming with bicycles, rickshaws, scooters, tongas and every other two- or three-wheeled vehicle imaginable, the streets of Saigon were like fast-flowing rivers.

From the floating markets of Bangkok where she ate shark's fin soup, to the verandah of the famous Raffles Hotel in Singapore, she kept heading towards India, to Gandhigram. Located midway between Trivandrum in the west and Madras in the east, it was a special community where the teachings of the Mahatma lived on in daily practice. Like Mildred, peacemakers from around the world were all making their way to Gandhigram, a holy place to them. Once there, they met under the banner of the War Resisters International.

Mildred at Dum Dum Airport, India, with a representative from Bharaf Airways.

People at Gandhigram.

The first night, a balmy December evening, they gathered in the prayer hall (men on one side, women on the other) and worshipped as Hindus, Buddhists, Muslims and Christians together. The prayer leader "spoke of the kingdom where there is no colour, caste, race or creed."[8] Over the following days, they examined the social obstacles to bringing about the Kingdom of God on Earth. They searched their respective faith traditions for practical insights into how to build justice in a flawed world. Together they visited orphanages, schools, family planning clinics, daycare centres, cottage industries and refugee camps. Their days were filled with discussions of wells, latrines and public hygiene. It was all part of the Indian National Congress party's plan to feed India's hungry millions.

Obviously Mildred could do nothing about the millions, but she wanted to make a difference at least for some. She decided to visit her friends K.K. and Mary Chandy, the Christian couple who led the Fellowship of Reconciliation in India, and who had founded and ran the Kerala Balagram, the home, school and job training centre for orphan boys. Mildred had been fundraising for the Balagram for a dozen years already, but she had never visited there. When she arrived, the Christmas tree was gaily decorated and the children were ready with a program of songs and folk dancing. Each of the boys received a glass tumbler and two candies for Christmas. They gave her a sari of green silk *khadi*.

At that time, the Balagram was home to thirty-five boys ranging in age from five to eighteen. Mildred felt keenly her commitment to all of them, and talked to each one individually. She was touched and shocked by their stories. Some had been abandoned and had no memory of their parents at all. Others lost their parents to disease or other natural causes. One boy told Mildred he ran away from home after his father killed his mother.[9]

On her 61st birthday, India gave Mildred a gift she would always cherish. That morning she went walking with some of the Balagram boys down through the rubber and coffee plantations to the white sand shores of Lake Periya. Coconut palms swayed on the sultry breeze, and she felt such joy just being with the children. Then, gradually, through the mist that hung over the water, they saw an elephant in the distance. Quietly they approached closer and closer, until they could see about twenty of them, both young and old. The massive, gentle beasts lumbered down to the water to drink, and the boys scampered and leapt about, thrilled to see so many all at once. With wide eyes, they told Mildred she must be very lucky to see them on her birthday. For her, it was one of the most enchanting moments she ever experienced in India, that most magical of places. Mildred never forgot the boys of the Balagram. She fundraised for them and cared for them until the end of her life.

From Kerala in the far south, Mildred then traveled northwards. Her destination was to be at the side of Vinoba Bhave, considered by many Indians

Balagram nursery school.

to be Gandhi's spiritual and political successor. As father of the Boodhan movement, Vinoba carried on the Mahatma's agrarian-based approach to peacemaking. Both men believed that the land should belong to those who worked it, and Vinoba's practical goal was to redistribute acreage from the few wealthy landowners to the many tenant farmers. So great was his moral suasion that thousands of landowners responded to his appeals that they simply relinquish large tracts of private land for the sake of their homeless fellow Indians — whether Muslim, Hindu, or Sikh. In the previous five years, more than five million acres had changed hands through his influence.

"Vinoba did not claim that the Boodhan movement would solve the economic problems of India, but that it would help to solve the land problem, and until the land problem was solved there could be no peace," Mildred wrote.[10] She finally caught up with him near the northern border, in the shadow of the Himalayas. Thousands of other pilgrims had also come to this village near Cooch Bihar to hear him speak. Most wore white homespun *khadi* — *saris* for the women, and *dhotis* like Gandhi wore for the men. Sitting up front, the women and children looked striking with their dark eyes outlined in black kohl. The men stood at the back, some wearing turbans and long beards, others with their faces painted.

"I sit near the platform & take pictures and soak in *darshan*," Mildred wrote. She started a new diary, bound in blue, and sketched two men wearing white turbans, sitting cross-legged upon a dais. Vinoba Bhave (speaking Hindi) and his translator (speaking Bengali) offered a message of hope and renewal to the village people. Mildred couldn't understand the words, but she felt blessed just to be there.

"I looked into his face and wept — so worn, so elderly, so gentle, so like my father, so committed. I looked into the sea of dark faces in front of me, intent & still, all fixed on the face in front. Children came with flowers. A man chanted & Vinoba kept time clapping his hands softly. The sun slipped behind a cloud as if not to shine too intently on this gentle face."[11]

Mildred joined up with the band of pilgrims walking with Vinoba. Some stayed a few days, while others had been walking for years. It was rough traveling. After evening prayers they bedded down on a concrete floor. All night long the wind whistled through the shutters, the mosquitoes droned and the men snored so loudly that when the alarm went off at 3 a.m., Mildred felt like she hadn't slept a wink. She struggled out of her sleeping bag, washed up and began walking.

Vinoba walked at the front of the procession between two men carrying lanterns. At the edge of town, people with flowers and garlands came to say farewell to their holy man. Many bowed to touch his feet. All day, from one small village to the next, crowds gathered to greet him under arches decorated with leaves and flowers. Some blew conch shells and others made a yodeling sound to herald his arrival.

That afternoon, when the Maharajah of the district arrived to greet Vinoba, Mildred sensed that the rich man was ill at ease. Later she understood why. In his speech Vinoba said: "In social life — like a bird — one wing is kindness, one a gift." He begged the landowners to give their land away, saying that people must be clean in body and in heart. At the end he asked whether the people wanted land to go to the landless. Everyone raised his hand, and then bowed his head in prayer. Like Gandhi, Vinoba succeeded partly because he always expected the best of his opponent. The Maharajah, who was invited to speak next, could hardly do anything else but what he did: announce he would give up half of his arable land — about fifty acres — to the Boodhan movement.[12]

Mildred had been fighting illness throughout much of the trip. She finally was diagnosed with hepatitis and so, in the summer of 1961, she returned to Vancouver to recuperate. Given that she had sold her home to get the money to go to India, she could have been facing a housing crunch. But she was able to move back into the old family home on West 8th, which was vacant now that her sister-in-law Connie Osterhout had remarried. Connie's new husband was a crusading lawyer named Bob McMaster, himself a widower. Between them, Connie and Bob had seven children. For two of them, it was a particularly special union.

Mildred's niece, Marion, was best friends with Beverley, Bob's eldest. At the age of nineteen, the young women became sisters in a deeper sense. Some of their younger siblings, though, had a hard time dealing with their deep losses. Connie often sought Mildred's advice and moral support in raising her two boys. Mildred loved all the kids, and let them know they were special to her. They, in turn, were influenced by her activism. She offered a compelling role model because she so clearly practised what she preached.[13]

In this period, Mildred helped launch the Peace by Peaceful Means Coordinating Committee so Vancouver-area peace groups could co-operate on actions. She spoke out whenever she could at schools, clubs, churches and demonstrations. "Violence speaks in loud and insistent voices. How can non-violence be heard?" she asked herself. Ever more convinced that war was the inevitable consequence of capitalist injustice, she questioned whether capitalism could exist in a peaceful world. Other recurring themes were humanity's very real capacity for total destruction, the threat to this and future generations from nuclear radiation, and the staggering cost of the arms race. With an ever-escalating litany of statistics, she tried to move people out of their apathy to action against such unconscionable waste. Peace through armed defence, she said, is "peace of the graveyard, peace of extermination. The nations must replace fear with trust, and abandon their terrible weapons of mass destruction."

As always, Mildred tried not to allow herself to feel daunted by the enormity of the peacemaker's task. She often quoted Gandhi: "A small body of dedicated spirits fired by an unquenchable faith in their mission can change the course of history." Now in her early sixties, Mildred would have loved to live and work in India for a couple of years. She wrote to both the Canadian and the American Friends Service Committees inquiring about overseas postings, but nothing came up in either India or Pakistan. She would have to look for somewhere else to put her Gandhian ideals into action. She found it in Mexico. "Mexico became my India," she often said.

Between 1963 and 1979, Mildred usually headed out in January. She traveled by bus, visiting friends in the Fellowship of Reconciliation in Washington, Oregon and California. Mildred enjoyed bus travel and, like Woodsworth and Gandhi, always rode with the people. In Mexico, that often meant riding with livestock, too. For a few months every winter, she worked at the *Casa de los Amigos*, the Quaker centre in downtown Mexico City. Located at Ignacio Mariscal 132, it was the former home of Jose Clemente Orozco, one of the great Mexican muralists. His studio became the Friends' worship hall.[14]

Mildred would take over for the directors of the *Casa*, allowing them time for home leave and vacation. Her duties included cooking breakfast for the guests, helping them get acquainted with Mexico City, running the front desk, doing the account books, supervising the Mexican women who cleaned up, and hosting evening dances and *folklorico* performances. Her days started early, with a quick stop in the kitchen to put on the coffee urn and a big pot of porridge. Then she'd head out to the market and load up on fresh bread, fruits and vegetables.

> I spend half my time checking people in and out, serving out 'entero vioform' pills for you know what … or if you don't you'll find out when you come to Mexico. Everyone gets a spell sooner or later. I had mine last week after eating a 40-cent meal in a nearby joint.

> Every day there is an emergency or an unusual event. Last week I had to rush out to the airport to meet a mother who had come because her daughter was in hospital with amoebic dysentery …

> The emergency at the moment is that the water has gone off … it happens quite often, when the city pressure is too low to bring it in. However everyone has to go to bed with a dirty neck and about 4 a.m. with a roar, the water comes rushing in so there is no excuse for unshaven faces at breakfast … although we do have them. Actually we have kept most of the hair cut and the beards trimmed this year … but not without well pointed hints and suggestions.[15]

Like everywhere else in North America, signs of the sexual revolution began to emerge, even in devoutly Roman Catholic Mexico. Pre-marital sex was becoming increasingly accepted in society, but at the *Casa* traditional standards were maintained. In 1967, Mildred wrote:

> The other day I had a boy and girl come and ask if they could have a double room. I said, "Are you married?"

> Reply, "no." My reply 'NO."[16]

Despite wide availability of "The Pill," it was not unusual for Mildred to have on her guest list a free-spirited American girl who got pregnant in Mexico. One year they visited a family planning clinic, which was "for the most part supported by the companies that make the magic pills … We also saw the Padre who comes in to advise these Catholics who are anxious to maintain good relations with the church."[17]

Mildred's enthusiasm for the *Casa* and all it stood for was infectious. Many of her socially-conscious friends, including Elizabeth Keeling, Mary Joubin and Jackie Mitchell, would come to enjoy the activity and fellowship, and stay to lend Mildred a hand. Mary was a particularly motherly person, so she was often called on to help with the "maternity cases."[18]

Although she spent months each year in Mexico, Mildred never really learned to speak Spanish, but simply carried on with a few cheerfully fractured phrases.

Mildred on the beach in Zihuatanejo, Mexico, undated.

Anyway, even without the language, the Mexican people could understand Mildred very well because of her transparent friendliness and sustained commitment to the work.

From the *Casa* in Mexico City, the American Friends Service Committee coordinated its rural development work: usually six or seven summer projects and two or three year-round ones. Instead of imposing their own solutions, the Friends simply put themselves at the service of the villagers. Their work included all the fundamentals of rural community development, the same kind of projects Gandhi launched in his villages. The volunteers dug wells for safe drinking water, and irrigation systems for vegetable gardens. They built primary schools and health clinics, organized libraries and crafts programs. Friends came from urban Mexico, the United States, Canada, Latin America and Europe. Ed Duckles, who served with his wife Jean as co-director for many years, explained that the volunteers' first point of arrival would be the *Casa*, where they would meet one another and receive their orientation before departing to the villages.

Mildred Fahrni was often the first person they met, and her warm and friendly personality made them feel welcome and calmed the anxieties which many of them felt as they were about to take on the new and challenging work ahead of them. Since she had also visited a number of the Friends Service Units, Mildred was also able to provide the new arrivals with important information about what to expect regarding life in small Mexican communities.[19]

Her "pet project" was the *Casa de Alfabetizacion*, a literacy program in Valle de Bravo, about one hundred kilometers west of Mexico City. The Friends offered programs for men, women, and children and also taught in the local prison. As well, they raised money for scholarships and trained some of the brightest young Mexicans as teachers. The school buildings were simple, hand-built structures with thatched roofs. Stationary, books and other supplies were scarce, but learning was not. Mildred became a loyal supporter of this and other projects of the American Friends Service Committee. Decades later Ed and Jean Duckles would write to her: "Once again we want to thank you for the innumerable services you have rendered to the Committee and the *Casa de los Amigos* in Mexico. We frankly don't see how the *Casa* could have gotten through the last few years without your help at the crucial times and emergencies."[20]

Mildred's loyalty to the *Casa* and its projects had a deep impact on her niece, Marion. "I remember going to the *Casa*, visiting Mildred one winter. There were students from work camps going in and out all the time. It was a real cosmopolitan place ... a very exciting place to be," she recalled.[21] And if that excitement was not enough to attract a young seeker like Marion, "there was also part of me that idolized her. I wanted to emulate her." So, at the age of twenty-two, Marion set off to work for a year with the Friends in Mexico. "I knew it was really important for who I was, to do that," she said.

One of a team of sixteen volunteers from many different countries, Marion served in a poor village in Tlaxcala. Marion had graduated from a Quaker school in the United States, so she was well-grounded in the philosophy underpinning the work and she felt comfortable in a communal home life. There was only one thing wrong: she simply couldn't stand one of her house mates, a volunteer from Panama.

"I realized I was trying to be this all-loving person at all times for everybody. I was putting out enormous energy trying to be ... the person I thought I should be." That Panamanian girl, however, touched off something in Marion's dark side. Shocked to discover that she was capable of hatred, Marion realized she either had to go home, or stop judging herself by Mildred's example and accept that she was only human.

"It was a real turning point in my life," Marion recalled. "I certainly had her on a pedestal. When I let myself off the pedestal I'd tried to put myself on, then Mildred became more of a person to me, too ... But I feel Mildred never really accepted her other side, her dark side."

* * *

If Mildred lacked self-awarenesss, it was at least in part due to extreme busy-ness. And nothing kept her busier than raising money to give away. From the late fifties and throughout the sixties, she sent between fifty and one hundred dollars a month to Mexico. This was on top of a larger sum she sent to India, sometimes as much as two hundred dollars monthly. To raise funds, she sold Mexican and Indian handicrafts through her wide circle of friends and contacts. Every summer she'd have a huge garden party and crafts sale, with all the proceeds going to the *Balagram* and the *Casa de Alfabetizacion*.

Many of her guests were like-minded women, veteran activists who were taking the leadership in a new national organization articulating women's demands for peace. Founded in 1960, it was called the Voice of Women.

"VOW gave voice, stature and credibility to a newly-conscious sector of Canadian women. They were primarily middle class, politically moderate and motivated to anti-nuclear action by a pressing anxiety about the welfare of their children and the children of the world. [Mildred] Fahrni became a key VOW spokeswoman in B.C., traveling to conferences within Canada and abroad, giving interviews and working to establish a VOW in Mexico."[22]

The Voices, as the women called themselves, were unlikely revolutionaries. Respectable in hats, gloves and pearls, they were educated, articulate and persuasive. The latest in a long tradition of "maternalist peacemakers," Mildred and her colleagues in the Voice of Women believed that the new women's peace campaign was uniquely suited to transcend political ideologies. Rejecting the rationalist, linear approach preferred by men, they advocated an integrated approach to peacemaking that spoke both to the hearts and minds of member activists, who were united by their common concerns as women and mothers.[23]

In September 1962, Mildred attended an international Voice of Women conference in Montreal, organized by Thérèse Casgrain, Muriel Duckworth and others. In an article published in an Indian journal, Mildred reported that "52 women from 17 countries met in closed session for four days and then joined 500 others in a three-day open session." Among the keynote speakers was American anthropologist Margaret Mead, who said: "There are no insurmountable barriers in the world's family. The tasks of women in caring for the basic needs of life are universal in essence and time. We can no longer defend *our* children unless we defend all. We must think of the Russians as defenders of our children, as we must be of theirs."[24]

Mildred agreed wholeheartedly with Mead. Whatever barriers of language and culture divided them, the women all shared a daily sense of dread. Her notes refer again and again to global fears — fear of annihilation, fear of being enslaved by others and by ourselves, fear of bacteriological war, and accidental war through technical error, fear of nuclear fallout from atmospheric testing, fear of being lied to and manipulated by propaganda, fear of the growing power of the military, fear of neo-Nazism and rearmament of Germany, and most of all, fear of Communism and of Russia.

To these worries, the western peacemakers had to add the fear of being smeared as Communists, which they decidedly were not. The women discussed the best ways to counter the charge, but they realized such efforts were ultimately futile. Merely to have been labeled a Communist was sufficient to discredit one in the public mind. In the end, Mildred simply noted: "Watch your language." This was not empty Cold War paranoia. Secret documents released in recent years reveal that indeed the RCMP security service did suspect that Voice of Women was being manipulated or infiltrated by Communists. The Mounties were keeping close check on this potentially subversive group. One RCMP informer at a VOW meeting in Parksville, B.C. told police some leaders were "very radical and appear to be against everything and seem intent on destroying the Canadian relations with the U.S.A."[25]

On the contrary, the Voices felt an enormous sense of urgency about building better relations with Americans and Russians alike. At the Montreal conference they adopted resolutions in support of "travel seminars, people-to-people visitations, contacts and correspondence with 'sister' towns and exchange of students."[26] They aimed to build trust, and thus enable people to overcome their fears, to connect again across the Iron Curtain. "To speak the truth in love" was their role. If that meant sometimes criticizing U.S. policy, so be it.

Within a month of the VOW conference, everyone's worst nightmare began to unfold as U.S. President John Kennedy provoked a terrifying standoff with Soviet Premier Nikita Khrushchev over Cuba. "WE'RE ON THE BRINK," shouted *The Vancouver Sun* of October 23, 1962. "The United States will lean out over the brink of war tonight by clamping a naval blockade on Cuba. President John Kennedy ... called it a quarantine action to halt shipments of Soviet missiles to Cuba."

The blockade was roundly condemned by the New Democratic Party's national leader, Tommy Douglas, who made headlines the same day for his landslide victory in a by-election in Burnaby-Coquitlam. Douglas charged that the U.S. was violating international law with the blockade. "It should not be forgotten that for the last fifteen years the West has been ringing the Soviet Union with nuclear bases and airports from which the Strategic Air Command could bomb any part," he said. "There should be some restraint on both sides before we hasten the world into a position from which it is impossible to retreat."[27]

When the superpowers stepped back from the brink, the whole world breathed a sigh of relief. Peaceful resolution of the crisis seemed to Mildred to be miraculous."Truly there is a creative spirit working in the world," she wrote.

Soon she received another small hopeful signal through the mail. On the day the crisis began, Gerard Daechsel, a Norwegian studying in London, wrote: "Dear Mrs. Fahrni, ... I first became a conscious pacifist ... at a meeting [at UBC] arranged by you."[28]

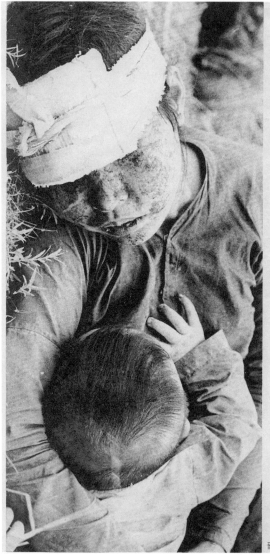

you are invited
to take part in

a
meal
of
reconciliation

an interfaith sharing
of rice and tea,
of reading and
of prayer,

a sign of unity
with each other
a sign of unity
with the war victims
● an act
of repentance
● an act
to help end the war
and to aid its victims

Send contributions or requests
for information:
Fellowship of Reconciliation
They Are Our Brothers Project
Box 271, Nyack, N.Y. 10960

Fellowship of Reconciliation poster advertising a 1960s event.

Chapter Seventeen: 1963

FLOWER POWER

Despite assurances from the U.S. military that the Vietnam war would be over by Christmas 1963, the conflict continued. By the end of the year, five hundred million American dollars and fifteen thousand American military advisors would be in South Vietnam. In Saigon and in Washington, people were growing ever more frustrated with the Diem regime. Through covert channels, the Americans encouraged another *coup d'état* and then claimed to be shocked when Diem was murdered instead of merely overthrown. After the news of his death was broadcast, enormous crowds of jubilant citizens celebrated in the streets of Saigon. Three weeks later, on November 22, 1963, President John F. Kennedy met his own assassin's bullet in the streets of Dallas. Americans (and Canadians) reeled from the shock and grief. Vice-President Lyndon Johnson was sworn in as millions mourned.[1]

They were painful but exhilarating times for Mildred. She saw so much promise in the growing anti-war movement, both in the United States and Canada. Students, trade unionists, church people and so many others formed an enormous peace force across the border. It was *Satyagraha* in action once again. Blacks joined in by the thousands after Martin Luther King began equating the anti-imperialist struggle of the Vietnamese people with the civil rights struggle of African-Americans. It was wonderful to see the creativity of the non-violent resisters, who staged teach-ins and love-ins, and placed flowers into the barrels of soldiers' guns.

They chanted: "Hey, hey, L.B.J.! How many kids did you kill today? Make love, not war. Ban the bomb. Burn the bra. Hell, no! We won't go!"

A classified ad in Vancouver's alternative newspaper, the *Georgia Straight*, read: "JOIN THE DODGE REBELLION. Americans: if you feel the draft, come to warm, safe Canada, the Land of Opportunity. If you are already caught and don't like killing people, by all means DESERT NOW! Don't hesitate. You have nothing to gain but your lives."[2]

By the end of the sixties more than 10,000 young American draft dodgers and deserters had fled to Canada and Scandinavia. There were an estimated 3,000 in Vancouver, with dozens more arriving every week via a new "underground railroad." The Committee to Aid American War Objectors championed their cause. Mildred and other supporters helped to feed and shelter the young men until they could get established in town. She wholeheartedly cheered their courage in resisting the draft, but their freewheeling attitude toward drugs she found deeply troubling. Mildred and other mature activists tried to bring more thoughtful perspectives to the public dialogue about war and peace.

> The rising tide of protest over the war in Viet Nam gives hope where frustration threatens to paralyze. Having a young 'Hippie' [live] with me for a couple of months was challenging. There is much of value in the revolt of the younger generation against conformity to the superficial and hypocritical in our civilization but it is difficult to understand their detachment from any sense of social responsibility.[3]

In contrast to the noisy demonstrations of the youth, a group of Vancouver pacifists chose to protest in silence. Among them were members of the Fellowship of Reconciliation, the Society of Friends, the Women's International League for Peace and Freedom, the Voice of Women, the B.C. Peace Council and the Canadian Coalition for Nuclear Responsibility. They all came together as the Vancouver Peace Action League. Beginning in the fall of 1966, they began holding a weekly vigil for peace in Vietnam. Every Saturday they'd gather downtown at the corner of Georgia and Granville Streets. They maintained the vigil every week without fail for more than seven years. One or two would pass out pamphlets and take questions from passersby, but the rest would remain silent. By their presence they tried to be a force for peace amid the conflict and the commerce. It wasn't easy. Most people passed quickly by, regarding them with suspicion or open contempt. One of their early pamphlets read: "(Kindly refrain from dropping this on the sidewalk. Thank you.)"

June Black of the Coalition for Nuclear Responsibility worked with Carolyn Kline and Sheila Young of the Women's International League to put out the weekly pamphlets. They updated developments in the conflict, exposed the military propaganda (which they called "Mythinformation") and examined the uncomfortably close relations between Washington and supposedly-neutral Ottawa. They stressed that Canadians, as major suppliers of arms and chemical weapons such as napalm, were also partly responsible for the carnage in Vietnam.[4] They pointed out that the war also had economic and social costs for Canada. Don't you see that we too are complicit? they asked. Can't you feel how it hurts us all? Most Canadians, accustomed to thinking of themselves as benign, honest brokers on the international stage, frankly weren't interested in that kind of question.

"Oh yes, there was a lot of hostility," June Black recalled. "The majority of people were in favour of the war. Everybody thought the U.S. could do no wrong. We got spat upon. People would scowl and growl 'Communist!' at us."

One of Mildred's letters to *The Vancouver Sun* provoked a similar response from an anonymous reader, who clipped out her letter to the editor and sent it back with the word COMMUNIST scrawled in red ink across the type. He added: "Been peddling this tripe for years. Get back to China. Don't pollute beautiful B.C."

Despite many such negative responses, the overall movement in society was positive. Mildred's peace work was beginning to be recognized. In February 1966, she was awarded Vancouver's Brotherhood Citizen Award. She was unable to attend the presentation ceremony because she was working in Mexico, but a lot of friendly mail came to the Casa congratulating her on the honour.

In 1967, Canada celebrated its centennial year with a flair and exuberance that was distinctly un-Canadian. The wildly successful Expo '67 attracted an astonishing fifty million people from around the world, including Mildred. Visitors from home and abroad delighted in the joyous, free atmosphere at the exposition, which contrasted sharply with Canada's reputation as a nice, but bland, nation. Journalist Robert Fulford wrote: "There was a sense during that remarkable summer that, as a people, we might never be the same again."[5] With perhaps typical Canadian understatement, Mildred wrote: "I was stimulated by the imagination and originality of the displays ... and the creative penetration into the future."[6]

In the afterglow of Expo '67, Canadians were ready for a new kind of leader, someone who would define their emboldened sense of national identity. Enter Pierre Elliott Trudeau, then Minister of Justice. A Jesuit-trained Quebecer, he was intensely cerebral, eloquently bilingual, widely travelled, and had an elusive kind of sex appeal. "Trudeaumania" swept the land, and on June 25, 1968 he was elected Prime Minister with a larger majority than any other Liberal government in decades. His dynamic reputation spread as far as India, whence a friend of Mildred's wrote: "I have been reading about Trudeau. He seems too good to be true, and certainly too good to be a politician — glamour boy & intellectual."[7]

Mildred and many others in the peace movement were optimistic their hip young prime minister would be open to new ideas and non-violent approaches. Some of the early signs were promising. Trudeau increased foreign aid, founded Canada World Youth, and spoke of the "global ethic of sharing." With the signature rose in his lapel and the fedora tilted just so, he cut a dashing figure on the international stage.

Mildred had been overjoyed when Martin Luther King won the 1964 Nobel Peace Prize. She felt that the world was beginning to hear Gandhi's message through his most famous disciple. She corresponded with Coretta King for several years after their first meeting during the bus boycott. In 1967, Coretta wrote to thank Mildred for a letter and donation:

> Ours is also a busy life. Martin travels, speaks, and writes a great deal. I have been busy presenting a Freedom Concert in cities across the United States and, last spring, in Toronto ... SCLC [Southern Christian Leadership Conference] continues its programs of voter registration and citizenship education. Our Operation Breadbasket, which was designed to increase the employment of Negroes by companies which rely on the Negro market, is quite successful. Last year was very rewarding and we look forward to next year.[8]

Ironically, next year would bring tragedy to her family, and martyrdom for her husband. On April 4, 1968, Dr. Martin Luther King Jr. was shot at his motel in Memphis, Tennessee. The shock of his death was compounded when, on June 5, Senator Robert Kennedy was also shot down during the California primary in Los Angeles. These political assassinations rocked America and were deeply felt in Canada as well. Mildred as usual tried to find the good outcome of the bad news:

> The way Gandhi went down, the way Martin Luther King went down — some people say, "What a tragedy!" Well, of course it was a terrible tragedy, but perhaps their thinking has been more widespread because of the tragedy they went through.[9]

Coretta King and Mildred Fahrni met once again in 1983 in Vancouver at the World Council of Churches Assembly. Their names stood together with those of Joan Baez, Daniel Berrigan and others on the 1987-88 list of advisors to the American Fellowship of Reconciliation. At the site of Rev. King's murder now stands a plaque bearing a quotation from Genesis: "Here comes the dreamer. Let us kill him and see what becomes of his dream."

King had been a member of the American Fellowship of Reconciliation, and that organization flourished as activists across the country worked to keep his dream alive. The American FOR had strong roots in the civil rights movement and was growing dramatically, with thousands of members in the Pacific Northwest alone. In Canada, however, it was a different story. Murray Thomson, an early member who later founded Peace Brigades International, said that FOR became "marginal in the sense that it never took off in Canada the way it did in the States." By 1966, FOR membership north of the border had dwindled to "about 225, mostly elderly" Canadians. Numbers continued to decline as some members passed away and others left to work with more dynamic groups such as the Campaign for Nuclear Disarmament and the Voice of Women. The organization was operating on a shoestring. With an annual budget of not more than nine thousand dollars, there was barely enough to pay one staff person a subsistence salary and to meet minimal office and organizing expenses.

There was much discussion among FOR members about the viability of continuing the work. Is it worthwhile to keep the FOR going? they asked themselves. Could we be more effective working with other peace groups? Some pointed out that the FOR was no longer the only voice for non-violence. "There are now various groups who share this witness with us. It is pointless for us to duplicate a job which is being done better elsewhere."[10] Others voiced "strong concern for an articulate pacifist Christian witness in this time and among the younger generations."[11] Everyone agreed the organization needed "new blood, new approaches and an overhaul of the executive committee."[12]

Between 1965 and 1969, three men led the Canadian FOR: Julian Griggs, Brewster Kneen and, finally, Rev. George Strong. In their different ways, they all tried to revitalize the group while contributing to the broader peace and disarmament struggles. However, as Mildred later wrote, "the results were disappointing and finally the National Council in Toronto broke us … as one by one the members became discouraged by methods used."[13] Mildred seems to have clashed with George Strong's leadership style. "He has ability and drive but it seems he must 'drive' alone," she wrote.[14]

Most western members felt they spent far too much time fundraising for national office in Toronto. In early 1969, when Mildred was next away in Mexico, the Vancouver group decided not to forward any more money to the national office because "the feeling is quite strong that he [Strong] does not represent us." George was annoyed since, as he expressed it, he had been working on the "witness now, pay later" principle. He felt he was owed back wages totaling fourteen hundred dollars, plus more than three hundred dollars expenses. The group simply didn't have the funds to pay him. Mildred wrote to George: "Unfortunately the executive had fallen apart, the members had become inactive and resources were at an end." By the end of 1969, Strong had resigned. The eastern chapter was soon defunct, leaving Mildred's little band in Vancouver as the only remaining chapter of the Fellowship in Canada.

"Organizationally the Canadian FOR has almost fallen apart but there is a thread of fellowship holding together those who have committed themselves to the way of active non-violence," Mildred wrote in her Christmas letter of 1971. By 1974, her list of Canadian FOR contacts was down to 32 individuals. Contrary to the expectations of many, that group still had a lot of life left in it.

mahatma gandhi centenary year
1969

war resisters' international
l'internationale des résistants à la guerre
internationale der kriegsdienstgegner
3 CALEDONIAN ROAD, LONDON, N.I, ENGLAND

War Resisters' International pamphlet, 1969.

The year Mildred turned sixty-nine was the hundredth anniversary of Gandhi's birth, in Porbandar on October 2, 1869. Celebrations to mark the centennial were planned across Canada and around the world. The Canadian Friends Service Committee coordinated events in Halifax, Toronto, Winnipeg and Vancouver. Mildred helped organize a weekend seminar on the theory and practical applications of non-violence. Among those working with her were Frank Dingman, a conscientious objector in the Second World War and crusading social worker who travelled to Vietnam with medical supplies for the North and South; Dick and Hazel Legge, a gentle Quaker couple active in the FOR and later in Veterans Against Nuclear Arms; Amy Dalgleish, a Unitarian women's rights activist and peace worker.[15]

They organized the gathering for Thanksgiving weekend at the United Church camp in Ocean Park, south of Vancouver just a few miles from the U.S. border. The camp, on a bluff overlooking Boundary Bay, had heated cabins and an excellent kitchen. They planned to serve Gandhian cuisine. They got letters of support from the likes of Joan Baez, Coretta King and Cesar Chavez, and they were excited when Mulford Sibley agreed to come as the keynote speaker. An eminent American socialist, pacifist and professor of political science, his most recent book was *The Quiet Battle: Writings on the Theory and Practice of Non-Violent Resistance*. Dr. Sibley gave a public lecture at UBC entitled "Revolution and Violence." The weekend seminar was called: "Gandhi's Non-Violence — Relevant Today?"

Obviously, to Mildred, Gandhi's non-violence was every bit as relevant in 1969 as when she first met him in 1931. To mark Gandhi's centenary in a personal way, Mildred returned to London where she visited Reg Reynolds, another of the volunteers who worked at Kingsley Hall during Gandhi's time there. Over the years they had both told the stories so many times of their encounters with Bapu that they had become personal legends, and the telling had taken on a quality of its own. Mildred and Reg made an audio tape for posterity. In her Christmas letter, she wrote: "It was in London that I first met Gandhi and this year of his Centenary has brought many memories and new insights into his philosophy. His commitment to Truth and Non-violence, his way of Love and Fearlessness are a continual challenge ... and very humbling to one who falls so far behind."

The close of the decade brought a watershed in human history: man walked on the moon. Mildred wrote: "1969 has been a big year for the scientists, who have left their footprints ... and the U.S. flag! ... on the moon. But what of hopes for peace on earth?"[16]

On the domestic front, events reached crisis point in October 1970 when the separatist *Front de Liberation du Quebec* kidnapped British Trade Commissioner James Cross and Quebec Labour Minister Pierre Laporte. A personal friend of Trudeau, Laporte was later murdered. Asked how far he would go to defeat the FLQ, Trudeau snapped: "Just watch me." He invoked the War Measures Act, which made membership in the FLQ illegal, suspended *habeas corpus*, and gave the police sweeping powers to detain and interrogate suspects without charge. Most Canadians applauded Trudeau's decisive response. Confronted with the sudden realization that political killings could happen here, too, they shrugged off the fact that a few hundred people were rounded up by mistake. Of nearly five hundred suspects arrested, only twelve were ever convicted.[17] For Mildred, the whole episode illustrated once again how violence inevitably begets more violence, and that everyone is hurt by such brutality. "We have seen ... new depths in the ignominy of the tiger cages in Vietnam and the murder in Montreal," she wrote.[18]

Mildred and the remaining members of the FOR in B.C. maintained close links with their counterparts in the numerous chapters of the FOR in Washington and Oregon. They held large annual meetings every July 4th weekend, giving the American pacifists a retreat from the overbearing jingoism of the U.S. national holiday. They met at the Seabeck Christian Conference Centre, located in wooded countryside on Hood Canal in northwest Washington state. Seabeck's idyllic setting contrasted with the presence nearby of the military base at Bangor, which later became the site of frequent FOR demonstrations.

Mildred was a central organizer of these conferences, which usually attracted more than two hundred people. Her days would start early, leading yoga exercises on the dock at 7 a.m., followed by a bracing morning swim. There were workshops morning and afternoon, punctuated by walks in the woods, salmon barbeques on the beach, and lots of singing — peace and protest songs, gospel tunes and favourite hymns. The gatherings were always stimulating, bringing together not only Christian pacifists, but also socialists, anarchists, agnostics, and environmentalists.

At Seabeck, Americans and Canadians planned co-operative strategies to assist conscientious objectors and draft dodgers, as well as joint actions at the Peace Arch on the Canada-U.S. border. At the 1964 meeting, Dorothy Gretchen Steeves, Mildred's friend from the days of the early CCF, spoke on "Cuba: A Canadian Perspective." The American peacemakers found her "eye witness report" refreshingly free of the anti-Castro propaganda to which they were so accustomed. In 1967, the theme was "Creative Revolution" and the keynote speaker was folk singer Joan Baez, who raised her exquisite, powerful voice in the struggle for peace in Vietnam and civil rights at home.

On April 29, 1975, with Communist rockets striking the Saigon airport, the last Americans were evacuated via helicopter from the U.S. embassy compound. That night elated North Vietnamese troops rolled into the city and through the gates of the presidential palace. The war was over; its costs were incalculable. When Jimmy Carter was elected president in 1976, one of his first acts was to pardon most of the 10,000 Vietnam war draft evaders.

For Mildred, the only good she could see coming from the whole nightmare was the increased awareness and political commitment of the young people. "Great hope is to be found in the 'drop out' movement of the youth, rejecting capitalism and militarism," she wrote. "Perhaps the new society will be germinated from the creative forces released among them."[19]

Chapter Eighteen: 1975

PEACE BEGINS AT HOME

Throughout her seventies, Mildred devoted herself to Servas, an international organization that promoted peace and understanding through travel and home stay. Servas was founded in Denmark in 1948 and, since then, Servas volunteers had developed a network of hosts and travellers in almost forty countries, all committed to furthering global goodwill. Servas emphasized non-profit, apolitical, interfaith and inter-racial principles.

"[It is] a peace-building program, opening doors into homes in other countries so that people who are travelling make friends and understand more of the culture and life instead of meeting only other tourists in hotels and campsites," Mildred said. "We want serious travellers, not just those looking for a pad or a cheap place to stay."[1]

In 1970 she travelled for the first time to South America, and part of the goal of the trip was to develop Servas contacts. From Mexico she headed south to Costa Rica, Panama City, Lima, Santiago, Buenos Aires, Montevideo, and then north again through Sao Paulo, Rio de Janiero, Tegucigalpa, Guatemala City and back to Mexico and home.

"The trip," she wrote, "brought me close to ferment in some areas, into countries where military governments repress and where foreign powers ... guess which ... support reactionary forces. I've had a glimpse of the problems of rapidly growing populations, urbanization, contrasts of wealth and poverty, exploitation, etc. And I've seen the Andes! Back home it takes time to adjust to our affluent West, to try to live without adding to conflict and exploitation, to find a middle way."

Mildred was the guest of Servas members in a number of alpine villages when she went to Switzerland for a 1974 conference, but it was as a host that she made her greatest contribution to Servas. Hosts were expected to provide a welcome along with free room and board for two or three nights. Travellers were screened in their home countries and, after approval, were given letters of introduction and host lists for their destination spots. They were supposed to write ahead of time to confirm their visits, but many simply arrived unannounced on Mildred's doorstep. None were turned away.

Mildred's open-door attitude was inspired by her deep belief in the unity of the human family. It was also a way for her to share what she considered her unearned privilege as a citizen of the affluent west. Hospitality is one form of worship, according to a Jewish proverb. In that light, Mildred lived an actively worshipful lifestyle. Entries in her visitor's book from the 1960s and '70s are by guests from throughout Canada and the United States, as well as England, Scotland, Northern Ireland, North and South Wales, Australia, New Zealand, France, The Netherlands, Belgium, Switzerland, Denmark, West Germany, Austria, Italy, Spain, Tunisia, Turkey, Sierra Leone, Trinidad, Thailand, Vietnam, Hong Kong, Japan, Uruguay, Costa Rica, Mexico, and, of course, India.

In 1970, Mildred's sister-in-law Connie was widowed again when her second husband, Bob McMaster, died. Within the year, Connie moved back into the Osterhout family home with Mildred. It was in some ways a difficult transition because there were times when Mildred had so many people coming and going through the house that Connie, like Mother Fahrni, felt out of place in her own home. However, the sisters-in-law were able to work out a peaceful co-habitation. Mildred was away each winter in Mexico and Connie was away each summer at the cottage on Vancouver Island, so they each could give the other her own space for significant periods of time.

"Mom always said she'd rather adjust to somebody else than have to live by herself," recalled her daughter, Marion. "She and Mildred were close companions."

In the mid-seventies, Connie and Mildred shared the house with two of Connie's step-daughters, Beverley and Nancy McMaster. "Connie respected Mildred but she didn't agree with some of the ways she lived," Bev recalled. "She felt Mildred was taken advantage of by all the so-called 'lame ducks' that leaned on her. And it bothered her that Mildred gave away all her money."

Content to spend less and less on herself, Mildred sent a significant amount of her pension to India and Mexico every month. "I'm grateful for the rewards of old age through the Pension benefits, which give us more to use and share," she wrote. Because she was always so aware of others without any shelter whatsoever, Mildred was usually reluctant to spend any money on the house. As a result, Connie quietly had necessary repairs done or bought needed household items when Mildred was away at the *Casa*.

In late 1977, Connie went to Hawaii on a dream vacation, but never returned. "She collapsed with a stroke and slipped away almost immediately," Mildred

Mildred at her desk, typewriter at hand, 1978.

wrote. In her will, Connie stipulated that Mildred should have use of the house for as long as Mildred needed to live in it. But Connie knew Mildred well enough to know that she should not bequeath legal title to her, particularly as property values in the neighbourhood were starting to rise. Sooner or later Mildred would have sold the house and donated the proceeds to one worthy cause or another. Thus, through Connie's love and good sense, Mildred had use of the family home, and security of housing, for the rest of her long life.[2]

Because Mildred lived so close to the University of B.C., student boarders found her place both convenient and congenial. Normally the three upstairs bedrooms were occupied by women students, and often a couple of young men were bunked in downstairs. Mildred believed that everyone should do some "bread labour" every day, so she kindly made it known she expected them to pitch in with the dishes or other household chores. Everyone knew where the key was kept (behind the thermometer on the back porch) but it was not needed because the door was never locked.

The students enjoyed Mildred's company, her unconventional style and politics. At age 72, she helped elect Dave Barrett and the New Democrats to the B.C. Legislature, ending the three-decade rule of Social Credit Premier W.A.C. Bennett. In a crowd her age, Mildred stood out in her Mexican sandals and embroidered blouses. She was an advocate of naturopathic healing and alternative foods, and was forever baking up "health cookies" to serve with herb tea. Cradling steaming mugs, Mildred's young friends talked to her about their studies, worries, dreams, and confided secrets about their love lives. Sometimes they dated one another, and at least one couple met and married at Mildred's. The bride was about five decades younger than the bridesmaid, but it mattered not.

"We planned the party and we went on down to the civil ceremony. We enjoyed that, and we enjoyed the rainstorm that broke out right at the critical time," recalled best man Tom Haythorne, another student boarder. "It was totally natural that Mildred was the bridesmaid. She was a very modern, together person, and sort of *complete* in a way which was a bit awe-inspiring."[3]

As well as the students, Servas travellers, friends and activists passing through town, Mildred continued to open her home to anyone in need of refuge. As a result, various financially and emotionally needy folk took up residence for a few days, or longer. Some friends and family members worried about Mildred's willingness to take absolutely anybody and everybody under her wing.

"She was too trusting," said Kathleen Barrett, a long-time friend who taught school with Mildred in the 1930s. "When I think of some of the wierdos she welcomed into her house! Although I don't think she was ever robbed, she was taken advantage of."

Mildred didn't worry about such things, however. Her tolerance combined with a ready sense of humour made it possible for her to abide guests that would have driven others to distraction. She genuinely loved people, and she cared for them with a motherly concern that was non-judgmental and accepting. In this way Mildred found what Hindus call *ananda*, the creative joy and uplift that comes from voluntary sacrifice and service.[4]

"No matter what, she never kicked people out. She'd try to help them," says Mrs. Barrett. "She always saw the best in everybody." Perhaps it was that quality at the root of Mildred's genius for relationships. The American pacifist John Heidbrink once wrote to her: "It is good to have you for a friend; you know how to be one."[5]

Certainly Mildred and others in the Fellowship of Reconciliation were building friendships and massing their creative forces for the next, anti-nuclear, phase of their peace work. Once again Gandhian non-violence and civil disobedience were the means to the end. In the mid-seventies, the U.S. military began construction of a nuclear submarine base at Bangor, near Seabeck. Two members of the Fellowship, Shelley and Jim Douglass, spearheaded the campaign against the Trident submarine and its apocalyptic cargo. They founded the Pacific Life Community at Bangor and many times went to prison for non-violent resistance to Trident, usually charged with trespassing on the base. They sometimes fasted in prison to drive home their total commitment to stopping the nuclear subs.

In the Douglasses and their willingness to accept suffering and imprisonment, Mildred once again saw Gandhi's spirit at work in the world. Mildred and Shelley first met when the younger woman was a student minister at West Point Grey United, just down the street from Mildred's home. When Shelley was in jail, Mildred often thought, "perhaps I should be there too." She wished she could have committed civil disobedience along with the younger people, but knew she couldn't have made it over the fence surrounding the base. Instead she did what she could in support of the Douglasses, and was pleased when the United Church of Canada expressed its solidarity with them and acknowledged "the validity of such non-violent prophetic witness in society."

In this period the government of India strayed farther from Gandhi's path than Mildred would ever have thought possible. India exploded its first nuclear device in 1974. Compounding the irony was that it had come about under the leadership of Prime Minister Indira Gandhi — daughter of Nehru, who had grown up at Bapu's knee. It was ghastly for Mildred to contemplate that the nation historically equipped to lead in the way of non-violence should employ the tool of ultimate destruction.

India's atomic test, Britain's decision to renew testing, continued development of nuclear weapons, the failure of the Strategic Arms Limitation Talks — many factors compounded global fears that the human race was intent upon self-annihilation. The *Bulletin of Atomic Scientists* sounded the alarm by moving the hands on its symbolic doomsday clock to zero minutes to midnight. Jim Douglass wrote: "A sense of ultimate violence was already abroad, and the doomsday clock only confirmed it ... In our own time ... we are living at the end of time."[6]

* * *

Vancouver City Hall, September 1, 1981: Mildred stepped up to the microphone to address the mayor and councillors, who were considering a resolution to declare Vancouver a nuclear-free zone. At the age of 81, she still had a strong speaking voice and a lot to say.

The resolution before us is one of top priority. It is one of life and death — not only yours and mine, but all humanity ...

Détente has not worked. We now have sophisticated weapons that could destroy the world many times ...

Our present concern is with the Neutron bomb, a demonic weapon that could change our beautiful world into a materialistic ghost planet, devoid of life. The global cost of military weapons is $1 million a minute ...

You ask, "What can be done about it?" Some say "nothing," and are willing to give up. I am not. I feel there is human potential for creative action that can reverse this insane race to extinction, and where better to start than here and now. Are you ready?[7]

Not only Vancouver, but the entire country, ought to become a nuclear-free zone, she urged. "Let our country become a mediator, recognizing that positive means will break fear and stimulate trust. Have faith that other nations will respond."

Unlike the federal government, which was singularly out of synch with voters' anti-nuclear sentiments, the municipal government under Mayor Mike Harcourt was actively co-operating with the peace movement. After the nuclear-free declaration was passed, the mayors of Hiroshima and Nagasaki wrote in salute and solidarity.

"When they join forces, the city government and the people, they will be helping ... to demonstrate that even the ashes of those devastated cities may yet produce a phoenix," wrote Linda Hossie in the *Vancouver Sun*.[8] That phoenix took the shape of a revitalized and immensely expanded anti-nuclear movement. After decades walking "the lonely path of peace," Mildred was delighted in her eighties to be joined by so many others. It gave her greater hope than she'd had in a long time, and a deep sense of confidence that the struggle would carry on long after she would. "Peace is still a distant hope ... but it is a hope and a *possible* improbable," she wrote.[9]

On a sunny Sunday in April 1982, Mildred and her friend Daisy Webster joined more than 30,000 other people in the first annual Vancouver peace walk. Endorsed by more than fifty different groups under the banner of End the Arms Race, the coalition had as its the slogan: "Abolish Nuclear Weapons, Fund Human Needs." From Kitsilano Beach, over the Burrard Bridge, through down-town Vancouver, and back down to the rally site at Sunset Beach on English Bay, Mildred and Daisy were overjoyed as they walked, arm in arm, surrounded by masses of other citizens non-violently affirming their will to build a peaceful planet. Along the way, they sang Holly Near's stirring anthem: "We are a gentle, angry people, and we are singing, singing for our lives."

The fear of nuclear annihilation had become so pervasive that the peace movement was attracting support from every walk of life: students, teachers, feminists, seniors, church people, trade unionists, retired soldiers, mothers with babies in strollers, dads with toddlers on their shoulders, doctors in white lab coats, hippies with flowers in their long hair, even Whores Against War turned out for the walk. In contrast to the wild garb of many younger peace walkers, Mildred was the picture of grandmotherly respectability with pearls at her ears and white gloves on her hands. She wore three different peace buttons on the lapels of her spring coat, and around her neck a hand-lettered sign decorated with doves. It read "PAX OR PERISH."

"I never thought I'd live to see this day," Mildred told a reporter for the *United Church Observer.*[10]

Compared to the early days in the peace movement, things had certainly come full circle. Peace was no longer considered a subversive pursuit. Peace was mainstream. Peace was the concern of all thinking people.

City council even proclaimed it "End the Arms Race Day," and the deputy mayor made a friendly speech. It was the first of twelve annual walks that contributed to Vancouver's reputation as "peace capital of Canada." Always held in April, the peace walks became one of the most exuberant signs of spring for a generation of young activists. Within a couple of years, the End the Arms race coalition had grown to 170 groups, and together they created a sensation. A massive turnout estimated at 115,000 people made Vancouver's 1984 peace walk the largest demonstration in Canadian history.

In North America, interest was further sparked by a provocative television drama entitled "The Day After," which dramatically depicted the impact of a nuclear blast. As well, many were inspired to action by an Academy Award-winning documentary on Australian peace activist Dr. Helen Caldicott. "If you love this planet," she said, "you've got to change the priorities of your life." Many did. Fortified by the passion of Dr. Caldicott and many others, Mildred carried on speaking and agitating and writing.

She kept up an active correspondence with politicians of all stripes, always urging them to "have the courage to disarm" and to commit themselves to non-violent leadership. She supported a "peace tax fund" that would allow citizens to channel their tax dollars that would otherwise go to the military into socially responsible ministries. She wrote to despots throughout the world, calling them to account for human rights abuses. She appealed to immigration authorities on behalf of a Chilean couple, refugees from the Pinochet dictatorship, and an Indian immigrant woman abused by her husband and threatened with deportation. She wrote to Soviet leader Leonid Brezhnev and American president Jimmy Carter. Over the years, she corresponded with Canadian prime ministers Pierre Trudeau, Joe Clark, John Turner, and Brian Mulroney. In 1985 she wrote to the latter, warning:

The Star Wars program is the most threatening of all ...

Are any commitments to the U.S. or NATO or any other country more important than your commitment to life? Of what value are trade relations or commercial advantages to a seared and devastated planet?

I beg you to listen to the voice of reason, to realize that preparing for war will never bring peace ... [11]

Mildred was never merely a correspondent of opposition. She took the politicians to task, but she also wrote to praise and thank them for good decisions. She wrote to congratulate Mulroney on his appointments of Stephen Lewis as Canada's Ambassador to the United Nations and Jeanne Sauvé as Governor General. She also praised him for coming to an honourable negotiated redress settlement with Japanese Canadians who suffered the injustices of 1942–1949.

Mildred wrote to U.S. President Ronald Reagan, whose belligerent policies in Central America she abhorred, but towards whom she expressed no rancor. She gave him her views on superpower disarmament, and then wished him a speedy recovery from the gunshot wounds he incurred in an assassination attempt. She also wrote to Nancy Reagan, appealing to her as a woman and a mother to use her influence for peace, and urging her to see "the Gandhi film."

Sir Richard Attenborough's epic had its premiere in Delhi in November 1982 — twenty years after the director first committed himself to the idea of bringing the Mahatma's struggle to the screen.[12] As soon as the film came to Vancouver, Mildred rushed to see it, full of high expectations. She was not disappointed. In the title role, actor Ben Kingsley brought her Bapu vividly to life. Mildred felt reconnected to Gandhi, and saw once again how imminent was his message for today. Members of the Fellowship of Reconciliation distributed leaflets at theatres showing the film, offering more information about Gandhi and his philosophy of non-violence.

Less than a year later, disturbing news came from Delhi. On October 30, 1984, Prime Minister Indira Gandhi was murdered. Mildred was saddened to see how Indira had contributed to the deterioration of Indian political life after the death of her father, the beloved Nehru, and how she utterly disregarded many of the democratic principals he held sacred. Mrs. Gandhi's final, fatal mistake was to order her government troops to make an assault on the Golden Temple of Amristar in an attempt to rout Sikh separatists holed up there. Two of the prime minister's long-time bodyguards shot her in retribution for this attack on Sikhism's holiest shrine. Jubilant Vancouver Sikhs celebrated her death by singing and dancing down Main Street to the sound of drums and fireworks.[13] Mildred's many Indo-Canadians friends, Sikhs and Hindus alike, mourned this latest eruption of sectarian violence in India, and prayed that it would not erupt in Canada as well.

India still held sway over Mildred's heart, and she continued working for the Balagram well into her eighties. She was still swimming and doing yoga, still driving her own car and digging her own garden, but there was no doubt that age was slowing her down. A friend sent her a funny poem on the trials of aging, which began: "How do I know my youth is all spent? Well, my get-up-and-go has got up and went!" Mildred chuckled ruefully to read that, and was forced to admit that there were some things that had become too much for her — the job of running the busy *Casa de los Amigos*, for example. In 1980, she let the directors know that this would have to be her last year. That didn't mean a final adios, of course, because she was still fundraising for the *Casa de Alfabetizacion* and always visited on future trips to Mexico.

In fact, Mildred's Latin American connections expanded in the 1980s, as Nicaragua became the battlefield in the latest east-west conflict. In 1979, the Sandinista National Liberation Front succeeded in overthrowing the dictator Anastasio Somoza, the second generation of his family to rule with an iron fist and lots of support from Washington. With wars of liberation already being waged against U.S.-backed regimes in El Salvador and Guatemala, the fate of the new Nicaragua became a powerful symbol throughout the Americas.

The Sandinista message inspired ardent support abroad. People from east and west volunteered to serve as carpenters, teachers, cotton pickers, fishers, labourers — whatever was needed. Had she been a few decades younger, Mildred would have been among them. As it was, she did all she could to support local solidarity initiatives such as the Tools For Peace coalition. As the Sandinistas struggled to redefine their society in the interests of the poor, one of the oft-repeated slogans was: "Relentless in the struggle, but generous in victory."

Mildred was profoundly moved by the actions of Tomás Borge, the only one of the FSLN's founders to survive the long war of liberation. Borge had been captured many times and endured atrocious treatment in prison. After the victory he confronted one of his torturers, saying: "Remember? I told you I would take revenge when I was free. Well, now I come for my revenge. For your hate and torture I give you love, and for what you did I give you freedom." And the man was released from prison.[14] Such astonishing acts of grace told Mildred that, although it was won by force of arms, this revolution would be built by soul force.

Meanwhile, the Sandinistas' wealthy opponents marshalled forces who emerged as the *contras*, a mercenary army largely comprised of ex-National Guardsmen and secret police. They were well-equipped, and paid in American dollars. The *contra* war posed the first big post-Vietnam challenge to pacifists, who had to counter a wave of Cold War-style propaganda about godless communists exporting revolution from Havana to Managua to San Salvador and beyond. While some Sandinista leaders were indeed Marxists, others were peasants and teachers and priests, and their revolution was as much spiritual as economic and political.

While the Nicaraguans fought to defend themselves and their revolution, their friends in El Salvador and Guatemala were still being killed or disappeared by government forces and paramilitary death squads. Mildred's heart went out to hear the anguished cry of San Salvador's Archbishop Oscar Romero — "In the name of God, in the name of this suffering people ... stop the repression!" His words echoed in her mind long after his assassination in 1980.

By 1984, there were an estimated 45,000 Salvadoran and Guatemalan refugees in Mexico City. Mildred responded generously to appeals from the Casa de los Amigos, which was desperately trying to help meet the basic physical and spiritual needs of at least a few of these unfortunate asylum seekers.[15] The wave of displaced Central Americans washed up on Canadian shores as well. Citizens and church groups organized to sponsor refugees. Mildred welcomed them into her home, offering sanctuary and empathy. One Salvadoran family stayed with her for about a year.

Chapter Nineteen: 1983

STILL SWIMMING

With all of her personal visitors and Servas travellers, Mildred's summers were always busy, but the summers of 1983 and 1986 were exceptional. In '83, the World Council of Churches held its sixth general assembly at the University of British Columbia. The World Council, representing about four hundred million Protestants from one hundred nations, was a powerful ally of progressive elements in the church and was considered akin to the anti-Christ by conservative evangelicals. The WCC had put women's rights and nuclear disarmament at the top of the agenda for this meeting, which was expected to attract four thousand delegates. The speakers list included Helen Calidcott and Coretta Scott King, as well as Archbishop Desmond Tutu from South Africa.

With her home only a few minutes from campus, Mildred was strategically located. FOR staff from New York wrote to ask if they could stay with her and she gladly said yes. The house filled up quickly, what with the refugees and several other international delegates. Among the visitors was Dr. Wee Chong Tan, teacher, scientist and theologian. He had first met Mildred in 1982, when she was invited to speak about Gandhi at Pearson College, an international school on Vancouver Island where Dr. Tan taught. He said his first impression of Mildred was of a "saintly" person.

"There's something there you can't explain," he said. "Her presence and quietness would be in line with the Quaker tradition ... but Mildred has that *ahimsa* quality to her."[1]

Dr. Tan was moved by the way Mildred opened her home to one and all. So deeply moved, indeed, that he was inspired to help refugees in his own community. He bought a small farm near Langford on Vancouver Island, and offered it to an exiled *campesino* family from Guatemala. It was only a few acres, but it was a home and chance to get on their feet in a new country. "I was inspired to do so by Mildred," Dr. Tan said.

Three years later, Mildred welcomed another wave of visitors when Vancouver hosted Expo '86, an international exposition on the theme of transportation. Vancouverites invited the world, and millions took them up on the offer. Thousands passed through the turnstiles daily and enjoyed attractions including the treasures of Ramses II, the Kirov Ballet, the world's largest hockey stick, the shiny new SkyTrain, and a mascot named Expo Ernie, a talking robot.

During the fair, United Church members helped to raise funds for their church camp by offering an economical bed-and-breakfast program for Expo visitors. Nearly 3,000 guests stayed an average of four nights in 180 different homes in the Lower Mainland.[2] Incredibly, about 100 of those guests stayed at Mildred's place the summer she was 86. Some of them later wrote with thanks and reflections:

> Peter and I wish to thank you so much for being our hostess at Expo … You have given us new ideas for serving in this world … Sincerely, Esther Addison.

> Dearest Mildred, I was enthralled by your stories about Gandhi, he being someone I have studied and admired for some time. The entire atmosphere in your home exuded a sense of peace … From Steve "Mask" Marvill.

> I have thought about you many times since I have been back, wondering if you had gained your equilibrium since that mad influx of company which the Exposition brought to you. I felt quite guilty imposing on you like that, yet, at the same time I was mighty grateful for your hospitality … I told my husband what an interesting home you had. It took me right back to my childhood … Thanks again, Mildred, for the friendship you extended and for your warm hospitality. Sincerely, Roxana Bodine.

> Dear Mildred, We send much positive love to the north, to your home. And we bask in the blessing of getting to know you. Thank you for opening your heart and home to us … Peace, Mimi and Michael.

Expo '86 was the biggest and flashiest of Vancouver's centennial projects, but there were other celebrations as well. To mark its 100th anniversary, the city honoured one hundred of its outstanding elders — Mildred among them — with the Distinguished Pioneer Award.

"I felt humble when my name was called and Gov. Gen. Jeanne Sauvé handed me the certificate," she told *The Vancouver Sun*. "Hundreds of pioneers and citizens in every part of the city are doing just as much, as volunteers. I can't imagine what our Canadian society would be if there were not causes and community projects."[3]

As she had done so often before, Mildred recounted how she met Gandhi and "learned the philosophy of peace and non-violence." She said: "That's been my purpose in life, my cause. It's been a long road. We've been attacked as peaceniks and Commies. But now things have changed. Peace is now a world issue. Thousands take part in parades. People are telling the politicians there's no future in nuclear war."

Mildred unveiling commemorative plaque in Tlaxco, Mexico, October, 1986.

The article came out with a charming picture of Mildred holding up her certificate. A friend sent a clipping to Mexico, and everyone happily passed the good news around the grapevine. When some of the people in the village of Tlaxco heard about it, they decided they wanted to honour Mildred in the same way. Her loyalty and consistency as a donor had made a significant difference to the Friends' work in the village. She was contributing her entire teacher's pension to the project and

Mildred never minded that there was a minor spelling mistake in her name!

251

Mildred with Rogelio Corra, Helen and Frank Dingman, Mexico, 1986.

in 1985, for example, that amounted to the equivalent of 415,072 pesos. It helped build a Quaker Centre for Service and Peace, as well as a *jaguey*, a little pool. The villagers asked their best ceramicist to make a large oval plaque bearing her name, to be glazed in ivory, surrounded by delicate handpainted flowers.

As she had many times before, Mildred travelled to Mexico in 1987 with her friend Jackie Mitchell, a lovely Quaker woman from Victoria. Together they had covered every bit of Mexico except the northeast region.[4] "Mildred always wanted to get to the beach. She was an ardent swimmer," Jackie said. "And she

Main gate of the new Children's Library and Cultural Centre at the Casa de Alfabetizacion in Mexico that Mildred's donations helped to build.

so loved the tropical fruits that she would have every shelf and windowsill of our hotel room stacked with papayas and mangoes and oranges."

The two women were very different by nature, but had a complementary relationship. "She was a Mary, not a Martha," Jackie said. "Mildred had to be in control, and I was definitely a follower. But I was happy to let her take control because I respected her objectives."

The two went together to Tlaxco, where they took turns unveiling one plaque honouring Mildred herself, and another for the Friends' centre. Mildred also helped plant a tree in the International Forest of Peace and Friendship, part of a reforestation project for the surrounding countryside.

The year 1986 brought more recognition for Mildred's life work. In May, she was made an honorary life member of the New Democratic Party. On behalf of Voice of Women, Mary Thomson wrote with additional congratulations. "We know that your years of service really represent the highest value for the NDP and this is their way of saying thank you. We in the Voice of Women and the peace world have also benefitted from the quality of your dedication."

In November, the United Nations' High Commissioner for Refugees presented the prestigious Nansen Medal to the Canadian people, in recognition of their "major and sustained contribution to the cause of refugees." It was the only time the prize had been awarded to "an entire generous and humanitarian people" who "set an enviable example through their willingness to share."

Mildred receiving life membership in the NDP from Grace MacInnis, 1986.

Certainly Mildred, who had opened her home to so many homeless exiles, was among those Canadians whose collective caring earned this honour for the whole nation.

Mildred remained vigorous into her later years, still doing yoga, swimming and walking miles on the beach and on the stump for the NDP. But increasingly her life centred on her home. In her garden, the peonies bloomed and the blue jays would come and feed from her open hand. She continued to host FOR meetings in her living room on the first Monday of every month, and a small but dedicated core group participated.

As her health declined, Hazel and Dick Legge took on the job of keeping the FOR going for Mildred's sake. They did the phoning to keep the twenty-odd members informed, arranged the speakers or visitors, went through the enormous amount of mail she received from peace organizations. At each meeting, Dick would offer a report on some of the more interesting or inspiring news from the FOR family, and update people on local events or campaigns of note. Discussions ranged from East Timor to South Africa, from Nanoose Bay to Oka.

In 1990, Mildred fell seriously ill with complications of pneumonia. She almost died, but was revived through some rather heroic efforts by her physician, Dr. Tom Perry Jr., son of Mildred's dear friends and fellow peace workers, Claire and Tom Perry Sr. Some said that Mildred should have been allowed to die, and not be kept alive "as a sort of walking ghost," but young Dr. Perry got the clear message from Mildred that she was not ready to go.

Certainly her nieces, Marion Irish and Bev McMaster, felt blessed to still have Mildred with them. She had always been so self-sufficient and so helpful to others that it was difficult for her to accept help until her very old age. Now, being able to give back to Mildred helped the younger women build a new kind of intimacy with her.

"As she's gotten older, she's more likely to reveal how she feels about things," Bev said. "I have more of a sense now of who's inside there. I feel closer to her in that way."

In the fall of 1990, Mildred was awarded the ninth annual Human Rights Award from MOSAIC, Vancouver's largest multicultural immigrant service agency. At that time I was serving on the human rights committee. Mildred's name was proposed, along with that of Marta Torres, a courageous Guatemalan lawyer and peace worker. Unable to choose one of these extraordinary women over the other, we decided to honour them both. Bringing them together, across generations and cultures, seemed to please them. Each said she was happier to share the award than to have received it solo. Mildred by then was quite frail, but she had not lost her sense of humour. After a letter of congratulations from then-premier Bill Vander Zalm was read aloud, she quietly quipped that she had never expected to receive something so nice from a Social Credit premier.

In the fall of 1991, Mildred was awarded the Vancouver Citizen's Peace Award, but by then she was not able to speak on her own behalf. She sat quietly as Dr. Carole Christopher, her close friend and neighbour, made some gracious remarks on her behalf.

As the season turned and the cold days and long nights approached, Bev and Marion began to worry that Mildred might not make it through the winter. They organized a Christmas tea and invited everyone, just as Mildred would have done in the old days. They served English and herbal teas, and dozens of festive sweets and savouries. Because it was so close to Mildred's birthday, the nieces also had a cake for her. Mary Thomson vividly described the scene at Mildred's last Christmas tea:

"We were clustered around the dining room table … The cake was put in front of her, but she just sat and looked at it. She didn't make any moves. She just kept on looking at it. So everybody just waited, and for some reason or other we all got the idea that that's what she wanted to do — just look at it, you know? And we all waited till the candles burned down. She didn't blow them out. It was kind of a magic time … It was like a meditation in a way."[5]

Within a few weeks, Mildred was in the UBC hospital for surgery to remove a blood clot from her right leg. Room 124 on Ward 1-A was brightened with purple cyclamen and pink primroses. She sensed my presence and looked up, smiling.

"Hello, dear," she said. She seemed distant, and a bit confused. "I'm just trying to figure out what I'm doing here. I'm looking for a friend with a car who could take me home." I explained about her operation and that she still had stitches in her leg so she needed to be in hospital. She seemed to accept my explanation, but still wasn't happy about the situation.

"But," she said. "I *am* glad to see you." Later: "Well, some things do work out. You promised you'd come and here you are." We chatted about her biography. I told her that I was thinking about her every day, enjoying the work and learning a lot. "What a book it will be," she said. "I don't know that I'll live to read it though." We both knew that was true, so after a moment I changed the subject and told her about reading one of her Mexico journals and realizing that we'd both swum on the same beach in Zihuatanejo. I told her I thought to myself, "Wouldn't it be neat if Mildred and I could go lie on the beach together and take a dip at *Playa La Ropa*." She said, "Don't go talking like that or you'll have me marching out of here in a minute!"

Mildred with her niece Marion (Osterhout) Irish and Marion's daughter, Wendy, 1991.

During another one of our visits we talked about India, and she encouraged me to go "to the slums, of course, and to the ashram." She fell quiet and we sat in friendly silence for a few moments, but then she began fretfully running her fingers through her hair. "It's strange, the things that come into your mind," she said. "I keep thinking, 'I *must* get to India. I've got to see Gandhi.' And I start pulling at my hair and it's *his* hair. It's like he's there, but I can't get through."

I told her I had had a dream about the spirits of her father and of Gandhi sitting together in her living room, Rev. Osterhout hooking a rug in his armchair by the fire and the Mahatma cross-legged on the floor, spinning. She laughed, as though the idea of the two men interacting was preposterous, but delightful to contemplate. "But don't forget that Marion won't let us have a fire in case we burn the house down," she added with a twinkle in her eye.

By February 1992, it was clear that in hospital Mildred was becoming resigned and withdrawn. Bev decided to have her discharged, knowing she could count upon the support of Mildred's many friends. She organized people to come over in shifts, so Mildred could live out her last days in her own home. As her life force faded, family, friends and neighbours pitched in to meet her physical and spiritual needs. Bev took primary responsibility for her care, but lots of other women offered consistent support. They'd drop in with healthy treats, and made sure that Mildred took a little nourishment. Some would give her a foot or hand massage, others would take her for a walk. Someone else would arrive with a few jokes. One woman, a music student, used to sing to her. Still others sat with her in silence. Everyone came with the gift of their time and concern for Mildred's continued independence and well-being.

The day before she died, Frank Dingman plucked a fresh rhododendron from his garden in White Rock and drove into town to see Mildred for the last time. She recognized him as soon as he sat down beside her. Much to Frank's surprise, Mildred sat right up in bed. "I'm not through yet," she told him with a smile and a hug.

Mildred in her dining room.

Epilogue: 1992

IN LIEU OF FLOWERS

Mildred Fahrni was 92 years old when she died quietly at home, about supper time on Sunday April 12, 1992. Her window was open to the Easter air and the pear tree outside was in bloom. She was not alone. Her dear niece, Beverley McMaster, and close friend, Mary Anne Cantillon, were present. The spirit of Mahatma Gandhi was with her too. His photograph hung low on the wall at the left of her bed, a single. Over the white coverlet, the women draped Mildred's turquoise kimono, the silk faded but still lustrous. They placed one cream-coloured rose across her breast. Rest in peace, their actions said. Later in the evening, as the candles burned low, the aroma of beeswax mingled with lilacs and lilies of the valley.

The day after she died, Mildred's presence in her house remained strong as friends and family gathered the next morning, a brisk spring day. At one point there were perhaps half a dozen women sitting and standing around the kitchen table, drinking tea and talking quietly, savouring the heady fragrance of hyacinths Daisy Webster had brought over.

Suddenly the back door swung open, and a fresh gust blew in. One of the women shut the door, but in less than a minute it whooshed wide open once again. As the clear April light flooded the room, everyone looked up together.

"Hello, Mildred?" someone called out.

Then we all laughed and smiled with the feeling that her spirit was rushing in on the breeze to say farewell and then to depart, carrying with her the essence of blue hyacinths.

"She was a law unto herself," said Daisy. "Now she is at peace."

Word of Mildred's death spread quickly. Even on the other side of the world, Marion sensed her passing. She was in Bali, staying in a small centre for the arts and music. That day, Marion had been invited to attend a cremation service for one of the respected matriarchs of the village. The men built her funeral pyre on a hill overlooking the valley, and the whole village — about seven thousand people — turned out for the ceremony. Grieving with the community, Marion became intuitively aware of her own loss. She was moved and shaken by the experience.

"The feelings were so powerful, and Mildred was so present, I said to myself, 'This is a sign. She has died.'" Marion phoned Vancouver right away. "I'm scared of what you're going to tell me," she said to Bev, who gave her the news. Marion and Bev — friends, sisters, nieces of Mildred, and now, in a sense, her daughters too — mourned together via long distance.

After they hung up, Marion walked for ages through the town, remembering Mildred. How she would have delighted in the birdsong on the air, the clear colours and cheerful cacophony of the marketplace! Amidst it all, Marion felt profoundly connected to Mildred. Later that evening, she created a little altar with a candle and some tropical flowers. Flame and fragrance, soul and senses — Marion said her prayers and her last farewell.

Beverley, too, held her own private memorial for Mildred the following Sunday by attending Easter services at West Point Grey United Church. It somehow seemed right that she died in spring, the time of rebirth. Surrounded by so many people Mildred knew and loved over the years, Bev felt their concern and caring in return. The swelling trumpet music uplifted her, and the healing began.

There were public farewells also. The day after Mildred died, three members rose in the British Columbia Legislature to pay her tribute. New Democrats Darlene Marzari and Tom Perry praised her as a distinguished Canadian, and a pioneer in the quest for peace and justice. "She had a certain dignity and peacefulness about her that anyone who knew her will never forget," Perry said. Liberal Val Anderson recalled hearing Mildred speak forty-five years earlier at the University of Saskatchewan. She had "a long-lasting effect on the lives of many students across Canada and around the world," he said, adding that he remained impressed by "her sincerity and her modesty and her supreme effectiveness."

Mildred's memorial service took place on June 20, 1992 at Point Grey United. Reverend Douglas Bacon welcomed the roughly two hundred friends and family members present. Most were from Vancouver, but some came from Toronto and Alberta, and a few FOR members came from Oregon and Washington too. Dr. Carole Christopher opened the celebration saying:

> We are here to remember Mildred, to mourn our own loss that Mildred is no longer with us as we have known her, to celebrate her truly magnificent life, and to rejoice that in a very real way Mildred will always be with us, because she has poured her super-abundant spirit out into all

of our lives and, indeed, the lives of people across the country and around the world …

Mildred — so humble of manner, so gracious of heart, so open and inviting in her spirit and her mind, and so deeply committed to human peace and solidarity — we are indeed grateful for her life.

Marion had asked me to speak about Mildred's life story in brief, and to read something from her archive. Soon afterwards, I found the quotation I was seeking scrawled on some notes from Bryn Mawr, 1931:

Why Strive

There is a chance that if we live courageously and honestly, putting enough intelligence and love into life, that we may be able to check the growth of ignorance & fear & hate, in fact may destroy it so that war will be impossible, so that men cannot kill each other by armaments or slow starvation.

There is a chance that our striving may swing the balance between the destruction of civilization & the building up of a better world in which it is worth while living — in which men do have equal opportunity.

And if there's even a chance, anyone who chooses to quit is a shirker & he who carries on even though he fails is a hero.

I challenge you with the statement that the adventure of throwing yourself into the struggle is worth the price. Those who climb mountains do so for the joy of struggling and achieving, for every step is an achievement even though they never reach the top …

The uncertainty of this struggle makes it more challenging. The amazing thing is that the insecurity of result does not take away the satisfaction of the struggle. It is worthwhile.

Soonoo Engineer spoke about Gandhi, and Mildred's enduring commitment to his ideals. They informed every aspect of her life to the very end, she said. "Mildred did not only believe in pacifism, she lived it every moment of her life."

Mary Anne Cantillon said that one of the most important lessons she learned from Mildred was "that one didn't have to find a babysitter to go out and make change on the planet. You could do it right at home."

"Mildred did not take a cheque book to eternity," Mary Anne said. "She took what Dom Helder Camara said was really important, and the only currency that's necessary in the presence of eternity. She took a life that was lived in love and in action."

She cautioned us not to place Mildred on a pedastal, but to celebrate her humanity. "Mildred was no plaster saint," Mary Anne said.

Mary Anderson wanted "to talk about the lightness of Mildred, and the quietness of Mildred ... Mildred never said: 'Be like me.' She never said: 'Do it the way I do it.' She listened far more than she spoke. We all wish that we were rather more like Mildred."

Franc Joubin agreed. "Mildred was an extraordinary woman," he said. "She was literally the guardian angel to many, many people."

Marion Irish and Bev McMaster reflected upon the richness of Mildred's final years. "In worldly eyes, she was diminished after her illness two and a half years ago, but Bev and I experienced a new depth in her love and affection for us both," Marion said.

"Her essential qualities stayed in place — her independent spirit, her passion for life. But it was her courage to take risks that challenged us. Could we risk, as well, to ensure that she had the space to keep that independent spirit alive and well?"

"We decided to take the risks on her behalf," Bev responded. "We succeeded in large part because of this community ... This community's extraordinary act of kindness over the last two years allowed Mildred to experience the continuity of her life to its end. Marion and I are deeply grateful to you all. Thank you."

* * *

April 12, 1993: a gusty grey morning that marked one year since Mildred's death. Before nine in the morning we sat down at her dining room table: Mildred's nieces, Marion and Bev, her friends, Carol and Mary Ann, and I. An ivory lace cloth was on the oval table and a slim blue candle burned faintly in the thin spring light. We drank coffee and tea, and ate muffins and croissants, kiwi, kumquats, and Chinese pears. We talked about the weather, and about how much further ahead the gardens were last year at this time.

Marion had put Mildred's ashes into a clay pot she had made herself, and placed it on the sideboard in the dining room, flanked by delicate white flowers in slim vases. When it was time to go, she wrapped the pot in a square of sturdy blue Indian cotton, all brightly embroidered. Then she tucked the bundle into her knapsack and slung it over her back. Marion was taking her Aunt Mildred home, to the beach, her final resting place.

As we walked out the door of 4536 West Eighth, someone recalled that it had been Mildred's home for more than half a century. Mildred was always both seeker and innkeeper. Her door was never locked. Over the decades, an untold number of visitors were warmed by her steadfast hospitality. Scores of foreign students lived with her, and refugees always found sanctuary at her hearth. Troubled souls found solace in her garden, and lots of weddings took place there, too.

Now only dirty grey water stains showed where flower boxes once had adorned the front windows. The spirits of geraniums and lobelia fluttered in the breeze. Little cards and special quotations were stuck all over the front door, a collage of doves, poems and hymns of peace. The tape was brittle and the paper yellowing, but her message was clear. Peace begins at home. The anniversary of Mildred's passing was made all the more poignant by the knowledge that this house (and Marion's childhood home) would remain standing a scant few weeks more. It had been sold and was slated for demolition. The survey stakes were already hammered into the lawn.

Walking down the steep hill towards Locarno Beach, we remarked upon the signs of new life everywhere: buds swelling on the branches, birdsong on the air. Down by the water, the wind picked up considerably, and it whipped our hair and scarves. We walked to the west along the water's edge, with the city skyline at our backs and the North Shore mountains on our right. Mildred herself walked many miles along this sand, and swam off these shores throughout her life. She came to this beach when she was troubled, and sometimes listened for God in the sound of waves or the cry of sea birds. She came here to celebrate, to have picnics, to laugh and sing around crackling bonfires. Many years she swam here on her birthday, January 2. We shivered and joked about how pioneers were made of sturdier stuff.

We came to a rocky outcrop Marion had chosen, and stopped. She unpacked her bundle and nestled the earthenware pot on the sand in the lee of the great stones. Then she began gathering talismans from the beach to place around it: a cluster of mussels and barnacles, trailing seaweeds. The rest of us gathered shells and stones, slips of greenery, and laid them in place. Mary Ann struggled to light a match in the wind, so we placed a few extra stones around the little blue candle. The flame flickered and danced, but stayed lit.

We gathered around. Marion held a framed copy of "The Indian Prayer," one Mildred had long cherished. She recalled how Mildred had read the same prayer at the outdoor memorial service for Bob Osterhout, her younger brother who died of cancer in 1987. Marion and Carol bent their heads together. Facing into the wind, they had to speak up as they took turns reading:

Do not stand at my grave and weep.
I am not there, I do not sleep.

I am a thousand winds that blow,
I am the diamond glint on snow.
I am the sunlight on ripened grain,
I am the gentle autumn rain.

When you walk in the morning hush,
I am the swift, uplifting rush
of quiet birds in circling flight.
I am the soft starlight at night.

Do not stand at my grave and cry.
I am not there, I did not die.

In March 1942, Mildred had grieved the death of her first pacifist hero, J.S. Woodsworth. As the family prepared to scatter his ashes on the same coastal waters, Mildred offered her thoughts and a poem of commemoration. More than half a century later, I simply changed the name and spoke her words:

> We commit these ashes to the boundless ocean. Following Mildred's request that her body be freed from any national boundaries, we cast these elemental remains to wind and wave, thereby making one last gesture of her commitment to the spirit of internationalism. And now her great spirit, released from the bonds of time and space, speaks to us in the words of Gibran's Prophet.

Should my voice fade in your ears, and my love vanish in your memory,
then will I come again.
And with a richer heart and lips more yielding to the spirit will I speak.
Yea, I shall return with the tide.
And though death may hide me and the greater silence enfold me,
yet again will I seek your understanding.
And not in vain shall I seek.
If aught I have said is truth that truth shall reveal itself in a clearer voice,
and in words more akin to your thoughts.
I go with the wind, but not into emptiness.
Know therefore, that from the greater silence I shall return.

Then, one by one, we each took a handful of her ashes and scattered them over the sand and into the water. We held our hands high, and the wind whisked the chalky grey ash away. We held our hands out to the sea, and the waves lapped up and swished it away. Handful by handful, moment by moment, we said goodbye to Mildred.

Vaya con Dios.

NOTES

Chapter One: 1900
A PRAIRIE CHILDHOOD

1. *Western Methodist Reporter*, January 1900.

2. Dr. Meredith Wadman, "Mildred Fahrni Memoirs Project," unpublished manuscript commissioned by the Mildred Fahrni Project, 1990.

3. Mildred's early years are recalled in interviews she conducted with Meredith Wadman, Carole Christopher and Irene Howard.

4. "Death Takes Pioneer Cleric," Obituary in the *Vancouver Daily Province*, July 18, 1940.

5. Gordon S. Fahrni, *Biography of Chris Fahrni: An Early Manitoba Settler*, (Winnipeg: Queenston Publishers, 1974), p. 23.

6. Author interview with Dr. Gordon Fahrni, Vancouver, December 13, 1991.

7. Randolph Carleton Chalmers, Th.D., *See the Christ Stand! A Study in Doctrine in the United Church of Canada*, (Toronto: The Ryerson Press, 1945),p. 90.

8. Frank H. Underhill, *James Shaver Woodsworth: Untypical Canadian*, (Toronto: Ontario Woodsworth Memorial Foundation, 1944),p. 11.

Chapter Two: 1914
A TEEN IN WARTIME

1. Author interview with Dr. Gordon Fahrni, December 13, 1991.

2. Carole Christopher interview with Mildred Fahrni, audiotape in Osterhout family collection.

3. Diary of Mildred Osterhout, April 21, 1918.

4. Diary, April 21, 1918.

5. Diary, April 26, 1918.

6. Diary, April 21, 1918.

7. Diary, September 5, 1918.

8. Diary, October 20, 1918.

9. Diary, March 7 and 16, 1919.

10. Hattie Osterhout to her family, April 12, 1919.

11. Diary of Mildred Osterhout, June 20, 1919.

Chapter Three: 1919
COMING OF AGE

1. "The Great Trek," Twenty-Fifth Anniversary commemorative booklet, University of British Columbia, October 29, 1947.

2. University of B.C. Annual, 1923.

3. *The Ubyssey*, November 9, 1922.

4. Diary of Mildred Osterhout, July 22, 1920.

5. Diary, September 29, 1920.

6. Diary, August 21, 1920.

7. Diary, January 2, 1921.

8. Diary, August 29, 1920.

9. Mildred Fahrni interviewed by Dr. Carole Christopher. Audiotape in Osterhout family collection.

10. Diary, August 1922.

11. Dr. Margaret Prang, Introduction to *All Things New*, Vol. 7, No. 1, pp. 1-2.

12. Marcia Toms, Transcript of interview with Mildred Fahrni, August 15, 1989.

13. *This One Thing: A Tribute to Henry Burton Sharman*, (Toronto: Student Christian Movement of Canada, 1959).

14. Diary, September 25, 1922.

15. Mildred Fahrni, in *The Way We Were*, (Vancouver: University of British Columbia Alumni Association, 1987), p. 27.

16. Author interview with Mary (Sadler) Kelly, October 29, 1991.

17. Author interview with Dr. Margaret Prang, February 22, 1993.

18. Frank H. Underhill, *James Shaver Woodsworth, Untypical Canadian*, (Toronto: Ontario Woodsworth Memorial Foundation, 1944), p. 17.

19. Diary, July 29, 1920.

20. Diary, February 13, 1921.

21. G. Jewell, *The History of the IWW in Canada*, Pamphlet, Vancouver Public Library reference division.

22. Olenka Melnyk, *No Bankers in Heaven: Remembering the CCF*, (Toronto & Montreal: McGraw-Hill Ryerson, 1989), p. 141.

23. Diary, January 28, 1923.

24. Author interview with Claude Campbell, October 28, 1992.

25. Letter from Mary Ballert, Dean of Women, June 10, 1924.

26. Author interview with former student Margaret Martin, Cultus Lake, August 1992.

27. Author interview with Kathleen Barrett, May 6, 1992.

28. Wadman, Dr. Meredith, "Mildred Fahrni Memoirs Project," p. 15.

29. Mildred's application letter to Bryn Mawr, undated 1930.

30. Ibid.

31. Carolyn G. Heilbrun, *Writing A Woman's Life*, (New York: Ballantine Books, 1988), p. 49.

Chapter Four: 1930
HEARING THE CALL

1. Diary of Mildred Osterhout, September, 29, 1930.

2. Diary, October 4, 1930.

3. Letter to Father, June 15, 1931.

4. Letter to Dearest Father and Vic, October 30, 1930.

5. Letter to Dearest Father and Uncle Phil, May 10, 1931.

6. Letter to Dearest Father, December 10, 1930.

7. Diary, June 12, 1931.

8. Undated page from a notebook, included with Mildred's letters home of the period.

9. Letter to Dearest Father and Vic, October 30, 1930.

10. Muriel Lester, *It Occurred To Me*, (New York and London: Harper & Brothers Publishers, 1937), p. 20.

11. Richard Deats, *Ambassador of Reconciliation: A Muriel Lester Reader*, (Philadelphia: New Society Publishers, 1991), p. 38.

12. Diary, January 1931.

13. Diary, June 14, 1931.

14. Letter to Father, June 23, 1931.

15. Letter to Father and Vic, May 19, 1931.

16. Letter to Father and Vic, undated.

17. Diary, June 20, 1931.

18. Reginald Singh to Mildred Osterhout, August 18, 1931.

19. Diary, August 17, 1931.

Chapter Five: 1931
A HERO(INE) EMERGES

1. Diary of Mildred Osterhout, August 28, 1931.

2. Diary, August 31, 1931.

3. Letter to Father, September 6, 1931.

4. Diary, September 4, 1931. A pocket-sized volume bound in red leather, it contains on a back page the signatures of the entire Indian delegation including the Mahatma, who shunned the honorific and signed simply "M.K. Gandhi." (A photograph of this page of the diary is on page 60.)

5. This is an undated clipping from an unnamed newspaper enclosed in Mildred's correspondence home from Kingsley Hall.

6. Letter from Mildred to Father and Vic, September 15, 1931.

7. Notes from Gandhi's "Talk On Prayer," later typed up by Mildred.

8. Letter to Father and Vic, September 15, 1931.

9. Ibid.

10. Ibid.

11. Letter to Father, October 15, 1931.

12. Vincent Sheean, *Mahatma Gandhi: A Great Life In Brief*, (New York: Alfred A. Knopf, 1954), p. 46.

13. Dream diary, March 11, 1932.

14. Letter to Father, November 2, 1931.

15. Diary, November 19, 1931.

16. Diary, November 5, 1931.

17. Sheean, p. 139.

18. Letter to Father, November 23, 1931.

19. William Shirer, *Gandhi: A Memoir*, (New York: Pocket Books, 1962), p. 19. In the years after he left India, Shirer wrote *The Rise and Fall of the Third Reich*, a classic study of WW2 and the Nazi Holocaust.

20. Carolyn G. Heilbrun, *Writing A Woman's Life*, (New York: Ballantine Books, 1988), p. 48.

21. Letter from Kingsley Hall, December 4, 1931.

22. Diary, December 5, 1931

23. Mildred Fahrni, audio tape interview with Dr. Meredith Wadman, November, 1989.

24. Diary, January 28, 1932.

Chapter Six: 1932
THE QUEST BEGINS

1. Radice, Lisanne, Beatrice and Sidney Webb: Fabian Socialists, The MacMillan Press, London, 1984, p. 9.

2. Letter to Father and Victor, March 8, 1932.

3. *The Indian Daily Mail*, February 29, 1932.

4. Father Verrier to Mildred Osterhout, February 23, 1932.

5. Dream diary, Spring 1932.

6. Letter to Father and Vic, February 16, 1932.

7. Europe diary, Spring 1932, p. 7.

8. Europe diary, p. 11.

9. Letter to Father, March 8, 1932.

10. Europe diary, March 29, 1932 and Letter to Father, April 2, 1932.

11. Letter to Father and Vic, April 7, 1932.

12. Europe diary, April 11, 1932.

13. Letter to Father, April 16, 1932.

14. Letter to Father, April 17, 1932.

15. Letter to Father, April 24, 1932.

16. Europe diary, May 1, 1932.

17. Dream diary, February 1932.

18. Dream diary, March 4, 1932.

19. Mildred to Father, November 1931.

20. Lisanne Radice, *Beatrice and Sidney Webb: Fabian Socialists*, (London: MacMillan Press, 1984), p. 303.

21. Letter to Father, July 20, 1932.

22. Letter to Father, July 26, 1932.

23. Letter to Vic and Father, December 24, 1932

24. Letter, August 4, 1932.

Chapter Seven: 1933
INTO THE FRAY

1. Author interview with Evelyn Harris, March 12, 1993.

2. Diary of Mildred Osterhout, 1933, undated.

3. Joan Sangster, *Dreams of Equality:Women on the Canadian Left 1920-1950*, (Toronto: McClelland & Stewart, 1989), p. 96.

4. S.P. Lewis, *Grace: The Life of Grace MacInnis*, Madiera Park, B.C.: Harbour Publishing, 1993), pp. 90-91.

5. Author interview with Frank MacKenzie, November 13, 1992.

6. Walter Young, *The Anatomy of a Party: The National CCF 1932-61*, (Toronto: University of Toronto Press, 1969), p. 45.

7. Ibid., p. 55.

8. Radio broadcast, CKMO, August 8, 1933.

9. Young, p. 45.

10. Olenka Melnyk, *Remembering the CCF: No Bankers in Heaven*, (Toronto & Montreal: McGraw-Hill Ryerson, 1989), p. 143.

11. *Vancouver Sun*, October 18, 1933, p. 13.

12. Ibid., October 19, 1933.

13. Mildred Osterhout, Speech MS, October 24, 1933.

14. *Vancouver Sun*, November 2, 1933, p. 20.

15. Letter to Dear Comrades, November 8, 1933.

16. Letter, March 11, 1934.

17. Daisy Webster, *Growth of the NDP in British Columbia 1900-1970: 81 Political Biographies*, (Vancouver: The New Democratic Party, 1970), p. 76.

18. M.J. Sparling to Mildred Osterhout, December 13, 1935.

19. Walter Fahrni to Mildred Osterhout, December 15, 1935.

20. Author interview with Paul Hucal, September 12, 1992.

21. Author interview with Dr. Gordon Fahrni, December 13, 1991.

22. Walter Fahrni to Mildred Osterhout, December 15, 1935.

23. Author interview with Paul Hucal, September 12, 1992.

24. Diary of Mildred Osterhout, January 1937.

25. Personal health inventory, October 17, 1938.

26. Clipping from unnamed newspaper of May 5, 1938.in Mildred's scrapbook of 1938 Dewdney by-election.

27. "On the Dewdney Front," undated clipping from CCF paper in Mildred's scrapbook from 1938 by-election.

28. Letter to Dear Comrades, May 23, 1938.

29. Journal of Mildred Osterhout, May 20, 1938.

30. Dear Comrades, May 23, 1938.

Chapter Eight: 1938
PILGRIMAGE TO INDIA, PRELUDE TO WAR

1. Mildred Osterhout to Dearest Father, Vic and Connie, November 2, 1938.

2. Trip diary, November 4, 1938.

3. Letter to family, November 1, 1938.

4. Letter to family, November 3, 1938.

5. Letter to family, November 4, 1938.

6. Trip diary, November 9, 1938.

7. Letter to family, November 9, 1938.

8. Letter to family, November 8, 1938.

9. Author interview with Ken Woodsworth, July 28, 1992.

10. Letter to family, December 7, 1938.

11. Trip diary, December 1938.

12. Christmas letter, December 1938.

13. Trip diary, December 2, 1938.

14. Trip diary, December 13, 1938.

15. Vincent Sheean, *Mahatma Gandhi, A Great Life In Brief*, (New York: Alfred A. Knopf, 1954), p. 137.

16. Trip diary, December 16, 1938.

17. Letter to family, December 23, 1938.

18. Author interview with Natverlal Thakore, October 14, 1993.

19. Trip diary, December 29, 1938.

20. Ibid.

21. Report by Mildred Fahrni to World Pacifist Meeting, 1950.

22. Trip diary, December 30, 1938.

23. Trip diary, Bapu with Muriel's group, undated, 1938.

24. Krishna Kripalani, *Gandhi, A Life*, (India: National Book Trust, 1968), p. 138.

25. Richard Attenborough, ed, *The Words Of Gandhi*, (New York: Newmarket Press, 1982), p. 46.

26. Letter to family, undated 1938.

27. Letter to family, January 8, 1939.

28. Letter to family, January 12, 1939.

29. Trip diary, January 14, 1939.

30. Ibid., January 1939.

31. Letter to family, January 31, 1939.

32. Letter to family, February 1, 1939.

33. Ibid.

34. Mildred Osterhout, "Palestine in Confusion," unpublished article, 1939.

35. Letter to family, February 24, 1939.

36. Ibid.

37. Letter to family, March 1, 1939.

38. Letter to family, March 19, 1939.

39. "From London to Glasgow by Foot and Thumb," p. 7.

40. Letter to family, March 22, 1939.

Chapter Nine: 1939
WAGING PEACE

1. Mildred Osterhout, Letter to the editor of the *Vancouver Daily Province*, August 29, 1939.

2. R.T. Elson to Mildred Osterhout, September 5, 1939.

3. Thomas P. Socknat, *Witness Against War: Pacifism in Canada 1900-1945*, (Toronto: University of Toronto Press, 1987), p. 192.

4. S.P. Lewis, *Grace: The Life of Grace MacInnis*, (Madeira Park, B.C.: Harbour Publishing, 1993), p. 125.

5. *Speeches of Mr. J.S. Woodsworth, Member for Winnipeg North Centre, on War, 1939 — Canada's Policy and War Budget*, Delivered in the House of Commons on Friday, September 8, and Tuesday, September 12, 1939, House of Commons Debates Official Report, p. 10.

6. Frank H. Underhill, *James Shaver Woodsworth: Untypical Canadian*. (Toronto: Ontario Woodsworth Memorial Foundation, 1944), p. 25.

7. Mildred Fahrni interviewed by Barbara Evans, p. 7.

8. Mildred Osterhout, Self-critique, 1939.

9. Charles J. Woodsworth to Irene Howard, February 21, 1986.

10. Author interview with Pat Hamill Barton, February 9, 2001.

11. Author interview with Elizabeth Keeling, June 9, 1992.

12. Mildred Osterhout, Christmas letter, 1940.

13. "Mildred Osterhout Announces Marriage," *CCF News*, July 31, 1941.

14. *Vancouver Daily Province*, August 2, 1941.

15. Mildred Fahrni, Christmas letter, 1941.

16. Mildred Fahrni interviewed by Dr. Carole Christopher, undated audio-tape in Osterhout family collection.

17. Author interview with Jean Fahrni, December 2, 1991.

18. Flora Bond to Mildred Osterhout, August 1941.

19. *Vancouver Sun*, December 9, 1941.

20. For a comprehensive history of the uprooting largely based upon the government's own documents, see Ann Gomer Sunahara's *The Politics of Racism*, (Toronto: James Lorimer & Company Publishers, 1981).

21. Thomas Shoyama to the author, March 16, 1992.

22. Author interview with Elizabeth Keeling, June 9, 1992.

23. Mildred Fahrni interview by Barbara Evans, p. 8.

24. Ibid.

25. Grace MacInnis, *J.S. Woodsworth, A Man to Remember*, (Toronto: MacMillan Company of Canada Limited, 1953), p. 330.

26. Ibid.

27. Mildred Fahrni, *In Memory of J.S. Woodsworth*, MS pp. 1-2.

Chapter Ten: 1943
WITH THE NISEI IN NEW DENVER

1. Roy Miki and Cassandra Kobayashi, *Justice In Our Time*, (Vancouver: Talonbooks, 1991), p. 30.

2. Thomas Shoyama to the author, March 16, 1992.

3. Gwen Suttie and Dorothy Blakey Smith, ed., "With the Nisei In New Denver," unpublished article.

4. Author interview with J.Stanley Rowe, New Denver, March 13, 1992.

5. Mildred Fahrni, Christmas letter to Dear Friends, December 1943.

6. Author interview with J. Stanley Rowe, New Denver, March 13, 1992.

7. Mildred Fahrni, "Lakeview Collegiate," in *The New Canadian*, November 13, 1943.

8. Author interview with Alice Murakami Tanaka, 1992.

9. Mildred Fahrni, Christmas letter 1943.

10. Author interview with Randolf and Frances Harding, Silverton, B.C., March 13, 1992. Harding retained his seat in Victoria till 1968, when he was elected NDP Member of Parliament from Kootenay West.

11. Author interview with J. Stanley Rowe, New Denver, B.C., March 13, 1992.

12. Mildred Fahrni letter, December 1944.

13. Mildred Fahrni interviewed by Marcia Toms, Vancouver, June 19, 1989.

14. Ibid.

Chapter Eleven: 1945
NOT UNDER A STAR, BUT A SWORD

1. Mildred Fahrni, Christmas letter, 1944.

2. Alan Reid, *A Concise Encyclopedia of the Second World War*, (Berkshire: Osprey Publishing Limited, 1974).

3. Of Things To Come: A Citizens' Forum, "What Kind of World Organization?" Transcript of CBC broadcast recorded in Vancouver, February 5, 1945.

4. Neil M. Morrison, CBC Supervisor of Talks and Public Affairs, to Mrs. Mildred Fahrni, February 7, 1945.

5. Mary Brim Scott to Mildred Fahrni, February 9, 1945.

6. Mildred Fahrni, Letter, April 13, 1945.

7. Bruce Hutchinson, *Vancouver Sun*, April 26, 1945, p. 1.

8. *CCF News*, May 3, 1945.

9. Diary of Mildred Fahrni, April 29 and May 7, 1945.

10. Mildred Fahrni, *CCF News*, August 16, 1945.

11. Mildred Fahrni, *CCF News*, June 14, 1945.

12. *CCF News*, July 12, 1945.

13. Del Finlay, *Vancouver Sun*, April 27, 1945, p. 1.

14. John Hersey, *Hiroshima*, (New York: Alfred A. Knopf, 1981). Reprinted from *The New Yorker*, August 31, 1946, p. 35.

15. Reid, p. 81.

16. *CCF News*, September 20, 1945.

17. Mildred Fahrni, Christmas letter, 1945.

18. "What Price Glory," undated pamphlet in Mildred Fahrni's personal papers.

19. *CCF News*, November 8, 1945

20. Mildred Fahrni to Riek Liesveld, undated letter, 1945.

21. Grace MacInnis, in the *CCF News*, December 1945.

22. Miki and Kobayashi, p. 55.

23. Mildred Fahrni, "Speech at King Edward High School," MS dated only May 6, year is likely 1946.

24. Riek Liesveld to Mildred Fahrni, April 4, 1946.

25. Mildred Fahrni, Radio broadcast, undated MS.

26. Irving Abella and Harold Troper, *None Is Too Many: Canada and the Jews of Europe 1933-48*. (Toronto: Lester & Orpen Dennys, 1983), p. vi.

27. Author interview with Dorothy MacDonald, Vancouver, January 14, 1992.

28. Author interview with Dr. Gordon Fahrni, Vancouver, December 13, 1991.

29. Author interview with Mary Thomson, Vancouver, May 20, 1992.

30. Mildred Fahrni, Letter, December 15, 1946.

31. Author interview with Marion Osterhout Irish, March 15, 1993.

32. Bob Sarti, "Atomic age protests long time on drawing board," *Vancouver Sun*, April 22, 1982.

33. Krishna Kripalani, *Gandhi: A Life*, (India: National Book Trust, 1968), p. 160.

34. Ibid., p. 163.

35. Ibid., p. 166.

36. Larry Collins and Dominique LaPierre, *Freedom At Midnight*, (New York: Avon Books, 1975), p. 309.

Chapter Twelve: 1947
BROADENING HORIZONS

1. Carolyn Kline and Peggy Stortz, eds., *Peace Lines*, a publication of the B.C. branch of the Women's International League for Peace and Freedom, to mark WILPF's 75th anniversary, (Vancouver: Press Gang Printers, 1990), pp. 10-11. Balch was actually WILPF's second Nobel laureate, the first being Jane Addams, its first president.

2. Mildred Fahrni, Guatemala reports, personal papers, April 1947.

3. Mildred Fahrni, Letter to My Dear Amigos, April 20, 1947.

4. Mildred Fahrni, [Impressions of Mexico] "At The End of Two Weeks," April 20, 1947.

5. Mildred Fahrni, Letter, April 21, 1947.

6. Mildred Fahrni, "Making Friends in Mexico," undated article, Spring 1947.

7. Mildred Fahrni, Letter, April 29, 1947. Mildred's cavalier attitude towards pesticides was typical of the times, but one shudders to imagine the long-term health consequences of these projects.

8. Mildred Fahrni, "A Village Awakens," Spring, 1947.

9. Ibid.

10. Mildred Fahrni, Bulletin on the Interamerican Congress of Women, Guatemala, August 12, 1947.

11. Mildred Fahrni, Letter, August 12, 1947.

12. Interamerican Congress of Women, Guatemala, August 19-27, 1947.

13. Mildred Fahrni, Letter, September 8, 1947.

14. Ibid.

15. Kripalani, p. 188.

16. Ibid., p. 193.

17. Ibid., pp. 193-4.

18. *Lucknow National Herald*, Saturday, January 31, 1948, p. 1.

19. *Vancouver Sun*, January 31, 1948.

20. Mildred Fahrni, "Tribute to Mahatma Gandhi," personal papers, February 1948.

21. Mildred Fahrni, Christmas letter, 1948.

22. Ibid.

23. Thomas P. Socknat, *Witness Against War: Pacifism in Canada 1900-1945.* (Toronto: University of Toronto Press, 1987), pp. 289-90.

24. Mildred Fahrni, Letter, April 25, 1949.

25. Mildred Fahrni, Letter, September 23, 1948.

26. Author interview with Franc Joubin, June 20, 1992.

27. Mildred Fahrni, World Pacifist Conference report, p. 2.

28. Mildred Fahrni, Letter, November 12, 1949.

29. Ibid.

30. Ibid.

31. Mildred Fahrni, audiotape interview by Dr. Carole Christopher.

32. Mildred Fahrni, World Pacifist Meeting report, p. 5.

33. Mildred Fahrni, Letter, December 31, 1949.

34. Mildred Fahrni, Letter, Christmas 1949.

35. Mildred Fahrni, Letter, January 6, 1950.

36. Ibid.

Chapter Thirteen: 1950
HOPE IN THE COLD

1. Mildred Fahrni, "Canadian F.O.R. and the International Situation," personal papers, December 1950.

2. Olenka Melnyk, *Remembering the CCF: No Bankers In Heaven*, (Toronto & Montreal: McGraw-Hill Ryerson), 1989, p. 138.

3. Mildred Fahrni, Christmas and New Year letter, 1950-51.

4. Mildred Fahrni, Letter, undated circa 1953.

5. Mildred Fahrni, "Blessed Are The Peacemakers," undated speech, 1950s.

6. "Arms Can't Kill Communism, Pearson Says," *Winnipeg Free Press*, June 5 1953.

7. Mildred Fahrni, F.O.R. Newsletter, February 1953.

8. Mildred Fahrni, Letter, Christmas December 1951.

9. Mildred Fahrni, "Peace And You," Speech delivered in St. John's, March 4, 1951.

10. Allena to Mildred Fahrni, September 28, 1952.

11. Mildred Fahrni interviewed by Dr. Carole Christopher.

12. Transcript of Victor Osterhout's funeral service, Mildred Fahrni papers.

13. Mildred Fahrni, "A Call For A More Disciplined and Revolutionary Pacifist Activity," 1953.

Chapter Fourteen: 1956
SATYAGRAHA IN THE DEEP SOUTH

1. Martin Luther King, "Our Struggle," reprinted from *Liberation*, April 1956, p. 2

2. Howell Raines, *My Soul Is Rested: The Story of the Civil Rights Movement in the Deep South*, (New York: Penguin Books, 1977), p. 61.

3. Bayard Rustin, "Montgomery Diary," in *Liberation*, April 1956, p. 10.

4. Pamphlet in Mildred Fahrni's papers from the Montgomery visit.

5. Rustin, p. 9.

6. L.D. Reddick, "The Southern Negro Speaks Up: The Bus Boycott in Montgomery," reprinted from *Dissent*, Spring 1956.

7. Mildred Fahrni, audiotape interview with Dr. Meredith Wadman.

8. Mildred Fahrni, Montgomery, Alabama, Trip diary, 1956

9. Marcia Toms interview with Mildred Fahrni, August 15, 1989.

10. Raines, p. 44.

11. Trip diary, Montgomery, Alabama, 1956.

12. Reddick, p. 5-6.

13. Trip diary, Montgomery, Alabama, 1956.

Chapter Fifteen: 1958
REBUILDING IN WIDOWHOOD

1. Mildred Fahrni, audiotape interview by Dr. Carole Christopher, 1988.

2. Ibid.

3. Mildred Fahrni, Letter, April 22, 1958.

4. Lucy Woodsworth to Mildred Fahrni, April 30, 1958.

5. Watson Thomson to Mildred Fahrni, June 19, 1958.

6. Letter from Bea, May 16, 1958.

7. Mildred Fahrni, Journal, 1958.

8. Mildred Fahrni, Journal, January 28, 1957.

9. Mildred Fahrni, Dream diary, January 8, 1958.

10. Mildred Fahrni, Christmas letter, 1958.

11. Author interview with Ursula Mueller-Schade, North Vancouver, June 10, 1992.

12. Author interview with Teruko and Noboru Omoto, May 29, 1992.

13. Author interview with Carolyn Kline, October 3, 1991.

14. Marcia Toms, "Into the Sunlight Of A New Day," Masters Thesis, Simon Fraser University, 1993, p. 177.

15. Mildred Fahrni, Pamphlet on Non-Violent Self-Discipline, 1958.

16. Undated clipping in Mildred's files, 1958.

17. Mildred Fahrni to Rev. Theo Roberts, July 11, 1958.

18. Marcia Toms, "Into the Sunlight of a New Day," p. 177.

19. Mildred Fahrni letter, November 1, 1959.

Chapter Sixteen: 1960
MEXICO, MY INDIA

1. Trip diary, October 22, 1960. This is a brown coil-bound notebook, illustrated with coloured pencil sketches of landscapes, bridges, market vendors, botanical gardens, and other sights from Vancouver to Vietnam.

2. Franc Joubin to Mildred Fahrni, March 28, 1961.

3. Diary, November 6, 1960.

4. Ibid.

5. Stanley Karnow, *Vietnam: A History*, (New York: Penguin Books, 1983), p. 235.

6. Ibid., p. 236.

7. Letter to Hazel, Dick, Joan & Betty, from Saigon, November 18, 1960.

8. India notebook, December 18, 1960.

9. Diary, undated, December 1960.

10. Letter, March 13, 1961.

11. Diary, February 27, 1961, Alipur Duar, India.

12. Trip diary, Baneswar, February 28, 1961.

13. Author interview with Beverley McMaster, October 2, 1991.

14. Interview with Ed and Jean Duckles, coordinators of AFSC projects in Mexico from 1945 to 1982.

15. Letter to friends, April 7, 1967.

16. Ibid.

17. Letter to *Muy Amables Amigos*, March 3, 1967.

18. Author interview with Franc Joubin, June 20, 1992.

19. Letter from Ed Duckles to the author, December 12, 1995.

20. Letter to Mildred from Jean and Ed Duckles, Comite de Servicio de los Amigos, Mexico, June 1968.

21. Author interview with Marion Osterhout Irish, June 1992.

22. Toms, p. 181.

23. Ibid., p. 183.

24. Mildred Fahrni, "Voice of Women International Conference, Montreal, September 9-16, 1962," in *Arunodayam*, November 1962, p. 9.

25. Dean Beeby, "RCMP spied on women's committee," *Vancouver Sun*, October 12, 1993, p. A10.

26. Mildred Fahrni in *Arunodayam*, p. 9.

27. "Douglas Attacks Cuban Blockade," *Vancouver Sun*, October 23, 1962, p. A7.

28. Gerard Daechsel to Mildred Fahrni, 23 October, 1963.

Chapter Seventeen: 1963
FLOWER POWER

1. Stanley Karnow, *Vietnam: A History*, (New York: Penguin Books), 1983.

2. *Georgia Straight*, November 24, 1967.

3. Mildred Fahrni, Christmas letter, 1967.

4. Author interview with June Black, June 1992.

5. Quoted in Richard Gwyn, *The Northern Magus*, (Toronto: McClelland & Stewart, 1980), p. 60.

6. Mildred Fahrni, Christmas letter, 1967.

7. Bhama Srinivasan to Mildred Fahrni, from Madras, July 3, 1968.

8. Mrs. Martin Luther King Jr. , Atlanta, Georgia, to Mildred Fahrni, January 5, 1967.

9. Mildred Fahrni interview with Marcie Toms, 1989.

10. Minutes, FOR executive committee meeting, Friends House, Toronto, June 20, 1967.

11. Peter Gorrie, FOR treasurer to Mildred Fahrni, January 1966.

12. Minutes, FOR executive committee, Friends House, Toronto, March 31, 1969.

13. Mildred Fahrni to Shelley Douglass, undated letter.

14. Mildred Fahrni to Bert and Irmgard, November 5, 1969.

15. Minutes of meetings of Gandhi Non-Violence Committee, May 31 to October 12, 1969, Courtesy of Frank Dingman.

16. Mildred Fahrni, Christmas letter, 1969.

17. Gwyn, p. 113.

18. Mildred Fahrni, Christmas letter, 1970.

19. Mildred Fahrni, Christmas letter, 1971.

Chapter Eighteen: 1975
PEACE BEGINS AT HOME

1. Quoted in *The Summerland Review*, October, 31, 1974.

2. Author interview with Bev McMaster, October 2, 1991.

3. Tom Haythorne, Remarks at Mildred's memorial service, June 20, 1992.

4. Amiya Chakravarty, "A Note on the Indian Philosophy of Pacifism," a pamphlet published for the World Pacifist Conference, Gandhigram, 1960.

5. John Heidbrink to Mildred Fahrni, from U.S. FOR head office in Nyack, New York, July 18, 1963.

6. Jim Douglass, *Lightening East To West*, (Portland, Oregon: Sunburst Press, 1980), p. 57.

7. Mildred Fahrni, to the Mayor and City Council, September 1, 1981.

8. Linda Hossie, "The City Council Votes For Sanity," *Vancouver Sun*, April 6, 1983.

9. Mildred Fahrni, Christmas letter, 1981.

10. Quoted in "That long road to peace," *The United Church Observer*, June 1982, p. 18.

11. Mildred Fahrni to Prime Minister Brian Mulroney, March 28, 1985.

12. Richard Attenborough, ed., *The Words of Gandhi*, (New York: Newmarket Press, 1982).

13. Dave Margoshes & Al Sheehan, "City Sikhs Cheer Gandhi's Death," *Vancouver Sun*, October 31, 1984.

14. Miguel D'Escoto, "Building a new Nicaragua," in *Sojourners*, March 16, 1983.

15. Juan Pascoe and Donald Campbell to Mildred Fahrni, Mexico, January 20, 1984.

Chapter Nineteen: 1983
STILL SWIMMING

1. Author's interview with Dr. Wee Chong Tan, Victoria, B.C., March 16, 1993.

2. Rev. Bob Burrows to B&B Hosts, October 15, 1986.

3. Bayley, Chuck, "A Lifetime Working for a Better World," *Vancouver Sun*, April 15, 1986, p. C2.

4. Author interview with Jackie Mitchell, March 15, 1993.

5. Author interview with Mary Thomson, May 20, 1992.

SOURCES

Mildred Osterhout Fahrni left such a rich written legacy that her biography is based in large measure on primary sources. Her personal papers include hundreds of letters and more than forty journals dating from 1918 to 1988, including a dream diary. They document her daily life and political work, as well as two trips around the world (1938 and 1949) and many other voyages through Europe, Asia and the Americas.

A portion of Mildred's personal papers are held in the Special Collections at the University of British Columbia, while an even more substantial collection remains in the possession of her family. Other relevant documents were to be found in the United Church of Canada archives, the City of Vancouver archives and the provincial archives.

Mildred had a courageous heart and an eye for detail, so she wrote compellingly of the people and places she encountered. As well, she illustrated many of her journals with pen and ink sketches and diagrams. They are marvelous artifacts, and I feel privileged to have had the opportunity to work with them. From 1931, for example, there is a small trip diary, bound in red leather, which tells of Mildred's months in London with Gandhi. The back page is autographed by the entire Indian delegation including the Mahatma himself, his son, secretaries and devotees. It's a potent piece of history that fits in the palm of your hand.

Interviews and correspondence with Mildred's family, friends and political colleagues, some unfortunately now deceased, helped immeasurably with the research. For their time and trouble, their candour and kindness, my thanks go to:

Win and Joe Awmack, Bela Banerjee, Kathleen Barrett, Pat Barton, June Black, Theodore Boggs Jr., Claude Campbell, Dr. Carole Christopher, Alice Coppard, Richard Deats, Frank and Helen Dingman, Ed and Jean Duckles, Soonoo Engineer, Dr. Gordon Fahrni, Jean Fahrni, Randolf and Francis Harding, Evelyn Harris, Sherryll Harris, Lydia Haythorne and her son John, Paul Hucal, Marion Irish, Franc Joubin, Chie Kamegaya, Elizabeth Keeling, Mary Kelly, Carolyn Lacey Kline, Margaret and Harold Knight, Vinoo Kripalani, Hazel and Dick Legge, Dorothy MacDonald, Frank McKenzie, Beverley McMaster, George Masuda, Dr. Roy Miki, Jackie Mitchell, Ursula Mueller-Schade, Edna Nash, Isabelle Showler, Noboru and Teruko Omoto, Mabel Parker, Dr. Margaret Prang, Dr. J. Stanley Rowe, Jean Scott, Dr. Tom Shoyama, Rev. Bob Smith, Alice Tanaka, Natverlal Thakore, Dr. Wee-Chong Tan, Mary Thomson, Murray Thompson, Ida Vyse, Daisy Webster, Harold Winch and Bruce Woodsworth.

BIBLIOGRAPHY

Abella, Irving & Harold Troper. *None Is Too Many: Canada and the Jews of Europe 1933-1948*. Toronto: Lester & Orpen Dennys, 1983.

Adams, David. *The American Peace Movements; History, Root Causes and Future*. New Haven, CT.: The Advocate Press, 1986.

Allen, Richard. *The Social Passion: Religion and Social Reform in Canada 1914-28*. Toronto: University of Toronto Press, 1971.

American Friends Service Committee. *In Place Of War: An Inquiry Into Nonviolent National Defense*. New York: Grossman Publishers, 1967.

Archer, Jules. *The Incredible Sixties: The Stormy Years that Changed America*. New York: Harcourt, Brace, Jovanovich Publishers, 1986.

Attenborough, Richard, ed. *The Words of Gandhi*. New York: Newmarket Press, 1982.

Banerjee, Bela. *Bringing Health To India's Villages*. Newton, Kansas: Wordsworth, 1988.

Berger, Thomas. *Fragile Freedoms: Human Rights and Dissent in Canada*. Toronto/Vancouver: Clark, Irwin, & Company Limited, 1981.

Berton, Pierre. *The Great Depression: 1929-1939*. New York: Penguin Books, 1990.

Borge, Tomás. *Carlos, The Dawn Is No Longer Beyond Our Reach*. Vancouver: New Star Books, 1984.

Brockman, S.J., and R. James. *The Violence of Love: The Pastoral Wisdom of Archbishop Oscar Romero*. San Francisco: Harper & Row Publishers, 1988.

Chalmers, Randolf Carleton. *See the Christ Stand! A Study in Doctrine in The United Church of Canada*. Toronto: The Ryerson Press, 1945.

Chandy, K.K. *Peace Culture Amidst Power Conflicts*. India: The Fellowship of Reconciliation, 1992.

Craig, John. *The Years of Agony: 1910/1920. Canada's Illustrated Heritage*, Toronto: Natural Science of Canada Ltd., 1977.

Collins, Larry and Dominique LaPierre. *Freedom at Midnight*. New York: Avon Books, 1975.

Deats, Richard, ed. *Ambassador of Reconciliation: A Muriel Lester Reader*. Philadelphia, PA: New Society Publishers, 1991

Fahrni, Gordon. *A Biography of Christian Fahrni*. Winnipeg: Princeton Queenstown Publishers, 1974.

Fisher, Louis. *Gandhi: His Life and Message for the World*. New York & Scarborough: New American Library, 1954.

Fowke, Edith, ed. *Toward Socialism: Selections from the writings of J.S. Woodsworth*. Toronto: Ontario Woodsworth Memorial Foundation, 1948.

Fromm, Erich. *The Art Of Loving*. New York: Harper & Brothers Publishers, 1956.

Goff, Richard, et al. *The Twentieth Century: A Brief Global History*. New York: McGraw-Hill, Inc., 1994.

Gwyn, Richard. *The Northern Magus: Pierre Trudeau and the Canadians*. Toronto: McClelland & Stewart, 1980.

Heilbrun, Carolyn G. *Writing A Woman's Life*. New York: Ballantine Books, 1988.

Hersey, John. *Hiroshima*. New York: Alfred A. Knopf, 1981. Reprinted from *The New Yorker*, August 31, 1946.

Howe, Irving, ed. *Essential Works of Socialism*. Third edition. New Haven and London: Yale University Press, 1986.

India and Disarmament: An Anthology of Selected Writings and Speeches. External Publicity Division, Ministry of External Affairs, Government of India, 1988.

Karnow, Stanley. *Vietnam: A History*. New York: Penguin Books, 1983.

King, Dr. Martin Luther. "Our Struggle," in *Liberation*, April 1956.

Kostash, Myrna. *Long Way From Home: The Story of the Sixties Generation in Canada*. Toronto: James Lorimer & Company, 1980.

Kloppenborg, Niwinski and Johnson, eds. *Vancouver: A City Album*. Vancouver/Toronto: Douglas & McIntyre, 1991.

Kripalani, Krishna. *Gandhi: A Life*. India: National Book Trust, 1968.

Krishna Murthy, Nadig. *Mahatma Gandhi And Other Martyrs of India*. Columbia, Missouri: Journal Press, 1948.

Lester, Muriel. *It Occurred To Me*. New York & London: Harper & Bros. Publishers, 1937.

Lester, Muriel. *Gandhi's Signature*. Los Angeles & New York: Fellowship of Reconciliation, 1949.

Lewis, S.P. *Grace: The Life of Grace MacInnis*. Madeira Park, B.C.: Harbour Publishing, 1993.

McAfee Brown, Robert. *Making Peace In The Global Village*. Philadelphia: The Westminster Press, 1981.

McClung, Nellie. *In Times Like These*. Toronto: University of Toronto Press, 1972.

MacGregor, G.H.C. *The New Testament Basis of Pacifism*. New York: Fellowship of Reconciliation, 1936.

MacInnis, Grace. *J.S. Woodsworth: A Man To Remember*. Toronto: MacMillan Company of Canada Limited, 1953.

Mayer, Peter, ed. *The Pacifist Conscience*. Chicago: Henry Regnery Company, 1967.

Melnyk, Olenka. *Remembering the CCF: No Bankers In Heaven*. Toronto & Montreal: McGraw-Hill Ryerson, 1989.

Miki, Roy and Cassandra Kobayashi. *Justice In Our Time*. Vancouver: Talonbooks, 1991.

Newman, Paul S. *Land of the Bible*. Norwalk, Connecticut: C.R. Gibson Company Publishers, 1974.

Phillips, Alan. *Into the 20th Century: 1900/1910*. Canada's Illustrated Heritage. Toronto: Natural Science of Canada Ltd., 1977.

Radice, Lisanne. *Beatrice and Sidney Webb: Fabian Socialists*. London: MacMillan Press, 1984.

Raines, Howell. *My Soul Is Rested: The Story Of The Civil Rights Movement In The Deep South*. New York: Penguin Books, 1983.

Reddick, L.D. "The Southern Negro Speaks Up; The Bus Boycott in Montgomery," reprinted from *Dissent*, Spring 1956.

Reid, Alan. *A Concise Encyclopedia of the Second World War*. Berkshire: Osprey Publishing Limited, 1974.

Sangster, Joan. *Dreams of Equality: Women on the Canadian Left 1920-1950*. Toronto: McClelland & Stewart Inc., 1989.

Sharman, Henry Burton. *Records Of The Life Of Jesus*. New Haven, Conn.: Yale Books, 1917.

Sheean, Vincent. *Mahatma Gandhi, A Great Life In Brief*. New York: Alfred A. Knopf, 1954.

Sheehan, Neil. *A Bright Shining Lie: John Paul Vann and America in Vietnam*. New York: Vintage Books, 1989.

Shirer, William. *Gandhi: A Memoir*. New York: Pocket Books, 1982.

Smith, Cameron. *Love & Solidarity: A Pictorial History of the NDP*. Toronto: McClelland & Stewart Inc., 1992.

Socknat, Thomas P. *Witness Against War: Pacifism in Canada 1900-1945*. Toronto: University of Toronto Press, 1987.

Sunahara, Ann Gomer. *The Politics of Racism*. Toronto: James Lorimer & Company, 1981.

Swomley, John M. Jr. *Press Agents of the Pentagon*. Washington, D.C.: National Council Against Conscription, July 1953.

"The South: Attack on the Conscience," *Time Magazine*, February 18, 1957, pp. 21-24.

Toms, Marcia Elizabeth. "Into The Sunlight Of A New Day: The Beliefs And Work Of Two Women Peace Activists In Vancouver During The Cold War," Master's Thesis, Simon Fraser University, 1993.

"Toward Security Through Disarmament," A report prepared for the American Friends Service Committee, Philadelphia, 1952.

Trocme, André. *The Politics Of Repentance*. New York: Fellowship Publications, 1953.

Underhill, Frank H. *James Shaver Woodsworth: Untypical Canadian*. Toronto: The Ontario Woodsworth Memorial Foundation, 1944.

Walker, Martin. *The Cold War: A History.* New York: Henry Holt and Company, 1993.

Webster, Daisy. *Growth of the NDP in British Columbia1900-1970: 81 Political Biographies.* The New Democratic Party, 1970.

Weinberg, Arthur and Lila, eds. *Instead of Violence: Writings By The Great Advocates of Peace And Non-Violence Through History.* Boston: Beacon Press, 1963.

Whittaker, Reg and Gary Marcuse. *Cold War Canada: The Making of a National Insecurity State.* Toronto: University of Toronto Press, 1994.

Woodcock, George. *British Columbia: A History of the Province.* Vancouver: Douglas & McIntyre, 1990.

Woodcock, George & Ivan Avakumovic. *The Doukhobours.* Toronto/New York: Oxford University Press, 1968.

Young, Walter. *The Anatomy of a Party: The National CCF 1932-61.* Toronto: University of Toronto Press, 1969.

Zinsser, William, ed. *Inventing The Truth: The Art And Craft Of Memoir.* Boston: Houghton Mifflin Company, 1987.